Encyclopaedic History of India Series

INDEPENDENT INDIA

Dr. Mahesh Vikram Singh
Professor, Deptt. of History
Mahatma Gandhi Kashi Vidyapeeth
Varanasi (UP)

Dr. Brij Bhushan Shrivastava
Head of Deptt., Ancient History, Archeology & Culture
SMMTPG College, Ballia (UP)

CENTRUM PRESS
NEW DELHI-110002 (INDIA)

CENTRUM PRESS
H.O.: 4360/4, Ansari Road, Daryaganj,
New Delhi-110002 (India)
Tel: 23278000, 23261597, 23255577, 23286875
B.O.: No. 1015, Ist Main Road, BSK IIIrd Stage,
IIIrd Phase, IIIrd Block, Bangalore-560085 (INDIA)
Tel: 080-41723429
Email: centrumpress@gmail.com
Visit us at: www.centrumpress.com

Independent India

First Edition, 2011

ISBN 978-93-80921-52-5

PRINTED IN INDIA

Printed at Mehra Offset Press, Delhi

प्रो. विपिन चंद्रा
अध्यक्ष
Prof. Bipan Chandra
Chairman

नेशनल बुक ट्रस्ट, इंडिया
नेहरू भवन
5 इंस्टीट्यूशनल एरिया, फेज़-II, वसंत कुंज, नई दिल्ली-110 070
फोन/ Phone: 011-26121880 फैक्स/ Fax: 011-26121883
NATIONAL BOOK TRUST, INDIA
Nehru Bhawan
5 Institutional Area, Phase II, Vasant Kunj, New Delhi-110 070
ई-मेल / E-mail: chairman@nbtindia.org.in
वेबसाइट / Website: www.nbtindia.org.in

FOREWORD

The term 'history' is derived from the Greek word 'historia' that means knowledge acquired through investigation. Obviously, this knowledge can be correct if the method of investigation is objective and not vitiated by any kind of bias. In other words, if the study of human past is comprehensive and obtained through scientific inquiry, it can provide perspective on the present day problems and help one plan for the future.

A true historian has to identify the sources that can be most useful in a given context. Documents, coins, archaeology, anthropology, geography, travel accounts, oral traditions, mythology and so on can be useful but they can be used only after their veracity is tested and they are critically examined. They should be checked and counter-checked.

Over the centuries, one finds the study and writing of history vitiated by biases. There are numerous instances in which historical data have been distorted to support or oppose certain preconceived ideas and purposes. Strictly speaking such history is just like fiction to accord with preconceived notions and serve some ulterior purposes.

The study of the past has never been static. Conclusions go on changing because of the discovery of new materials and tools of investigation. To give a concrete example, the carbon 14 or radiocarbon dating test has revolutionized the study of civilizations and settlements, especially of prehistoric times, for which written documents, coins, etc. are seldom available. This method has enabled historians to determine more accurately than before the time period of a particular civilization or settlement. This method was discovered only 70 years ago by American scientists.

In our country, excavations brought to light the Indus Valley Civilization and its various features, hitherto unknown. Similarly, no complete text of Kautilya's Arthashastra was available before it was discovered by Shamasastry, the chief of the Mysore Government Oriental Library in the first decade of the last century. Likewise, people's knowledge of the history of the Buddhist period got extended after excavations at Sarnath and the ruins of the Asokan period at Patna. In the future, if the Harappan inscriptions are deciphered, our knowledge of the Indus Valley Civilization will increase enormously. All these instances underline the fact that our knowledge of history is never static and its frontiers go on extending.

In the light of what has been said above the encyclopedic history is going to be of great help to students interested in Indian history. It is comprehensive and as far as possible free from biases. It includes the latest materials, and objective conclusions.

Prof . Bipan Chandra

Professor Emeritus, JNU

Chairman, National Book Trust, India

Contents

Preface

The people of India have had a continuous civilization since 2500 B.C., when the inhabitants of the Indus River valley developed an urban culture based on commerce and sustained by agricultural trade. This civilization declined around 1500 B.C., probably due to ecological changes. During the second millennium B.C., pastoral, Aryan-speaking tribes migrated from the northwest into the subcontinent. As they settled in the middle Ganges River valley, they adapted to antecedent cultures.

The political map of ancient and medieval India was made up of myriad kingdoms with fluctuating boundaries. In the 4th and 5th centuries A.D., northern India was unified under the Gupta Dynasty. During this period, known as India's Golden Age, Hindu culture and political administration reached new heights. Islam spread across the Indian subcontinent over a period of 500 years. In the 10th and 11th centuries, Turks and Afghans invaded India and established sultanates in Delhi. In the early 16th century, descendants of Genghis Khan swept across the Khyber Pass and established the Mughal (Mogul) Dynasty, which lasted for 200 years. From the 11th to the 15th centuries, southern India was dominated by Hindu Chola and Vijayanagar Dynasties. During this time, the two systems—the prevailing Hindu and Muslim—mingled, leaving lasting cultural influences on each other.

The first British outpost in South Asia was established in 1619 at Surat on the northwestern coast. Later in the century, the East India Company opened permanent trading stations at Madras, Bombay, and Calcutta, each under the protection of native rulers. The British expanded their influence from these footholds until, by the 1850s, they controlled most of present-day India, Pakistan, and Bangladesh. In 1857, a rebellion in north India led by mutinous Indian soldiers caused the British Parliament to transfer all political power from the East India Company to the Crown. Great Britain began administering most of India directly while controlling the rest through treaties with local rulers.

In the late 1800s, the first steps were taken toward self-government in British India with the appointment of Indian councillors to advise the British viceroy and the establishment of provincial councils with Indian members; the British subsequently widened participation in legislative councils. Beginning in 1920, Indian leader Mohandas K. Gandhi transformed the Indian National Congress political party into a mass movement to campaign against British colonial rule.

—Authors

1

Economic Planning after Independence

Five-year Plans of India

The economy of India is based in part on planning through its five-year plans, developed, executed and monitored by the Planning Commission. With the Prime Minister as the *ex officio* Chairman, the commission has a nominated Deputy Chairman, who has rank of a Cabinet minister. Montek Singh Ahluwalia is currently the Deputy Chairman of the Commission. The tenth plan completed its term in March 2007 and the eleventh plan is currently underway.

First Plan (1951-1956)

The first Indian Prime Minister, Jawaharlal Nehru presented the first five-year plan to the Parliament of India on December 8, 1951. The first plan sought to get the country's economy out of the cycle of poverty. The plan addressed, mainly, the agrarian sector, including investments in dams and irrigation. The agricultural sector was hit hardest by partition and needed urgent attention. The total plan budget of 206.8 billion INR (23.6 billion USD in the 1950 exchange rate) was allocated to seven broad areas: irrigation and energy (27.2 percent), agriculture and community development (17.4 percent), transport and communications (24 percent), industry (8.4 percent), social services (16.64 percent), land rehabilitation (4.1 percent), and other (2.5 percent).

The target growth rate was 2.1 percent annual gross domestic product (GDP) growth; the achieved growth rate was 3.6 percent.

During the first five-year plan the net domestic product went up by 15 percent. The monsoon was good and there were relatively high crop yields, boosting exchange reserves and the per capita income, which increased by 8 percent. National income increased more than the per capita income due to rapid population growth. Many irrigation projects were initiated during this period, including the Bhakra Dam and Hirakud Dam. The World Health Organization, with the Indian government, addressed children's health and reduced infant mortality, indirectly contributing to population growth.

At the end of the plan period in 1956, five Indian Institutes of Technology (IITs) were started as major technical institutions. University Grant Commission was set up to take care of funding and take measures to strengthen the higher education in the country.

Contracts were signed to start five steel plants; however these plants did not come into existence until the middle of the next five-year plan

Second Plan (1956-1961)

The second five-year plan focused on industry, especially heavy industry. Domestic production of industrial products was encouraged, particularly in the development of the public sector. The plan followed the Mahalanobis model, an economic development model developed by the Indian statistician Prasanta Chandra Mahalanobis in 1953. The plan attempted to determine the optimal allocation of investment between productive sectors in order to maximise long-run economic growth. It used the prevalent state of art techniques of operations research and optimization as well as the novel applications of statistical models developed at the Indian Statiatical Institute. The plan assumed a closed economy in which the main trading activity would be centred on importing capital goods.

Hydroelectric power projects and five steel mills at Bhilai, Durgapur, and Rourkela were established. Coal production was increased. More railway lines were added in the north east.

The Atomic Energy Commission was formed in 1957 with Homi J. Bhabha as the first chairman. The Tata Institute of Fundamental Research was established as a research institute. In 1957 a talent search and scholarship program was begun to find talented young students to train for work in nuclear power.

Third Plan (1961-1966)

The third plan stressed on agriculture and improving production of rice, but the brief Sino-Indian War in 1962 exposed weaknesses in the economy and shifted the focus towards defence. In 1965-1966, The war led to inflation and the priority was shifted to price stabilisation. The construction of dams continued. Many cement and fertilizer plants were also built. Punjab begun producing an abundance of wheat.

Many primary schools were started in rural areas. In an effort to bring democracy to the grassroot level, Panchayat elections were started and the states were given more development responsibilities.

State electricity boards and state secondary education boards were formed. States were made responsible for secondary and higher education. State road transportation corporations were formed and local road building became a state responsibility.

Harrod–Domar Model

The Harrod–Domar model is used in development economics to explain an economy's growth rate in terms of the level of saving and productivity of capital. It suggests that there is no natural reason for an economy to have balanced growth. The model was developed independently by Sir Roy F. Harrod in 1939 and Evsey Domar in 1946. The Harrod–Domar model was the precursor to the exogenous growth model.

Overview

According to the model there are three concepts of growth:

- Warranted growth
- Natural growth
- Actual growth.

Mathematical Formalism

Let Y represent output, which equals income, and let K equal the capital stock. S is total saving, s is the savings rate, and I is investment. $\ddot{a}$ stands for the rate of depreciation of the capital stock. The Harrod–Domar model makes the following *a priori* assumptions:

1. Output is a function of capital stock

2. The marginal product of capital is constant; the production function exhibits constant returns to scale. This implies capital's marginal and average products are equal.
3. Capital is necessary for output.
4. The product of the savings rate and output equals saving, which equals investment
5. The change in the capital stock equals investment less the depreciation of the capital stock.

Derivation of output growth rate: An alternative (and, perhaps, simpler) derivation is as follows, with dots (for example,) denoting percentage growth rates.

First, assumptions (1)–(3) imply that output and capital are linearly related (for readers with an economics background, this proportionality implies a capital-elasticity of output equal to unity). These assumptions thus generate equal growth rates between the two variables. That is,

Since the marginal product of capital, *c*, is a constant, we have

Next, with assumptions (4) and (5), we can find capital's growth rate as,

In summation, the savings rate times the marginal product of capital minus the depreciation rate equals the output growth rate. Increasing the savings rate, increasing the marginal product of capital, or decreasing the depreciation rate will increase the growth rate of output; these are the means to achieve growth in the Harrod–Domar model.

Conclusions

Although the Harrod–Domar model was initially created to help analyse the business cycle, it was later adapted to explain economic growth. Its implications were that growth depends on the quantity of labour and capital; more investment leads to capital accumulation, which generates economic growth. The model also had implications for less economically developed countries; labour is in plentiful supply in these countries but physical capital is not, slowing economic progress. LDCs do not have sufficient average incomes to enable high rates of saving, and therefore accumulation of the capital stock through investment is low.

The model implies that economic growth depends on policies to increase investment, by increasing saving, and using that investment more efficiently through technological advances. The model concludes that an economy does not find full employment and s growth rates naturally, similar to the Keynesian beliefs.

Criticisms of the Model

The main criticism of the model is the level of assumption, one being that there is no reason for growth to be sufficient to maintain full employment; this is based on the belief that the relative price of labour and capital is fixed, and that they are used in equal proportions. The model explains economic boom and bust by the assumption that investors are only influenced by output (known as the accelerator principle); this is now widely believed to be false.

In terms of development, critics claim that the model sees economic growth and development as the same; in reality, economic growth is only a subset of development. Another criticism is that the model implies poor countries should borrow to finance investment in capital to trigger economic growth; however, history has shown that this often causes repayment problems later.

The endogenity of savings: Perhaps the most important parameter in the Harrod–Domar model is the rate of savings. Can it be treated as a parameter that can be manipulated easily by policy? That depends on how much control the policy maker has over the economy. In fact, there are several reasons to believe that the rate of savings may itself be influenced by the overall lever of per capita income in the society, not to mention the distribution of that income among the population.

Mahalanobis Model

The Mahalanobis model is a model of economic development, created by Indian statistician Prasanta Chandra Mahalanobis in 1953. Mahalanobis became essentially the key economist of India's Second Five Year Plan, becoming subject to much of India's most dramatic economic debates.

The Feldman–Mahalanobis Model

The essence of the model is a shift in the pattern of industrial investment towards building up a domestic consumption goods sector. Thus the strategy suggests in order to reach a high standard in consumption, investment in building a capacity in the production of capital goods is firstly needed. A high enough capacity in the capital goods sector in the long-run expands the capacity in the production of consumer goods. The distinction between the two different types of goods was a clearer formulation of Marx's ideas in Das Kapital, and also helped people to better understand the extent of the trade off between the levels of immediate and future consumption. These ideas were however first introduced in 1928 by G.A. Feldman, a Soviet economist working for the GOSPLAN planning commission; presenting theoretical arguments of a two-department scheme of growth. There is no evidence that Mahalanobis knew of Feldman's approach, being kept behind the borders of the USSR. Due to the similarity of the two theories, the model is often referred to as the Feldman-Mahalanobis model.

Implementation of the model

The model was created as an analytical framework for India's Second Five Year Plan in 1955 by appointment of Prime Minister Jawaharlal Nehru, as India felt there was a need to introduce a formal plan model after the First Five Year Plan (1951-1956). The First Five Year Plan stressed investment for capital accumulation in the spirit of the one-sector Harrod–Domar model. It argued that production required capital and that capital can be accumulated through investment; the faster one accumulates, the higher the growth rate will be. The most fundamental criticisms came from Mahalanobis, who himself was working with a variant of it in 1951 and 1952. The criticisms were mostly around the model's inability to cope with the real constraints of the economy; it's ignoring of the fundamental choice problems of planning over time; and the lack of connection between the model and the actual selection of projects for governmental expenditure. Subsequently Mahalanobis introduced his celebrated two-sector model, which he later expanded into a four-sector version.

Assumptions

The assumptions under which the Mahalanobis model holds true are as follow:

- We assume a closed economy.
- The economy consists of two sectors: consumption goods sector C and capital goods sector K.
- Capital goods are *non-shiftable*.

- Full capacity production.
- Investment is determined by supply of capital goods.
- No changes in prices.
- Capital is the only scarce factor.
- Production of capital goods is independent of the production of consumer goods.

Basics of the Model

The full capacity output equation is as follows:

$$Y_t = Y_0 \left\{1 + \alpha_0 \frac{\lambda_k \beta_k + \lambda_c \beta_c}{\lambda_k \beta_k} \left[(1 + \lambda_k \beta_k)^t - 1\right]\right\}$$

In the model the growth rate is given by both the share of investment in the capital goods sector, ë$_k$, and the share of investment in the consumer goods sector, ë$_c$. If we choose to increase the value of ë$_k$ to be larger than ë$_c$, this will initially result in a slower growth in the short-run, but in the long run will exceed the former growth rate choice with a higher growth rate and an ultimately higher level of consumption. In other words, if this method is used, only in the long run will investment into capital goods produce consumer goods, resulting in no short run gains.

Criticisms

One of the most common criticisms of the model is that Mahalanobis pays hardly any attention to the savings constraint, which he assumes comes from the industrial sector. Developing countries however do not have this tendency, as the first stages of saving usually come from the agricultural sector. He also does not mention taxation, an important potential source of capital. A more serious criticism is the limitation of the assumptions under which this model holds, an example being the limitation of foreign trade. This cannot be justifiable to developing countries today. Also another criticism is that a country to use this model would have to be large enough to contain all the raw resources needed to be sustainable, so therefore this would not apply to smaller countries.

Empirical Case

Essentially the model was put into practise in 1956 as the

theoretical pathway of India's Second Five Year Plan. However after two years the first problems started to emerge. Problems such as unexpected and unavoidable costs contributed to increased money supply and growing inflation. The biggest problem was the fall in the foreign exchange reserve due to liberalised import policy and international tension, leading to modifications in the Second Plan in 1958. It was finally abandoned and replaced by the Third Five Year Plan in 1961.

Planning Commission (India)

The Planning Commission is an institution in the Government of India, which formulates India's Five-Year Plans, among other functions.

History

Rudimentary economic planning, deriving the sovereign authority of the state, first began in India in 1930s under the British Raj, and the colonial government of India formally established a planning board that functioned from 1944 to 1946. Private industrialists and economist formulated at least three development plans in 1944.

After India gained independence, a formal model of planning was adopted, and the planning commission, reporting directly to the Prime Minister of India was established. Accordingly, the Planning Commission was set up on 15 March 1950, with Prime Minister Jawaharlal Nehru as the chairman.

The first Five-year Plan was launched in 1951 and two subsequent five-year plans were formulated till 1965, when there was a break because of the Indo-Pakistan Conflict. Two successive years of drought, devaluation of the currency, a general rise in prices and erosion of resources disrupted the planning process and after three Annual Plans between 1966 and 1969, the fourth Five-year plan was started in 1969.

The Eighth Plan could not take off in 1990 due to the fast changing political situation at the Centre and the years 1990-91 and 1991-92 were treated as Annual Plans. The Eighth Plan was finally launched in 1992 after the initiation of structural adjustment policies.

For the first eight Plans the emphasis was on a growing public sector with massive investments in basic and heavy industries, but since the launch of the Ninth Plan in 1997, the emphasis on the public sector has become less pronounced and the current thinking on planning in the country, in general, is that it should increasingly be of an indicative nature.

Organisation

The composition of the Commission has undergone a lot of change since its inception. With the Prime Minister as the ex-officio Chairman, the committee has a nominated Deputy Chairman, who is given the rank of a full Cabinet Minister. Mr. Montek Singh Ahluwalia is presently the Deputy Chairman of the Commission.

Cabinet Ministers with certain important portfolios act as part-time members of the Commission, while the full-time members are experts of various fields like Economics, Industry, Science and General Administration.

The Commission works through its various divisions, of which there are three kind:

- General Planning Divisions
- Programme Administration Divisions.

The majority of experts in the Commission are economists, making the Commission the biggest employer of the Indian Economic Services.

India Planning

India planning is undertaken by the Planning Commission of India in order to improve the standard of living of the people belonging to the country. To improve the quality of life of the people, the resources of the country have to be utilized efficiently.

India planning has been done in various areas such as sports, education, labour, health, village industry, urban development, rural development, agriculture, industry, information technology, environment, real estate, infrastructure, and finance. The India Planning Commission has been set up in March, 1950 and it undertook to draw up 5 year plans for developing the Indian economy. In these plans the Planning Commission of India, emphasized particular spheres such as industry, employment, agriculture, education, and health. Till 2007, there have been 10 five year plans. All these plans have helped improve the quality of life of the people of India. In order to improve sports in India, the Sports Authority of India has been set up by the Indian government. This body sees to it that the infrastructure required for sports is upgraded regularly and kept in good condition. It also formulates new projects and gets funding from the government in order to promote sports in the country. Under India planning, education forms the most important area for it determines the future growth of the country. The department of higher education oversees all levels of education in India and is subsidized by the government of India heavily

For rural planning, India planning has set up a Rural Planning and Credit Department which is under the Reserve bank of India. This department formulates policies which help in rural development. It also extends credit for employment programs and agricultural activities in rural areas. Under India planning, local bodies have been set up in all states in order to develop urban areas. These urban local bodies such as the municipal corporation and the Panchayat see to it that the services and basic infrastructure are well maintained.

India planning has helped improve the quality of life of the people. The Indian government must make efforts so that it continues to do. India Planning has facilitated the utilization of the resources of the country for the common good of the people and also to develop the country.

India Planning Commission

India Planning Commission was set up in March, 1950 by the resolution of the Indian government. The Commission for India Planning was established in order to bring about a steady and swift rise in the living standards of Indian citizens.

The government sought to uplift the condition of India's teeming millions by exploiting the country's rich resources (natural and otherwise) efficiently, providing employment opportunities to all, and by increasing the production levels in the agricultural as well as industrial sectors.

The various functions of India Planning Commission are:

- To assess the country's resources
- To formulate 5 year plans that make an effective use of the country's resources

- To determine national priorities and allot resources to the plans
- To decide the machinery required to make the plans successful
- To make appraisals of the plans periodically in order to check their progress.

The composition of the India Planning Commission has changed a lot since its inception. At the head is the Prime Minister of the country who acts as the ex-officio chairman. The India Planning Commission has a deputy chairman who is nominated and the cabinet members who act as part-time members. The full-time members of the Indian Planning Commission are experts from various fields such as industry, science, general administration, and economics.

In 1951, the 1st 5 year plan was announced and the then Prime Minister, Jawaharlal Nehru was the chairman of that India Planning Commission. Till 1965, 2 consecutive 5 year plans had been formulated. After that, there was a pause in the launch of 5 year plans in India due to the Indo-Pakistan war. Again, in 1969, the 4th five year plan was launched and by 1992, the 8th five year plan was started. In all these 8 plans emphasis has been laid on the public sector, with huge investments being made in heavy and basic industries. But in 1997, with the launch of the 9th five year plan, the emphasis shifted from the public sector and became more indicative in nature. India Planning Commission has helped in the better utilization of the country's resources for the common good of the citizens. The Planning Commission is considered by many as the backbone of the country's progress and all-round development.

First Five Year Plan India

The first five year plan India (1951-1956) had been presented by the then Prime Minister Jawaharlal Nehru in the Indian Parliament on 8th December, 1951. The first five year plan had been made by the planning commission whose objective was to improve the standard of living of the people by effective use of the country's resources. In India, the first five year plan's total outlay was estimated to been worth Rs. 2,069 crore. In the first five year plan, this amount was allocated to various areas.

They are:

- Community and agriculture development
- Energy and irrigation
- Communications and transport
- Industry
- Land rehabilitation
- Social services.

The target of GDP growth in the first five year plan of India was 2.1% per year and the actual growth of GDP that was achieved had been 3.6% per year. This shows the extent to which the first five year plan in India had been successful. During the period of India first five year plan, many projects related to irrigation had been started, such as the Mettur Dam, Bhakra Dam, and Hirakud Dam. In the first five year plan of India, provisions have been made for the rehabilitation of agricultural workers who were landless. Apart from that financial allocation was also made for conservation of soil, experiments, and training in cooperative organizations. Increased provisions have also been made for the improvement of roads, civil aviation, railways, telegraphs, and posts. For the development of the basic industry which includes the manufacture of fertilizers and electrical equipment, provisions have been made in the Indian first five year plan. Emphasis has also been given to small scale and village indust

Second Five Year Plan India

Second five year plan India (1956-1961) intends to increase and carry forward the development that had been started by the first five year plan in India. These five year plans are formulated by the planning commission whose objective is to utilize the country's resources effectively, so that the standard of living of the people improves.

The various tasks of the second five year plan in India are:

- To increase by 25% the national income
- To make the country more industrialized
- To increase employment opportunities so that every citizen gets a job.

In India, the second five year plan focused on industry-more specifically on the heavy industry. The domestic production of industrial goods in the public sector was encouraged by the second five year plan in India. The total amount for development given allocated under the second five year plan in India was Rs. 4,800 crore. This money has been distributed under the second five year plan in India for the development of various sectors. They are:

- Mining and industry
- Community and agriculture development
- Power and irrigation
- Social services
- Communications and transport
- Miscellaneous.

During the second five year plan India, 5 steel plants in Jamshedpur, Durgapur, and Bhilai had been established, apart from a hydro-electric power project which was also undertaken and implemented. The production of coal increased during this period. Also, more railway lines were added in the northeast part of the country, during the Indian second five year plan. Land reform measures have been taken during the period of the second five year plan India, in order to remove the socioeconomic constraints of the rural population. The second five year plan India has, to a large extent, improved the living standards of the people.

Third Five Year Plan India

The third five year plan India (1961-1966) intended to make a more determined effort to develop the nation, carrying forward the legacy set by the previous two five year plans. These five year plans are formulated by the planning commission, the aim of which is to increase the quality of life of the citizens through effective use of the country's resources.

The various tasks of the third five year plan India are:

- To increase the national income by 5% per year
- To increase the production of agriculture so that the nation is self sufficient in food grains
- To provide employment opportunities for every citizen of the country
- To establish equality among all the people of the country.

In the earlier 2 five year plans, agriculture was not given a great deal of importance in spite of the fact that India's economy is still primarily agrarian. But in the third five year plan of India, more stress had been given to agriculture because increase in agricultural production would lead to the growth of the Indian economy. Sufficient sops and subsidies were allowed by the government for the agricultural sector under the third five year plan of India. In an effort to invite increased state participation to the India third five year plan, more responsibility was given to the states. Also, various organizations such as the Panchayat and Zila Parishads were set up at the block and district level in order to increase rural development. In India, the third five year plan have also laid emphasis on soil conservation, irrigation, afforestation, and dry farming. Many fertilizer and cement plants were built during the period of the third five year plan India. Stress had been given to the development of social services and education in India. The third five year plan in India had, to a large extent, improved the quality of life of Indian citizens, and played a crucial role in the growth and development of the country.

The Planning Commission was set up by a Resolution of the Government of India in March 1950 in pursuance of declared objectives of the Government to promote a rapid rise in the standard of living of the people by efficient exploitation of the resources of the country, increasing production and offering opportunities to all for employment in the service of the community. The Planning Commission was charged with the responsibility of making assessment of all resources of the country, augmenting deficient resources, formulating plans for the most effective and balanced utilisation of resources and determining priorities. Jawaharlal Nehru was the first Chairman of the Planning Commission.

The first Five-year Plan was launched in 1951 and two subsequent five-year plans were formulated till 1965, when there was a break because of the Indo-Pakistan Conflict. Two successive years of drought, devaluation of the currency, a general rise in prices and erosion of resources disrupted the planning process and after three Annual Plans between 1966 and 1969, the fourth Five-year plan was started in 1969.

The Eighth Plan could not take off in 1990 due to the fast changing political situation at the Centre and the years 1990-91 and 1991-92 were treated as Annual Plans. The Eighth Plan was finally launched in 1992 after the initiation of structural adjustment policies.

2

Industrialisation in India

To discuss the topic "The Indian approach to industrialisation", this essay is divided into several parts. Firstly, the reasons for, and policies of industrialisation are discussed. The theoretical framework is finished by identifying indicators to be used in the evaluation of the success of such policies. The second section gives a rough overview of the development of industrialisation in India since independence. The third section goes into more detail and provides information about some specific and important areas for industrialisation. The fourth section uses the defined indicators to measure the success of India's two main approaches to industrialisation and evaluates the results. The fifth section describes the main problems India faces today and in the future. Last but not least, the sixth section informs about current trends in Indian policy.

Theoretical Framework for Industrialisation

Before analysing the Indian approach, we want to introduce the aims of industrialisation, give a rough overview of the industrialisation strategies for Less Developed Countries (LDCs) and identify indicators for the evaluation of the success of industrialisation policies.

Why Industrialisation?

What are the ultimate objectives of economic development? Different governments may have different objectives in mind. Generally, however, they will include a faster growth of national income, alleviation of poverty, and reduction of income inequalities.

But how is industrialisation expected to contribute to these goals? The experience of industrial economies shows a close association between development and industrial expansion. But industry is also thought to provide certain spillovers which would benefit other activities: enhancement of skills, training of managers, dispersion of technology, etc. Moreover, pessimism about the prospects of food and raw materials made the substitution of domestic for imported manufactured goods seem the most promising route to development for many countries.

Industrialisation and Foreign Trade

Economists and policymakers in the developing countries have long agreed on the role of government in providing infrastructure and maintaining stable macroeconomic policies. But they have disagreed on policies toward trade and industry. The form of government intervention in this area is the distinguishing feature of alternative development strategies.

A convenient and instructive way to approach the complex issues of appropriate trade policies for development is to set these specific policies in the context of a broader Less Developed Countries strategy of looking outward or inward. Outward-looking development policies encourage not only free trade but also the free movement of capital, workers, enterprises, the multinational enterprise, and an open system of communications. By contrast, inward-looking development policies stress the need for LDCs to evolve their own styles of development and to control their own destiny. Within these two broad philosophical approaches to development, a lively debate has been carried out between the free traders, who advocate outward-looking export promotion strategies of industrialisation, and the protectionists, who are proponents of inward-looking import substitution strategies.

The advocates of import substitution (IS) – the protectionists – believe that LDCs should substitute domestic production of previously imported simple consumer goods and extend this later to a wider range of more sophisticated manufactured items – all behind the protection of high tariffs and quotas on imports. In the long run, IS advocates cite the benefits of greater domestic industrial diversification and the ultimate ability to export previously protected manufactured goods, as economies of scale, low labour costs, and the positive externalities of learning by doing cause domestic prices to become more competitive with world prices.

By contrast, advocates of export promotion (EP) of both primary and manufactured goods cite the efficiency and growth benefits of free trade and competition, the importance of substituting large world markets for narrow domestic markets, the distorting price and cost effects of protection, and the tremendous success of the East Asian export-oriented economies of South Korea, Singapore, and Hong Kong.

The balance of the debate has swung back and forth, with the protectionists predominating in the 1950s and 1960s, and the export promoters gaining the upper hand in the late 1970s and in the 1980s and 1990s, especially among Western and World Bank economists.

Indicators for Measuring Economic Development

Of course, any development policy has to be assessed by measuring the economic development it effects. India's first Prime Minister Jawaharlal Nehru declared on the eve of the departure of the British, on 14 August 1947, that India's task in the future included "the ending of poverty and ignorance and disease and inequality of opportunity".

These measures will be used to determine the success of the inward-looking policies he initiated, as well as to compare their success with the success of the reform policies. Therefore, growth of income per capita, alleviation of poverty and reduction of income inequalities are amongst the most important indicators.

To measure advances regarding inequality of opportunity and ignorance, several indicators pertaining to education and health will be used. These are two important public goods to which every individual is entitled; both for their intrinsic importance and for their enhancement of instrumental personal, social and process roles, and also empowerment and distributive roles.

History of Industrialisation in India

This section gives a rough overview of the history of industrialisation in India. Several areas will be discussed in more detail in the following section.

Colonial Rule

Under colonial rule, India, as with most other developing countries, followed a non-industrial model. But many Indians believed that progress was retarded by this. It was believed that true economic progress lay in industrialisation; Smith's and Ricardo's ideas of international specialisation and mutually advantageous free trade were rejected, at least until India became an exporter of more sophisticated goods.

Industrialisation Since Independence

India's first Prime Minister, Jawaharlal Nehru, Premier from 1947 to 1964, saw industrialisation as the key to alleviating poverty. Industrialisation not only promised self-sufficiency for his nation that had just regained political sovereignty, but also offered external economies accruing from technical progress. Believing the potential of agriculture and exports to be limited, Indian governments taxed agriculture by skewing the terms of trade against it and emphasising import substitution, thus giving priority to heavy industry.

Nehru believed a powerful state with a centralised planned economy to be essential if the country was to industrialise rapidly. The Industries (Development and Regulation) Act (IDRA) in 1951 laid the foundations for this administrative control on industrial capacity. But, over time, the licensing requirements became increasingly stringent and were accompanied by a gamut of procedures that required clearance by a number of disparate and uncoordinated ministries.

In order to pursue IS, the Import Trade Control Order of 1955 subjected almost all imports to quantitative restrictions in the form of import licenses. These were supplemented by tariffs at rates that were among the highest in the developing world.

Indian state intervention in industrial development has been extensive. Unlike many East Asian countries, which used state intervention to build strong private sector industries, India opted for state control over key industries. At different times, nationalised industries included chemicals, electric power, steel, transportation, life insurance, portions of the coal and textile industries, and banking. To promote these industries the government not only levied high tariffs and imposed import restrictions, but also subsidised the nationalised firms, directed investment funds to them, and controlled both land use and many prices.

Under Prime Minister Indira Gandhi (1966-77), two major shifts took place in the role of the state. First, the neglect of agriculture was reversed through state activism in subsidising new seeds and fertilisers, agricultural credit, and rural electrification. The green revolution took off and by the mid-1970s India was self-sufficient in grain. The second shift was the further tightening of state control over every aspect of the economy. Banks were nationalised, trade was increasingly restricted, price controls were imposed on a wide range of products, and foreign investment was squeezed.

In 1973, dealings in foreign exchanges as well as foreign investment came to be regulated by the Foreign Exchange and Regulation Act (FERA). The act virtually shut out the inflow of new technology from abroad in the 1970s and 1980s, particularly when these involved large equity participation.

The Indian system of state planning went far beyond the usual inward-looking industrialisation policies that most developing countries pursued after World War II. The government regulated the most basic business decisions for all firms above a certain size: borrowing, investment, capacity utilisation, pricing and distribution.

The over-restrictive, and often self-defeating nature of the regulatory framework, began to become evident by the late 1960s and early 1970s. Comprehensive planning was increasingly criticised as planned targets were not met and many plans were not even implemented. The lack of success in some dimensions led to a new and more restrictive set of regulations. One example is the attempt to reserve sectors for small industries and to restrict the growth of large firms.

Beginning in the early 1980s, a mild trend towards deregulation started. Economic reforms were introduced, starting to liberalise trade, industrial and financial policies, while subsidies, tax concessions, and the depreciation of the currency improved export incentives. These measures helped GDP growth to accelerate to over 5% per year during the 1980s, compared to 3.5% during the 1970s, and reduced poverty more rapidly. However India's most fundamental structural problems were only partially addressed. Tariffs continued to be among the highest in the world, and quantitative restrictions remained pervasive.

Moreover, a significant government influence continued in the allocation of credit to firms and a discouragement of foreign investment. Relatively inefficient public enterprises, controlling nearly 20% of GDP, remained a drag on economic growth.

The government expanded antipoverty schemes, especially rural employment schemes, but only a small fraction of the rising subsidies actually reached the poor. Competition between political parties drove subsidies up at every election. The resulting fiscal deficits (8.4% of GDP in 1985) contributed to a rising current account deficit. India's foreign exchange reserves were virtually exhausted by mid-1991 when a new government headed by Narasimha Rao came to power.

In July 1991, India launched a second major economic reform program. The government committed itself to promoting a competitive economy that would be open to trade and foreign investment. Measures were introduced to reduce the government's influence in corporate investment decisions. Much of the industrial-licensing system was dismantled, and areas once closed to the private sector were opened up. These included electricity generation, areas of the oil industry, heavy industry, air transport, roads and some telecommunications. Foreign investment was suddenly welcomed.

Greater global integration was encouraged with a significant reduction in the use of import licenses and tariffs (down to 150% from 400%), an elimination of subsidies for exports, and the introduction of a foreign-exchange market. Since April 1992, there has been no need to obtain any license or permit to carry out import-export trade.

As of April 1, 1993, trade is completely free, barring only a small list of imports and exports that are either regulated or banned. The WTO estimated an average import tariff of 71% in 1993 which has been reduced to 40% in 1995. With successive additional monetary reforms, the rupee, since 1995, can nearly be considered a fully convertible currency at market rates. India now has a much more open economy.

Special Areas of Economic Policy

After giving a rough overview of the history of industrialisation, this chapter provides more detailed information about the areas of human factors for industrialisation, structure of foreign investment, and the process of privatisation.

Human Factors for Industrialisation

A very necessary ingredient for promoting industrialisation and technological change is the investment in human capital. India's current average adult literacy rate is low at 52%. There are large inequalities between males (literacy: 64%) and females (literacy: 39%), between urban and rural areas, and between different social classes. Low levels of female education in India are due to the gender division of labour. Females are expected to spend most of their life in domestic work and child rearing. Secondly, the practice of dowry and the ideology of hypergamous marriage can turn female education into a liability. An educated girl is likely to be more expensive to marry off, thus female education tends to be a threat to the social order. Illiteracy is widespread not only in older groups, but also among young boys and girls, particularly in rural areas. The remarkable neglect of elementary education in India is all the more striking given the widespread recognition, in the contemporary world, of the importance of basic education for economic development. Primary education in India is not compulsory. However those who receive primary education and make it through secondary school have an excellent chance of getting a high-class University education. India has a huge supply of people with more education than they can use.

Amartya Sen argued that there were deep-seated class biases in the pressures that have determined Indian educational priorities, and that the inequalities in education are, in fact, a reflection of the inequalities of economic and social powers of different groups in India. India's hierarchical, Brahmin-dominated society has been noticeably casual about primary education; resources have been poured into the higher education that benefits the upper class.

The persistence of endemic illiteracy and educational background in India generally limits the freedom and well-being of the Indian masses and has a direct role in the relative deprivation of women in particular. Elementary education is extremely important for a successful integration in the world market and if the process of growth were more 'participatory' it could raise the income-earning power of large parts of the nation. Even if India's high technology industries, such as modern computer software or engineering products had an accelerated growth, the bulk of the Indian population would benefit only marginally.

Foreign Investment Policy Instruments

Since independence, new foreign investment has been rigidly controlled in line with established development thinking. Investment was mostly restricted to industries where it was felt that the acquisition of foreign technology was important, or where the promise of exports was convincing. The FERA was a landmark. In most industries, foreign shareholdings in rupee companies had to be reduced to 40%. The relative importance of foreign ownership in the private corporate sector fell significantly in the next decades. The attitude towards foreign investment began to change in 1985 as a part of Gandhi's drive for advanced technology. Despite this, looking at 1988 shows how poorly India fared in attracting private foreign investment. Net Private Foreign Investment to India (in million US$) was $280. This is compared to her Asian competitors with figures of $2344 (China), $1093 (Thailand) and $986 (Philippines).

Since the liberalisation in, mid-1991 India has become a magnet for foreign investment. A noteworthy feature is the dramatic speed of approvals, some taking only a week. Automatic approval of projects in 34 industrial sectors is permitted. The constraint that foreign investment should reach only 40% was relaxed to 51%. In certain sectors, such as infrastructure and computer software, the ownership can also be as high as 74%. In some sectors such as transport infrastructure, full foreign ownership is permitted and even encouraged.

Foreign direct investment rose from $170 million in 1991-92 to $1.3 billion in 1994-95. India is targeting foreign direct investment of at least $10 billion annually by the turn of the century. It attracted a total of $2.4 billion in 1996-97 and $3.4 billion in 1997-98. Foreign direct investment is nearly 25 times higher than it was before the economy was liberalised.

The government in New Delhi is continuing to work toward reforming long-standing policies to make the country more "investor friendly"; a move that continues to heighten US interest in the country. A growing number of US companies, motivated by an increasingly favourable investment climate and the country's huge reserves of both human and natural resources, have seriously begun to consider investing there. US investment has been more than 24% of the total investment since 1991. In 1995 approximately

$3.5 billion of US foreign investment flowed into India. The US continues to be the leading investor in India. The US is followed by other more 'traditional' investors like the U.K. (6.4%), Israel (5.9%), Mauritius (4.6%), Japan (4.2%) and Germany (4.1%). Most of the investment interest has been in the telecommunications, oil refining, automobile and transportation sectors, with other projects developing in the electronics, software and electrical equipment industries.

Revitalisation of the Indian Private Sector

India has always been a trading nation. Centuries of alien rule and decades of socialism did not stamp out the Indian entrepreneurial spirit. The Statement of Industrial Policy 1991 reduced the list of industries reserved for the public sector from 17 to 6. In 1992/93, 104 out of a total of 237 central public sector enterprises made losses. With few exceptions, the inefficiency of public enterprises, which generate 17% of GDP, has continued to be a serious issue. It is clear that there is a *prima facie* case for privatisation on grounds of efficiency. However, the strength of the case for privatisation varies with the type of industry.

Now exposed to international competition, Indian companies are forming alliances with each other to face the challenges of the future. It is now even possible for Indian firms to merge with other companies. Procter & Gamble merged its operations with Godrej Soaps. Coca Cola acquired Parle, its erstwhile competitor, thus extending the cola wars to new exotic lands. Companies are enjoying the benefits of economies of scale and synergy. As larger and stronger groups emerge, they will have the resources necessary to invest in upgrading technology and will become more competitive.

Evaluation of Industrialisation in India

The indicators named above will be used to evaluate the success of Indian industrialisation policies. A distinction will be made between the period from Independence until 1980, characterised by inward-looking policies such as IS, and the period from 1980 until today, characterised by reforms and the opening up of the Indian economy. The following analysis with indicators compares the achievements of these two periods only. Absolute statements of Indian achievements follow later on.

It must be emphasised that the analysed data conceals sharp disparities within India between development-oriented states and laggards, between women and men, between adults and children, and between city and countryside. Different states have progressed at differing paces and, even within states, different regions have achieved markedly varied results. Even more noticeable than geographic differences in poverty reduction are the inequalities that persist across gender, caste and ethnic groups. Social indicators for women – literacy, for example – are distinctly lower than for men, and the level of scheduled castes and tribes in both economic and social achievements is still well below the national average.

Growth of National Income

Growth of national income in GNP per capita in India was about 1.4% in the years from 1960 to 1980. The effects of the reforms of the 1980s are reflected in growth figures: the average GNP per capita growth increased to 3.25%. And with further opening up in the 1990s, the GNP per capita reaches new heights with 3.8% average growth in the period from 1987 to 1997.

Alleviation of Poverty

In the early 1950s, about half of India's population was living in poverty. Since then, poverty has been declining slowly. The poverty reduction was given new impetus by the reforms: falling from around 55% in 1974 to just under 35% in 1994 by a headcount index. In the 1980s and 1990s, poverty reached historically low levels. Still, because of India's rapid population growth rate, the relative reduction of poverty has not been sufficient to reduce the absolute number of poor which increased from about 164 million in 1951 to 312 million in 1993-94.

Reduction of Income Inequalities

The reduction of income inequalities has only made slight advances. The biggest advances were made mostly before the reforms. On the other hand, one of the biggest increases in inequality happened in the late 1970s, and the developments for the late 1980s/early 1990s. Compared to other low-income economies, the inequality is relatively low.

Education

From 1960 to 1977 the reduction of illiteracy was only 11%.

From 1978 to 1995, it was 25%, thus much higher. Of course, there are also long-term developments involved here, so that the higher reduction in the second period might be partially due to actions taken in the first period.

Health

Life expectancy, used as an indicator of health, has increased constantly since independence. During the period from 1960 to 1980, it increased from 43 years to 52 years, which is an increase of 21% in 20 years. From 1980 to 1995 it grew to 62 years, which is a 19% increase in only 15 years. This means that the growth of this indicator has increased by a rate of 24% compared to the previous period.

Even clearer is the improvement in the reduction of infant mortality. This was reduced by 25% in the period 1960 to 1995 and a further reduction of 45% took place from 1980 to 1995. This is partially due to better education of mothers, as well as to an improved economic situation of parents.

Independence-1980

The system of state planning constrained growth of the private sector by allowing it to expand only with government permission. But despite the massive interventions, economic progress was made during the period following independence. The per capita GDP grew at a respectable rate of 1.4% per annum from the late 1940s into the 1970s. Both famine and poverty were significantly reduced during this period.

Nevertheless, most economists argued that the interventions lowered India's economic growth rates to a level which was not adequate for a country that saved and invested over one-fifth of its GDP. With few major producers of many key industrial products, the concentration of domestic production was very high, inviting monopolistic pricing.

Moreover, as the world economy grew and as beneficial opportunities for growth through trade expanded, India paid an increasing price for its economic isolation.

The Indian system of state planning has been described as combining "the worst of socialism and capitalism, by suppressing growth while failing even to deliver the social welfare that communist systems provided".

1980 – Mid-1990s

The liberalisation that started in the 1980s and gained further momentum in mid-1991 proved the critics of the old system right.

Per capita GNP reached historically high growth rates; industrial output-growth averaged 8.4% in 1994-95; exports were up by 27%; inflation dropped below 10%; the current account deficit is below 1% of GDP; foreign-exchange reserves are high at $20 billion; and food stocks have hit an all-time high of 37m tonnes.

The long neglected private sector today generates two-thirds of India's GDP. The World Bank describes the change of the state's role from that of principal investor to that of facilitator of entrepreneurship. Thus, over the course of a few years, the old national consensus on socialism has given way to a new consensus on liberalisation.

India – A Perspective

It should not be forgotten, that despite all mentioned advances, India is still a low-income, developing country. It has an economy slightly smaller than Belgium's with a GNP per capita of $390. Only about half of its 960 million people can read. Only 14% of the population has access to clean sanitation-a lower proportion than anywhere else except for parts of Sudan and Burkina Faso. According to the World Bank, 63% of India's under-five-year olds are malnourished. The infant mortality rates of two Indian states is above the sub-Saharan average. About 40% of the world's desperately poor live in India.India's progress in fighting poverty is modest when compared with some of its Asian neighbours. Between 1970 and 1993, the proportion of Indonesia's population living in poverty dropped from 58% to 8% – a greater decline in a shorter period of time. According to the World Bank,

"it is through rapid growth that India will be able to reduce poverty and generate the resources to invest in the health and education of its people who will in turn sustain this growth, [as] overall growth accounted for the lion's share of poverty reduction: 80% of the decline in the number of households below the poverty line between 1951 and 1970, and almost 100% since 1970".

But India, like many developing countries that adopted a philosophy of government intervention with import substitution policies, is finding that economic reform can often be a slow, incremental process. Complications continue. Domestic producers will resist tariff reductions that subject them to increased competition. Government bureaucrats will try to maintain the power and influence they acquired during periods of substantial government involvement in economic decision making. The reforms so far are a positive step but must be extended and accelerated if India is to catch up with the East Asian tigers.

It is not possible to condemn the inward-looking policies as totally wrong. Some advances were made and no one can say what would have happened if India had followed another strategy. In our opinion, the idea that industrialisation was important for India in the 1950s was right, as the share of commodities in world trade is constantly decreasing. However, the view that exports are not important and that India could go its own way was wrong. By protectionism and interventions, India fostered the establishment of industries. India didn't create an efficient private sector but a huge, inefficient public sector, and protectionism lowered the competitiveness of India's economy. Furthermore, the neglect of exports led to the fact that India's share of world trade decreased from 2% in 1950 to 0.5% in 1990.

In our opinion, India should have followed an EP-strategy as the Asian tigers did and shouldn't have created the system of state planning and such a large public sector; both of which led to huge inefficiencies. The success of the recent opening up of the economy illustrates the potential India has. Therefore, India should proceed in this direction to encourage further economic growth.

Still, economic growth alone is not enough. Amartya Sen emphasises that growth must be "high and participatory". But even today, India's "have-nots are treated virtually as are-nots" due to the caste-system and are neglected. Sen toured India in January 1999 to communicate his message that Indians are woefully underfed, undereducated and sickly, even by the standards of poor countries. The impact remains to be seen. India's biggest current problems will be covered in the following section.'

India's Current Problems Regarding Industrialisation

After evaluating important indicators for industrialisation and giving a summary of industrialisation since independence, we will now take a more detailed look at some specific areas for future industrial development in India.

Infrastructure

Perhaps the biggest problem for doing business in India is the woeful state of its infrastructure. Consider this: it takes four days for a truck to travel the 900 miles between India's national capital New Delhi and its commercial capital Bombay. It takes months to get connected to the power supply in any Indian city, and several years to get a telephone connection in large cities.

Poor infrastructure is acting as a drag on the Indian economy, and the Indian government is now attracting private domestic and foreign investment to build the backbone of a modern economy. A recent report estimated that investment in infrastructure would rise from 5.5% of GDP in 1997, to about 7% in 2000/01. This includes massive improvements in telecommunications, power, energy, and transport.

India has recognised the vital role telecommunications play in the growth of the economy. The Indian telecom sector was wholly under government ownership and control until recently and was characterised by under-investment and outdated equipment. There is vast potential for extending these services in India, which has one of the world's smallest telephone densities of 1.3 per 100 people, compared with the world average of 10 per 100. Advanced communication services such as fax, data transmission, and leased circuits are becoming increasingly common. Foreign collaboration is also being encouraged in cellular phones and paging systems. In the telecommunications sector, estimates for regional investment needs range from $40 billion a year, to as high as $70 billion a year by the end of the century.

The power problems are severe in India with three-hour-a-day power cuts and damaging voltage fluctuations that require companies to generate their own power. Investment in energy is a sound way of increasing manufacturing activity. If all 49 proposed private sector power projects are implemented, these would add a total of 20,000 megawatts to India's current capacity of 66,000mW. However it should be noted that India's energy demand is growing at 8-10% a year.

As part of India's liberalisation efforts, the transportation sector has been opened to private investment. The government is offering incentives to invest $4.7 billion to construct and operate bypass roads, highways, bridges, railways, and ports.

Health and Education

HIV/AIDS is a newly emerging threat to India's public health. About 3 million people in India may be affected. Malnutrition also continues to impede India's development. Prejudices against women and girls are reflected in the demographic ratio of 929 females for every 1,000 males.

To support India's goal of achieving universal primary education, the World Bank is supplementing increased state government expenditure. This has boosted school enrolment, particularly among girls and disadvantaged children, and is improving the quality of instruction and learning achievement.

Amartya Sen reckons that India could enrol all its children in primary school by spending an additional 0.5-1% of GDP. Providing basic health and education is not expensive where labour is cheap. But health and education indicators, while showing some progress, still remain among the world's lowest.

Public Sector

Another big problem is India's notoriously bloated and inefficient public sector. The World Bank has turned down applications for power loans worth $750 million for projects in some states because of mismanagement in their government. Many electricity boards have become insolvent as a result of providing electricity at extremely subsidised rates and ignoring large-scale thefts of electricity. State governments have been unable or unwilling to take the politically unpalatable decisions needed to make their electricity boards viable.

The most telling evidence of the cost of delaying reform is the sheer effort companies have to expend to cope with the country's labyrinthine bureaucracy. For example, foreign investors continue to seek permission from the Foreign Investment Promotion Board, even though their plans are covered by the automatic approvals system.

Corruption

An immediate threat to India's governance is not the tottering coalition governments or the BJP, but corruption. The combination of a state-run economy and weak political institutions created all too many opportunities for crooked politicians and bureaucrats.

Worse still for the business community is that the government itself is the fountain-head of corruption. This is particularly serious in view of the huge importance of the government sector in India's economy.

Corruption has become ubiquitous at all levels and is accepted by everyone. Many Indian businessmen feel that liberalisation of the economy will have no impact on reducing the corruption that has become so well entrenched. The influx of foreign companies is already unleashing a new wave of even greater corruption. A survey of 183 US firms conducted by the US embassy in 1995 revealed that US investors rated corruption in India as the third worst problem they faced after red tape and a lack of electric power.

The blame for the deluge of corruption in India lies in the lack of transparency in the rules of governance, extremely cumbersome official procedures, excessive and unregulated discretionary power in the hands of politicians and bureaucrats, who are prone to abuse it, and a lax judiciary.

Tax Problems

Tax reforms have been seeking to transform India's tax system from one with high differential tax rates falling on a narrow base, into one with tax rates at moderate levels falling on a broad base. The 1995 fiscal budget reduced taxes on corporate income, and a major reform of excise taxes has been implemented to make it resemble a value-added tax more closely.

But the government's income is also constricted by an inefficient taxation system. Rural areas are not taxed because they contain such a large pool of voters and no government has had the political will to change this. Income tax is skilfully dodged. This leaves the government with excise and customs duties, which represent two thirds of all taxes.

Labour Market

India needs greater labour market flexibility to make its companies more competitive and its economy more productive. Politically powerful labour unions have stifled most efforts at serious reform or privatisation of India's largest public sector enterprises, including most banks, all insurance companies, and many major industries, even though privatisation would probably cost the jobs of no more than 1.1% of the urban labour market. India's labour laws hinder efficiency and growth.

Financial Sector

India's financial sector still cannot effectively mobilise and mediate capital to respond to economic changes. The resulting high cost of capital makes Indian industry and exports less competitive. In spite of recent improvements, India's equity markets are still too thin and volatile to inspire great confidence on the part of domestic or foreign investors. Bond markets are practically non-existent. Liberalisation of the insurance industry, which would greatly improve the investing of India's substantial savings, now 26% of GDP, has been stymied. India's banking system remains flawed, with the dominant state-owned banks still carrying bad loans amounting to 15 to 25% of their total.

Outlook

The arrival of a BJP-led government in March looked like a setback for freer trade. It took two steps away from trade liberalisation. Firstly, India's anti-dumping procedures were tightened. Secondly, the Finance Minister imposed an extra tariff of 4% in June. However, it is too early to conclude that India is returning to protectionism. The government insists that tariffs were increased to raise revenue, not to protect Indian business.

BJP Strategy Regarding Foreign Investment

BJP party leaders seem keen to limit foreign investment in all areas other than infrastructure. They are worried that Indian culture will be eroded by western consumerism such as food habits brought in by Kentucky Fried Chicken or McDonald's. Such sentiments cause alarm.

"Foreign investors are not exactly queuing up to enter India, and this attitude will scare away those who are weighing up the possibilities of doing business here," cautions a top executive with a foreign investment bank in Bombay. In its defence, the BJP says that while it seeks to protect domestic industry and reserve "India for Indians", it does not intend to take back the reforms. But approved and actual foreign direct investment already shrank between January and July 1998. Approvals totalled only $4.7 billion, compared with $7.1 billion in the same period in 1997 and actual inflows slid to $1.6 billion from $1.9 billion.

Furthermore the BJP's decision to conduct five nuclear tests in May 1998 underscored India's reputation for unpredictability and highlighted the vulnerability of infrastructure investment to international and domestic political pressures. The sanctions imposed by the US on India include bans on private banking assistance to the Indian government and pressure on multinational lenders such as the International Monetary Fund to withhold loans. The sanctions hit the Indian economy and Indian companies generally, and were potentially very onerous for foreign developers.

On the other hand, the government recently encouraged foreign direct investment. In July 1998 it put forward a plan allowing foreign companies to take stakes of up to 26% in Indian insurance companies, having resisted opening the insurance market to foreigners in the past. "Automatic" approval of foreign investment of up to 100% was extended to more sectors of industry.

Recent Development of the Macroeconomic Situation

The macroeconomic situation is also causing concern. After a year of patting itself on the back for escaping the Asian crisis, the Indian government is now sitting up at some spine-chilling signs that the economy hasn't been unscathed after all.

India's gross fiscal deficit will rise to 6.6% of GDP from a planned 5.7% in 1998, forcing the government to keep borrowing and pushing up interest rates. But the government's infighting and inability to push through much-touted economic reform bills raises doubts as to whether it can tackle these problems.

The ballooning trade deficit comes on top of sluggish industrial production, high inflation (a 9% annual rate in the first half of November), and an expanding budget deficit. Currency devaluations in the rest of Asia have made Indian exports even less competitive than they were previously.

The current deficit of $2 billion has been pushed to the highest level since 1991. The rising deficit is financed by foreign-exchange reserves, and is expected to put upward pressure on the rupee.

On the other hand, GDP growth is forecast to move upwards to 6.4% in 1999. This follows a slowdown to 5.1% in 1998 due to a 1.5% decline in agricultural production, slowing exports, and industrial growth. Factor-cost GDP is forecast to expand by an annual average of 6.7% until 2002-2003.

Overall, it remains to be seen how entrenched the reforms are in India in the face of more difficult and troubled economic conditions.

Government of India Ministry of Industry

Statement on Industrial Policy

Pandit Jawaharlal Nehru laid the foundations of modern India. His vision and determination have left a lasting impression on every facet of national endeavour since Independence. It is due to his initiative that India now has a strong and diversified industrial base and is a major industrial nation of the world. The goals and objectives set out for the nation by Pandit Nehru on the eve of Independence, namely, the rapid agricultural and industrial development of our country, rapid expansion of opportunities for gainful employment, progressive reduction of social and economic disparities, removal of poverty and attainment of self-reliance remain as valid today as at the time Pandit Nehru first set them out before the nation. Any industrial policy must contribute to the realisation of these goals and objectives at an accelerated pace. The present statement of industrial policy is inspired by these very concerns, and represents a renewed initiative towards consolidating the gains of national reconstruction at this crucial stage.

2. In 1948, immediately after Independence, Government introduced the Industrial Policy Resolution. This outlined the approach to industrial growth and development. It emphasised the importance to the economy of securing a continuous increase in production and ensuring its equitable distribution. After the adoption of the Constitution and the socioeconomic goals, the Industrial Policy was comprehensively revised and adopted in 1956. To meet new challenges, from time to time, it was modified through statements in 1973, 1977 and 1980.

3. The Industrial Policy Resolution of 1948 was followed by the Industrial Policy Resolution of 1956 which had as its objective the acceleration of the rate of economic growth and the speeding up of industrialisation as a means of achieving a socialist pattern of society. In 1956, capital was scarce and the base of

entrepreneurship not strong enough. Hence, the 1956 Industrial Policy Resolution gave primacy to the role of the State to assume a predominant and direct responsibility for industrial development.

4. The Industrial Policy statement of 1973, inter alia, identified high-priority industries where investment from large industrial houses and foreign companies would be permitted.

5. The Industrial Policy Statement of 1977 laid emphasis on decentralisation and on the role of small-scale, tiny and cottage industries.

6. The Industrial Policy Statement of 1980 focused attention on the need for promoting competition in the domestic market, technological upgradation and modernisation. The policy laid the foundation for an increasingly competitive export based and for encouraging foreign investment in high-technology areas. This found expression in the Sixth Five Year Plan which bore the distinct stamp of Smt. Indira Gandhi. It was Smt. Indira Gandhi who emphasised the need for productivity to be the central concern in all economic and production activities.

7. These policies created a climate for rapid industrial growth in the country. Thus on the eve of the Seventh Five Year Plan, a broad-based infrastructure had been built up. Basic industries had been established. A high degree of self-reliance in a large number of items-raw materials, intermediates, finished goods-had been achieved. New growth centres of industrial activity had emerged, as had a new generation of entrepreneurs. A large number of engineers, technicians and skilled workers had also been trained.

8. The Seventh Plan recognised the need to consolidate on these strengths and to take initiatives to prepare Indian industry to respond effectively to the emerging challenges. A number of policy and procedural changes were introduced in 1985 and 1986 under the leadership of Shri Rajiv Gandhi aimed at increasing productivity, reducing costs and improving quality. The accent was on opening the domestic market to increased competition and readying our industry to stand on its own in the face of international competition. The public sector was freed from a number of constraints and given a larger measure of autonomy. The technological and managerial modernisation of industry was pursued as the key instrument for increasing productivity and improving our competitiveness in the world. The net result of all

these changes was that Indian industry grew by an impressive average annual growth rate of 8.5% in the Seventh Plan period.

9. Government is pledged to launching a reinvigorated struggle for social and economic justice, to end poverty and unemployment and to build a modern, democratic, socialist, prosperous and forward-looking India. Such a society can be built if India grows as part of the world economy and not in isolation.

10. While Government will continue to follow the policy of self-reliance, there would be greater emphasis placed on building up our ability to pay for imports through our own foreign exchange earnings. Government is also committed to development and utilisation of indigenous capabilities in technology and manufacturing as well as its upgradation to world standards.

11. Government will continue to pursue a sound policy framework encompassing encouragement of entrepreneurship, development of indigenous technology through investment in research and development, bringing in new technology, dismantling of the regulatory system, development of the capital markets and increasing competitiveness for the benefit of the common man. The spread of industrialisation to backward areas of the country will be actively promoted through appropriate incentives, institutions and infrastructure investments.

12. Government will provide enhanced support to the small-scale sector so that it flourishes in an environment of economic efficiency and continuous technological upgradation.

13. Foreign investment and technology collaboration will be welcomed to obtain higher technology, to increase exports and to expand the production base.

14. Government will endeavour to abolish the monopoly of any sector or any individual enterprise in any field of manufacture, except on strategic or military considerations and open all manufacturing activity to competition.

15. The Government will ensure that the public sector plays its rightful role in the evolving socioeconomic scenario of the country. Government will ensure that the public sector is run on business lines as envisaged in the Industrial Policy Resolution of 1956 and would continue to innovate and lead in strategic areas of national importance. In the 1950s and 1960s, the principal instrument for controlling the commanding heights of the economy

was investment in the capital of key industries. Today, the State has other instruments of intervention, particularly fiscal and monetary instruments. The State also commands the bulk of the nation's savings. Banks and financial institutions are under State control. Where State intervention is necessary, these instruments will prove more effective and decisive.

16. Government will fully protect the interests of labour, enhance their welfare and equip them in all respects to deal with the inevitability of technological change. Government believes that no small section of society can corner the gains of growth, leaving workers to bear its pains. Labour will be made an equal partner in progress and prosperity. Workers' participation in management will be promoted. Workers cooperatives will be encouraged to participate in packages designed to turn around sick companies. Intensive training, skill development and upgradation programmes will be launched.

17. Government will continue to visualise new horizons. The major objectives of the new industrial policy package will be to build on the gains already made, correct the distortions or weaknesses that may have crept in, maintain a sustained growth in productivity and gainful employment and attain international competitiveness. The pursuit of these objectives will be tempered by the need to preserve the environment and ensure the efficient use of available resources. All sector of industry whether small, medium or large, belonging to the public, private or cooperative sector will be encouraged to grow and improve on their past performance.

18. Government's policy will be continuity with change.

19. In pursuit of the above objectives, Government have decided to take a series of initiatives in respect of the policies relating to the following areas.

A. Industrial Licensing.

B. Foreign Investment

C. Foreign Technology Agreements.

D. Public Sector Policy

E. MRTP Act.

A package for the Small and Tiny Sectors of industry is being announced separately.

Industrial Licensing Policy

20. Industrial Licensing is governed by the Industries (Development & Regulation) Act, 1951. The Industrial Policy Resolution of 1956 identified the following three categories of industries: those that would be reserved for development in public sector, those that would be permitted for development through private enterprise with or without State participation, and those in which investment initiatives would ordinarily emanate from private entrepreneurs. Over the years, keeping in view the changing industrial scene in the country, the policy has undergone modifications. Industrial licensing policy and procedures have also been liberalised from time to time. A full realisation of the industrial potential of the country calls for a continuation of this process of change.

21. In order to achieve the objectives of the strategy for the industrial sector for the 1990s and beyond it is necessary to make a number of changes in the system of industrial approvals. Major policy initiatives and procedural reforms are called for in order to actively encourage and assist Indian entrepreneurs to exploit and meet the emerging domestic and global opportunities and challenges. The bedrock of any such package of measures must be to let the entrepreneurs make investment decisions on the basis of their own commercial judgement. The attainment of technological dynamism and international competitiveness requires that enterprises must be enabled to swiftly respond to fast changing external conditions that have become characteristic of today's industrial world. Government policy and procedures must be geared to assisting entrepreneurs in their efforts. This can be done only if the role played by the government were to be changed from that of only exercising control to one of providing help and guidance by making essential procedures fully transparent and by eliminating delays.

22. The winds of change have been with us for some time. The industrial licensing system has been gradually moving away from the concept of capacity licensing. The system of reservations for public sector undertakings has been evolving towards an ethos of greater flexibility and private sector enterprise has been gradually allowed to enter into many of these areas on a case by case basis. Further impetus must be provided to these changes which alone can push this country towards the attainment of its entrepreneurial

and industrial potential. This calls for bold and imaginative decisions designed to remove restraints on capacity creation, while at the same, ensuring that over-riding national interests are not jeopardised.

23. In the above context, industrial licensing will henceforth be abolished for all industries, except those specified, irrespective of levels of investment. These specified industries (Annex-II), will continue to be subject to compulsory licensing for reasons related to security and strategic concerns, social reasons, problems related to safety and over-riding environmental issues, manufacture of products of hazardous nature and articles of elitist consumption. The exemption from licensing will be particularly helpful to the many dynamic small and medium entrepreneurs who have been unnecessarily hampered by the licensing system. As a whole the Indian economy will benefit by becoming more competitive, more efficient and modern and will take its rightful place in the world of industrial progress.

Foreign Investment

24. While freeing Indian industry from official controls, opportunities for promoting foreign investments in India should also be fully exploited. In view of the significant development of India's industrial economy in the last 40 years, the general resilience, size and level of sophistication achieved, and the significant changes that have also taken place in the world industrial economy, the relationship between domestic and foreign industry needs to be much more dynamic than it has been in the past in terms of both technology and investment. Foreign investment would bring attendant advantages of technology transfer, marketing expertise, introduction of modern managerial techniques and new possibilities for promotion of exports. This is particularly necessary in the changing global scenario of industrial and economic cooperation marked by mobility of capital. The government will therefore welcome foreign investment which is in the interest of the country's industrial development.

25. In order to invite foreign investment in high priority industries, requiring large investments and advanced technology, it has been decided to provide approval for direct foreign investment upto 51% foreign equity in such industries. There shall be no bottlenecks of any kind in this process. This group of

industries has generally been known as the "Appendix I Industries" and are areas in which FERA companies have already been allowed to invest on a discretionary basis. This change will go a long way in making Indian policy on foreign investment transparent. Such a framework will make it attractive for companies abroad to invest in India.

26. Promotion of exports of Indian products calls for a systematic exploration of world markets possible only through intensive and highly professional marketing activities. To the extent that expertise of this nature is not well developed so far in India, Government will encourage foreign trading companies to assist us in our export activities. Attraction of substantial investment and access to high technology, often closely held, and to world markets, involves interaction with some of the world's largest international manufacturing and marketing firms. The Government will appoint a special board to negotiate with such firms so that we can engage in purposive negotiation with such large firms, and provide the avenues for large investments in the development of industries and technology in the national interest.

Foreign Technology Agreement

27. There is a great need for promoting an industrial environment where the acquisition of technological capability receives priority. In the fast changing world of technology the relationship between the suppliers and users of technology must be a continuous one. Such a relationship becomes difficult to achieve when the approval process includes unnecessary governmental interference on a case to case basis involving endemic delays and fostering uncertainty. The Indian entrepreneur has now come of age so that he no longer needs such bureaucratic clearances of his commercial technology relationships with foreign technology suppliers. Indian industry can scarcely be competitive with the rest of the world if it is to operate within such a regulatory environment.

28. With a view to injecting the desired level of technological dynamism in Indian industry, Government will provide automatic approval for technology agreement related to high priority industries within specified parameters. Similar facilities will be available for other industries as well if such agreements do not require the expenditure of free exchange. Indian companies will

be free to negotiate the terms of technology transfer with their foreign counterparts according to their own commercial judgement. The predictability and independence of action that this measure is providing to Indian industry will induce them to develop indigenous competence for the efficient absorption of foreign technology. Greater competitive pressure will also induce our industry to invest much more in research and development and they have been doing in the past. In order to help this process, the hiring of foreign technicians and foreign testing of indigenously developed technologies, will also not require prior clearance as prescribed so far, individually or as a part of industrial or investment approvals.

Public Sector Policy

29. The public sector has been central to our philosophy of development. In the pursuit of our development objectives, public ownership and control in critical sector of the economy has played an important role in preventing the concentration of economic power, reducing regional disparities and ensuring that planned development serves the common good.

30. The Industrial Policy Resolution of 1956 gave the public sector a strategic role in the economy. Massive investments have been made over the past four decades to build a public sector which has a commanding role in the economy. Today key sectors of the economy are dominated by mature public enterprises that have successfully expanded production, opened up new areas of technology and built up a reserve of technical competence in a number of areas.

31. After the initial exuberance of the public sector entering new areas of industrial and technical competence, a number of problems have begun to manifest themselves in many of the public enterprises. Serious problems are observed in the insufficient growth in productivity, poor project management, over-manning, lack of continuous technological upgradation, and inadequate attention to R&D and human resource development. In addition, public enterprises have shown a very low rate of return on the capital invested. This has inhibited their ability to re-generate themselves in terms of new investments as well as in technology development. The result is that many of the public enterprises have become a burden rather than being an asset to the Government.

The original concept of the public sector has also undergone considerable dilution. The most striking example is the take over of sick units from the private sector. This category of public sector units accounts for almost one third of the total losses of central public enterprises. Another category of public enterprises, which does not fit into the original idea of the public sector being at the commanding heights of the economy, is the plethora of public enterprises which are in the consumer goods and services sectors.

32. It is time therefore that the Government adopt a new approach to public enterprises. There must be a greater commitment to the support of public enterprises which are essential for the operation of the industrial economy. Measures must be taken to make these enterprises more growth oriented and technically dynamic. Units which may be faltering at present but are potentially viable must be restructured and given a new lease of life. The priority areas for growth of public enterprises in the future will be the following.

- Essential infrastructure goods and services.
- Exploration and exploitation of oil and mineral resources.
- Technology development and building of manufacturing capabilities in areas which are crucial in the long term development of the economy and where private sector investment is inadequate.
- Manufacture of products where strategic considerations predominate such as defence equipment.

At the same time the public sector will not be barred from entering areas not specifically reserved for it.

33. In view of these considerations, Government will review the existing portfolio of public investments with greater realism. This review will be in respect of industries based on low technology, small scale and non-strategic areas, inefficient and unproductive areas, areas with low or nil social considerations or public purpose, and areas where the private sector has developed sufficient expertise and resources.

34. Government will strengthen those public enterprises which fall in the reserved areas of operation or are in high priority areas or are generating good or reasonable profits. Such enterprises will be provided a much greater degree of management autonomy through the system of memoranda of understanding. Competition

will also be induced in these areas by inviting private sector participation. In the case of selected enterprises, part of Government holdings in the equity share capital of these enterprises will be disinvested in order to provide further market discipline to the performance of public enterprises. There are a large number of chronically sick public enterprises incurring heavy losses, operating in a competitive market and serve little or no public purpose. These need to be attended to. The country must be proud of the public sector that it owns and it must operate in the public interest.

Monopolies and Restrictive Trade Practices Act (MRTP Act)

35. The principal objectives sought to be achieved through the MRTP Act are as follows:

i. Prevention of concentration of economic power to the common detriment, control of monopolies, and
ii. Prohibition of monopolistic and restrictive and unfair trade practices.

36. The MRTP Act became effective in June 1970. With the emphasis placed on productivity in the Sixth Plan, major amendments to the MRTP Act were carried out in 1982 and 1984 in order to remove impediments to industrial growth and expansion. This process of change was given a new momentum in 1985 by an increase of threshold limit of assets.

37. With the growing complexity of industrial structure and the need for achieving economies of scale for ensuring high productivity and competitive advantage in the international market, the interference of the Government through the MRTP Act in investment decisions of large companies has become deleterious in its effects on Indian industrial growth. The pre-entry scrutiny of investment decisions by so called MRTP companies will no longer be required. Instead, emphasis will be on controlling and regulating monopolistic, restrictive and unfair trade practices rather than making it necessary for the monopoly house to obtain prior approval of Central Government for expansion, establishment of new undertakings, merger, amalgamation and takeover and appointment of certain directors. The thrust of policy will be more on controlling unfair or restrictive business practices. The MRTP Act will be restructured by eliminating the legal requirement for

prior governmental approval for expansion of present undertakings and establishment of new undertakings. The provisions relating to merger, amalgamation, and takeover will also be repealed. Similarly, the provisions regarding restrictions on acquisition of and transfer of shares will be appropriately incorporated in the Companies Act.

38. Simultaneously, provisions of the MRTP Act will be strengthened in order to enable the MRTP Commission to take appropriate action in respect of the monopolistic, restrictive and unfair trade practices. The newly empowered MRTP Commission will be encouraged to require investigation suo moto or on complaints received from individual consumers or classes of consumers.

Decisions of Government

39. In view of the considerations outlined above Government have decided to take a series of measures to unshackle the Indian industrial economy from the cobwebs of unnecessary bureaucratic control. These measures complement the other series of measures being taken by Government in the areas of trade policy, exchange rate management, fiscal policy, financial sector reform and overall macro economic management.

Industrial Licensing Policy

i. Industrial licensing will be abolished for all projects except for a short list of industries related to security and strategic concerns, social reasons, hazardous chemicals and overriding environmental reasons, and items of elitist consumption. Industries reserved for the small scale sector will continue to be so reserved.

ii. Areas where security and strategic concerns predominate, will continue to be reserved for the public sector.

iii. In projects where imported capital goods are required, automatic clearance will be given

   a. in cases where foreign exchange availability is ensured through foreign equity or

   b. if the CIF value of imported capital goods required is less than 25% of total value of plant and equipment, upto a maximum value of Rs. 2 crore. In view of the current difficult foreign exchange situation, this scheme (i.e. (iii) b) will come into force from April, 1992.

In other cases, imports of capital goods will require clearance from the Secretariat for Industrial Approvals (SIA) in the Department of Industrial Development according to availability of foreign exchange resources.

iv. In locations other than cities of more than 1 million population, there will be no requirement of obtaining industrial approvals from the Central Government except for industries subject to compulsory licensing. In respect of cities with population greater than 1 million, industries other than those of a non polluting nature such as electronics, computer software and printing will be located outside 25 kms. of the periphery, except in prior designated industrial areas. A flexible location policy would be adopted in respect of such cities (with population greater than 1 million) which require industrial re-generation. Zoning and Land Use Regulation and Environmental Legislation will continue to regulate industrial locations. Appropriate incentives and the design of investments in infrastructure development will be used to promote the dispersal of industry particularly to rural and backward areas and to reduce congestion in cities.

v. The system of phased manufacturing programmes run on an administrative case by case basis will be applicable to new projects. Existing projects with such programmes will continue to be governed by them.

vi. Existing units will be provided a new broad banding facility to enable them to produce any article without additional investment.

vii. The exemption from licensing will apply to all substantial expansions of existing units.

viii. The mandatory convertibility clause will no longer be applicable for term loans from the financial institutions for new projects.

Procedural Consequences

ix. All existing registration schemes (Delicensed Registration, Exempted Industries Registration, DGTD registration) will be abolished.

x. Entrepreneurs will henceforth only be required to file an information memorandum on new projects and substantial expansions.

xi. The lists at Annex II and Annex III will be notified in the Indian Trade Classification (Harmonised System).

Foreign Investment

i. Approval will be given for direct foreign investment upto 51 percent foreign equity in high priority industries. There shall be no bottlenecks of any kind in this process. Such clearance will be available if foreign equity covers the foreign exchange requirement for imported capital goods. Consequential amendments to the Foreign Exchange Regulation Act (1973) shall be carried out.

ii. While the import of components, raw materials and intermediate goods, and payment of know-how fees and royalties will be governed by the general policy applicable to other domestic units, the payment of dividends would be monitored through the Reserve Bank of India so as to ensure that outflows on account of dividend payments are balanced by export earnings over a period of time.

iii. Other foreign equity proposals, including proposals involving 51% foreign equity which do not meet the criteria under (I) above, will continue to need prior clearance. Foreign equity proposals need not necessarily be accompanied by foreign technology agreements.

iv. To provide access to international markets, majority foreign equity holding upto 51% equity will be allowed for trading companies primarily engaged in export activities. While the thrust would be on export activities, such trading houses shall be at par with domestic trading and export houses in accordance with the Import Export Policy.

v. A special Empowered Board would be constituted to negotiate with a number of large international firms and approve direct foreign investment in select areas. This would be a special programme to attract substantial investment that would provide access to high technology and world markets. The investment programmes of such firms would be considered in totality, free from predetermined parameters or procedures.

Foreign Technology Agreements

i. Automatic permission will be given for foreign technology agreements in high priority industries upto a lumpsum payment of Rs. 1 crore, 5% royalty for domestic sales and 8% for exports, subject to total payment of 8% of sales over a 10 year period from date of agreement or 7 years from commencement of production. The prescribed royalty rates are net of taxes and will be calculated according to standard procedures.

ii. In respect of industries other than those in Annex III, automatic permission will be given subject to the same guidelines as above if no free foreign exchange is required for any payments.

iii. All other proposals will need specific approval under the general procedures in force.

iv. No permission will be necessary for hiring of foreign technicians, foreign testing of indigenously developed technologies. Payment may be made from blanket permits or free foreign exchange according to RBI guidelines.

Public Sector

i. Portfolio of public sector investments will be reviewed with a view to focus the public sector on strategic, high-tech and essential infrastructure. Whereas some reservation for the public sector is being retained there would be no bar for areas of exclusivity to be opened up to the private sector selectively. Similarly the public sector will also be allowed entry in areas not reserved for it.

ii. Public enterprises which are chronically sick and which are unlikely to be turned around will, for the formulation of revival/rehabilitation schemes, be referred to the Board for Industrial and Financial Reconstruction (BIFR), or other similar high level institutions created for the purpose. A social security mechanism will be created to protect the interests of workers likely to be affected by such rehabilitation packages.

iii. In order to raise resources and encourage wider public participation, a part of the government's shareholding in the public sector would be offered to mutual funds, financial institutions, general public and workers.

iv. Boards of public sector companies would be made more professional and given greater powers.

v. There will be a greater thrust on performance improvement through the Memoranda of understanding (MOU) systems through which managements would be granted greater autonomy and will be held accountable. Technical expertise on the part of the Government would be upgraded to make the MOU negotiations and implementation more effective.

vi. To facilitate a fuller discussion on performance, the MOU signed between Government and the public enterprise would be placed in Parliament. While focussing on major management issues, this would also help place matters on day to day operations of public enterprises in their correct perspective.

MRTP Act

i. The MRTP Act will be amended to remove the threshold limits of assets in respect of MRTP companies and dominant undertakings. This eliminates the requirement of prior approval of Central Government for establishment of new undertakings, expansion of undertakings, merger, amalgamation and takeover and appointment of Directors under certain circumstances.

ii. Emphasis will be placed on controlling and regulating monopolistic, restrictive and unfair trade practices. Simultaneously, the newly empowered MRTP Commission will be authorised to initiative investigations suo moto or on complaints received from individual consumers or classes of consumers in regard to monopolistic, restrictive and unfair trade practices.

iii. Necessary comprehensive amendments will be made in the MRTP Act in this regard and for enabling the MRTP Commission to exercise punitive and compensatory powers.

The MRTP Act, 1969

The Monopolistic and Restrictive Trade Practices Act, 1969, was enacted :

1. To ensure that the operation of the economic system does not result in the concentration of economic power in hands of few,
2. To provide for the control of monopolies, and
3. To prohibit monopolistic and restrictive trade practices.

The MRTP Act extends to the whole of India except Jammu and Kashmir. Unless the Central Government otherwise directs, this act shall not apply to:

1. Any undertaking owned or controlled by the Government Company,
2. Any undertaking owned or controlled by the Government,
3. Any undertaking owned or controlled by a corporation (not being a company established by or under any Central, Provincial or State Act,
4. Any trade union or other association of workmen or employees formed for their own reasonable protection as such workmen or employees,
5. Any undertaking engaged in an industry, the management of which has been taken over by any person or body of persons under powers by the Central Government,
6. Any undertaking owned by a cooperative society formed and registered under any Central, Provincial or state Act,
7. Any financial institution.

3

Jawahar Lal Nehru and Industrial Policy

Economic Policies

Nehru presided over the introduction of a modified, Indian version of state planning and control over the economy. Creating the Planning commission of India, Nehru drew up the first Five-Year Plan in 1951, which charted the government's investments in industries and agriculture. Increasing business and income taxes, Nehru envisaged a mixed economy in which the government would manage strategic industries such as mining, electricity and heavy industries, serving public interest and a check to private enterprise.

Nehru pursued land redistribution and launched programmes to build irrigation canals, dams and spread the use of fertilizers to increase agricultural production. He also pioneered a series of *community development programs* aimed at spreading diverse cottage industries and increasing efficiency into rural India. While encouraging the construction of large dams (which Nehru called the "new temples of India"), irrigation works and the generation of hydroelectricity, Nehru also launched India's programme to harness nuclear energy.

For most of Nehru's term as prime minister, India would continue to face serious food shortages despite progress and increases in agricultural production. Nehru's industrial policies, summarised in the Industrial Policy Resolution of 1956, encouraged the growth of diverse manufacturing and heavy industries, yet state planning, controls and regulations began to impair productivity, quality and profitability. Although the Indian economy enjoyed a steady rate of growth, chronic unemployment amidst widespread poverty continued to plague the population.

Mixed Economy

A mixed economy is an economic system that includes a variety of private and government control, or a mixture of capitalism and socialism.

There is not one single definition for a mixed economy, but relevant aspects include: a degree of private economic freedom (including privately owned industry) intermingled with centralized economic planning and government regulation (which may include regulation of the market for environmental concerns, social welfare or efficiency, or state ownership and management of some of the means of production for national or social objectives).

For some states, there is not a consensus on whether they are capitalist, socialist, or mixed economies. Economies ranging from the United States to Cuba have been termed mixed economies.

The mixed economy as an economic ideal is supported by social democrats as a compromise between socialism and free-market capitalism, among others.

Economic Policies of Jawaharlal Nehru

The economic policies of Jawaharlal Nehru have been subject to much controversy in the past few decades. However, it is important to place Nehru's economic policies in context for a proper appreciation of his policies. Nehru's commitment to the cause of India's development remains unquestioned, and it is no doubt that much of his plans and speculations were jeopardized by the unexpected partition that came along with the independence of India, which brought about an unprecedented fissure in the economic resources of the Indian mainland. Nehru himself confessed that the partition brought about a large share of problems, including a great rift in the agricultural and the industrial sectors.

A large portion of the most productive agricultural lands fell in Pakistan whereas the corresponding industries remained in Indian dominion. The problem faced by the Jute industry soon after Independence can be stated as a case in the point. The jute producing areas were in Pakistan whereas the Jute processing factories remained in India, thereby affecting jute productions on both sides of the border.

Early Economic Reforms of Nehru: Nehru started his career as the Prime Minister of independent India in 1947, and immediately launched a number of economic reforms. Nehru was a firm believer in state control over the economic sectors. His socialist ideals revealed themselves in the way he introduced laws for land redistribution, in order to curtail the economic disparity in India among the landed and the landless classes. One of Nehru's key economic reforms was the introduction of the Five Years Plan in 1951. It was introduce to determine the mode of government expenditure and grants in important development sectors like agriculture, industries and education.

The Ideology guiding Nehru's Economic Policies: Nehru's economic policies have often been considered to be Socialist in nature. It is no doubt that Socialism did play a very important role in Nehru's ideological make-up. But at the same time, it is also important to consider that Nehru himself denied any kind of overt Socialist tendencies in the economic policies adopted by him. Nehru advocated a kind of mixed economy. Any kind of unquestioned ideological adherence to any form of economic tenet, or 'ism', he realized, would be detrimental to India's growth. He wanted a practical approach in framing the Indian economy, which would suit best the country's needs. On the one hand, as a devoted Gandhian, he had strong belief in the betterment of rural economy. On the other hand, he had a strong belief that heavy industrial development would be the best way to serve India's economic interests.

Nehru's Industrial Policies: Nehru wanted to create a balance between the rural and the urban sectors in his economic policies. He stated there was no contradiction between the two and that both could go hand in hand. He denied to carry forward the age old city versus village controversy and hoped that in India, both could go hand in hand. Nehru was intent to harness and fully exploit the natural resources of India for the benefit of his countrymen. The main sector he identified was hydroelectricity, and he constructed a number of dams to achieve that end. The dams would not only harness energy, but would also support irrigation to a great degree. Nehru considered dams to be the very symbol of India's collective growth, as they were the platforms where industrial engineering and agriculture met on a common platform. Nehru also considered the possibility of nuclear growth during his tenure as the prime minister of India.

Nehru and Foreign Investment: Nehru inspired the industrialists to provide a fillip to India's economy. However, he had strict reservations on the question of foreign investment. Nehru was wary of foreign investment. Nehru's nationalist ideals confirmed in him the belief that India was self-sufficient to bolster her own growth. Although he did not officially decry the possibility of foreign investment in direct terms, he did stress that the sectors of foreign investment would be regularized, and the terms and conditions of investment and employment would be strictly controlled by government rules in case there were possibilities of a foreign investment. Nehru, moreover, emphasized that the key sectors will always be in government hand. This step of Nehru is much criticized now. Yet, it cannot be denied that Nehru aptly looked forward to long term investments for which he banked more on Indian industries. It is also often suggested that his endeavour to harness international support to develop India's infra-structural profile between 1947 and 1955 did not meet with much success. It, however, remains a fact that Nehru's regime was not one of great economic growth for India. Although his economic policies are blamed for the failure of India to turn into a major economic force in the aftermath of independence, yet Nehru was probably thinking on a more long term basis. It is often inferred that the economic liberation of the later years was possible only because of Nehru's policies in the initial stages.

The State Control in Nehru's Economic Policies: The most distinctive, and often debated feature of Nehru's economic policies, was the high level of state and central control that was exercised on the industrial and business sectors of the country. Nehru emphasized that the state would control almost all key areas of the country's economy, either centrally or on a state-wise basis. His Socialist emphasis on state control somehow seemed to undermine his stress on industrial policies. The rigorous state laws and License rules put a great degree of restrain on the free execution of industrial policies. Even the farmers, along with the business personnel, found themselves to be at the receiving end of rigorous state control policies and high taxation. Poverty and unemployment were widespread throughout Nehru's governance.

Nehru's Views on Rural Economy: Nehru's policy towards the rural economy of India was also significant. Nehru felt for the rural self-development of India very strongly. He tried to boost India's cottage industries. Much on the lines of Gandhi, Nehru believed that the rural and cottage industries of India played a major role in the economic fabric of the country. But most of his cottage industry development programs were meant as a part of community development. He was also of the belief that small scale industries and cottage industries were effective solutions to the massive employment problems that remained a perpetual issue of concern throughout his tenure.

The economic policies of Nehru are often blamed for the poor economy of India in the subsequent years. However, it cannot be denied that his decisions were necessitated by the needs of the times. India needed to effectively harness its domestic means as well as strengthen its governmental control to lay the base for future privatization. It is often speculated that Nehru would have embraced the economic reforms and economic liberalization of the late twentieth century if he was alive.

India knows it has something to celebrate Wednesday, the 60th anniversary of its independence from Britain. That may sound obvious, but it isn't, because 10 years ago many people said they were not sure what there was to be proud of on the 50th anniversary.

People bemoaned the country's failure to get to grips with endemic social and infrastructure problems, especially poverty, education, health, roads, and power. There had been a spate of economic reforms after a humiliating international financial crisis in 1991, but they had sputtered to a virtual halt. Business was not doing anything very dramatic, and there were only glimmerings of the information technology-led boom and more recent manufacturing renaissance.

Today, many of the problems – especially social – are little improved. Vast proportions of the country's 1.1 billion people are undernourished and hungry, as well as poorly educated and illiterate. Blighted by a lack of drinking water and proper sanitation, many are plagued with poorly-treated ill health.

But the country's overall self-confidence, and its economic performance, is being transformed. In the past four or five years, a spirit of "can-do" has inspired businesspeople – big and small, ranging from names like Ratan Tata, Mukesh Ambani, Azim Premji and the Infosys founders to small niche players – who invest, manage, deliver, and grow both at home and abroad. Funds are more often than not raised legitimately, rather than via a friendly politician's influence on a pliant public sector bank.

Companies operate in a mostly open market, knowing that they must manage efficiently and deliver quality or fail. Many of the names at the top of the business league tables have changed in the 10 years from old Marwari trading caste families, which thrived in a controlled economy, to new entrepreneurs. Family control of companies is still widespread, but the newcomers have an ambition to succeed in India and abroad that was previously often lacking. That has been shown most dramatically by the recent surge of takeovers overseas, spearheaded by the Tata group and by IT and pharmaceutical companies. Similarly, the growth in the number of executives from abroad who are prepared to work in India – foreign as well as of Indian origin and not just on lucrative postings – reflects both the availability of internationally competitive salaries and a more conducive working environment.

Consequently, economic growth has risen in the 10 years from around 6% to almost 10%. The Mumbai stock market's Sensex index has gone from under 3,500 to a peak last month of over 15,800. The rupee has recovered a decades-long slide and is now strengthening against world currencies (not just because of the declining dollar), and foreign exchange reserves have rocketed from $26 billion to around $230 billion.

India is also earning new respect as an international player, not least with the United States, which is on the brink of signing a nuclear deal that will transform the two countries' diplomatic and business relationship

One the flip side, some things are getting worse. The quality of governance is declining, especially in the states, because many politicians and bureaucrats are becoming more corrupt and self-serving. Parts of the country are appallingly run, especially Uttar Pradesh and Bihar, which for years have been almost as bad as Pakistan in terms of political failure – and their economies are worse. Maoist Naxalite rebels control vast areas of other states.

There is little urban planning or respect for regulations: construction of new buildings takes little account of environmental standards or the need, for example, for adequate drainage and other services.

Even more seriously, the economic boom is leading to intense pressure on land in a country where 70% of the population relies on it for its living. In the next ten years, it is quite possible that social unrest will be caused more frequently by land disputes than by traditional religious and ethnic differences.

Ten years ago that work ethic had not materialized. Today it is operating in the private sector, generating most of the successes.

India's Fifty Years of Economic Development

When India gained its independence after a long period of subjugation, its land and people were a picture of distress, removed from great events of its past glory and splendour. A whole creative side of Indian civilisation had shrunk under the foreign rule. Common man, burdened by poverty, hunger and ignorance, had lost the will to exercise its productive might. Out of the dust, they had to be raised by men of great vision, like Gandhi and Nehru. In his memorable speech, delivered to the Constituent Assembly on 14th. August, 1947, Nehru said: "The future is not all of ease and resting, but of incessant striving..."

India was a stagnant economy at the time of independence. The economy was predominantly agrarian with little industrial development. Most people lived in villages, in hunger and despair. Bullock carts, wooden ploughs, spinning wheels and thatched huts-life made of small things, unimaginatively hard, dull and cruel. Agricultural growth was around 0.3% per annum in the first half of this century. The colonial government took little interest in the improvement of cultivation practices, except in the case of export crops like cotton, jute and tea. The railway system was built only for connecting the ports with the export production centres and the import markets; all other infrastructural facilities were lacking. Local enterprise was confined largely to trade and commerce, mainly in and around port cities like Bombay, Calcutta and Madras. A few industrial centres grew around these cities through private entrepreneurship. There had been an adverse impact on the artisan sector under British rule.

The old crafts were left to languish and decay-ill prepared to modernise. Large factories, few in number, produced mainly consumer goods, like textiles and sugar. Intermediates like steel, cement and jute machinery were mostly imported. The extremely narrow base of industrialisation remained confined to a very few cities and states and was the monopoly of a few privileged families. The export strategy was not conducive to the country's interests. Exports were seen as a mechanism to transfer raw materials cheaply to the metropolitan cities in the United Kingdom, which, in turn, processed them into final goods for exporting back to the colonies.

Social indicators were equally poor; illiteracy was as high as 84%; public health services were inadequate to face even epidemics such as influenza, malaria and cholera. Some efforts were made by the state to prevent epidemics like malaria which continued to revisit again and again. The mortality rate remained high at around 27 per thousand in 1947. Children cried for milk but mothers could not feed them. Famines devastated human lives, adding to the interminable misery in a barren wasteland.

The first task of the Indian Government, in the immediate post-independence period, was to improve the material and human conditions of life by motivating rapid growth in a stagnant economy and to set the country on a path for higher growth with social justice. The objective of India's development strategy has been to establish a socialistic pattern of society through economic growth with self-reliance, social justice and alleviation of poverty. These objectives were to be achieved within a democratic political framework using the mechanism of a mixed economy where both public and private sectors co-exist.

India initiated planning for national economic development with the establishment of the Planning Commission, in 1950. The aim of the First Five Year Plan (1950-56) was to raise domestic savings for growth and help the economy resurrect itself from the twisted wreckage cause by colonial exploitation and the aftermath of Partition. The real break with the past in planning came with the Second Five Year Plan, celebrated as the Nehru-Mahalanobis Plan). The industrialisation strategy, articulated by Professor Mahalanobis, placed emphasis on the development of heavy industries and envisaged a dominant role for the public sector in the economy.

The entrepreneurial role of the state was evoked to develop the industrial sector. Commanding heights of economy were entrusted to the public sector. In brief, the emphasis of the first three Five Year Plans, was on economic growth with marginal stress on institutional changes like land reforms. The objectives of industrial policy were:-a high growth rate, national self-reliance, reduction of foreign dominance, building up of indigenous capacity, encouraging small-scale industry, bringing about balanced regional development, prevention of concentration of economic power, reduction of income inequalities and control of the economy by the state.

During the Second Plan period, the emphasis was to build heavy industries which would lay down the basis of rapid industrialisation ("machines to build machines"). The planners and policy makers suggested the need for using a wide variety of instruments, licensing and other regulatory controls to steer Indian industrial development on a closed economic basis.

The strategy underlying the first three Plans assumed that, once the growth process gets established, the institutional changes would ensure that benefits of growth would trickle down to the poor. But doubts were raised in the early 70's about the effectiveness of the "trickle down" approach and its ability to banish poverty. Further, the growth itself generated by the planned approach, remained too weak to create adequate surpluses-a prerequisite for the "trickle down" mechanism to work. Public sector did not live up to the expectations of generating surpluses to accelerate the pace of capital accumulation and help reduce inequality.

Agricultural growth remained constrained by perverse institutional conditions. Unchecked population explosion made the twin historic tasks of industry more difficult. Though the growth achieved in the three Five Year Plans was not insignificant, yet, it was not sufficient to meet the aims and objectives of development. A diversified industrial structure was established. Professional, managerial and technical manpower and skills were created. Similarly, in the field of agriculture, land under cultivation and irrigation increased, but their impact on economic growth and human development remained marginal. These brought into view the weakness of economic strategy. A shift of policy was called for. The country had also witnessed calamities of nature, war and oil-shocks.

Continuing the Fourth Plan's targeted programmes, the Fifth Plan (1974-79) corrected its course by initiating a programme emphasising growth and distribution. To accelerate the process of production and to align it with contemporary realities, a mild version of economic liberalization was started in the mid-1980's. Three important committees were set up in the early 1980's...- (1) Narimham Committee on the shift from physical to fiscal controls... (2) Sen Gupta Committee on the public sector and the... (3) Hussain Committee on trade policy.

The Committees recommended a shift from physical controls to fiscal controls, promotion of greater public sector autonomy and more freedom to business and financial institutions. The result of such thinking was to reorient our economic policies. As a result, there was some progress in the process of deregulation during the 1980's. Two kinds of delicensing activity took place. First, 32 groups of industries were delicensed without any investment limit. Second, in 1988, all industries were exempted from licensing except for a specific negative list of 26 industries. Entry into the industrial sector was made easier but exit still remained closed and sealed.

The Eighth Five Year Plan (1992-97), was launched against the backdrop of a balance of payments crisis, leading to the debt trap experienced in 1991. The crisis led to a second rethinking about our economic strategies and far reaching changes were effected. India launched a major programme of economic liberalization (stabilization and structural adjustment) in July 1991, under the able stewardship of Dr. Manmohan Singh, the Finance Minister in Narasimha Rao's Government.

Trade and exchange controls were further liberalized and structural adjustments were carried out in the industrial sector through delicensing and accompanying measures. The reforms, as they emerged, gave primacy to employment-related growth as a means of providing credible solutions to the problem of mass poverty, an expanded role to the private sector, both domestic and foreign, import liberalization, disinvestment in public enterprises, increased public investment in agriculture, physical infrastructure and social sector.

These reforms also led to reduction in fiscal deficits, control of inflation, and reform of the tax system to encourage efficiency and productivity through constant technological upgrading and determined improvements in capital output ration. During the Eighth Plan, efforts were also made toward towards decentralisation through the 73rd and 74th Amendments of the Constitution, identifying "human development" as its focus.

The Ninth Five Year Plan (1997-2002) is now being launched in the 50th year of India's independence with an ambition to achieve 7%-8% rate of economic growth. The Ninth Plan, without minimising the value of industrialisation, gives priority to agriculture and rural development, provision of basic minimum services, creation of productive employment, empowerment of women and other weaker sections, promotion of Panchayati Raj Institutions etc.. The performance of India's economic plans speak of both our success and certain setbacks and reveals the extent to which we plug the gaps in our development. The long term growth rate of Gross Domestic Product (GDP) during the period 1950-51 to 1994-95 was around 3.8% per annum while population increased at the rate of 2%.

The turn around in growth rates for macro aggregates started in the 1980's and continues in the 1990's. During the period 1980-95, GDP growth was more than 5% per annum. Regarding the period of economic reforms, after showing negative growth in the first year of the reform period (1991-92), GDP growth recovered in 1992-93. The GDP growth has been around 7% since 1994-95. Thus, the Eighth Plan is likely to end with an average growth rate of 6.5% per annum. More important for the future is the fact that the average growth during the last three years is 7 %, probably placing India among the top ten performers in the world during this period. The economy seems to be on a new path of higher growth.

India's 50 years of Economic Development-Continued:-The importance of agriculture in the Indian economy is well known. There appears to be a general consensus that agricultural policies have an economic-wide impact and that there is a direct correlation between Indian Agricultural Perfórmance and the standards of living of a majority of our population. In terms of growth, the performance of agriculture has been quite impressive in the post-independence period (a long-term growth on 2.7 % growth per annum) as compared with the pre-independence period (0.3% per annum) An important feature of the 1980's and the 1990's, however, is that there has been much more equitable spread of agricultural growth.

Not having done well during the early years of the Green Revolution, many of the states like Assam, Bihar, Orissa, Madhya Pradesh and West Bengal, showed significant growth in the 1980's. Oilseeds have also gained in the dry belt of Rajasthan, Madhya Pradesh, Karnataka and Maharashtra. Thus, there seems to be a reduction in regional disparities in output growth during the 1980's and 1990's. The Ninth Five Year Plan projects to achieve 4.5 % growth in agriculture.

India is considered as the tenth industrially developed nation in the world. The share of industry in overall GDP, has increased substantially since independence, from 15% to 28% in recent years. The long-term growth rate of the GDP in the secondary sector, and GDP in the manufacturing sector during the period 1950-51 to 1994-95, has been around 5% per annum. In the first 15 year period after independence-1950-65-the growth-rate of manufacturing was around 6.5 %, after which it became somewhat sluggish. The "turn-around" in industrial growth seems to have started in the 1980's. In the Seventh Plan, the growth-rate was around 8.5 %. Since 1993-94, the industrial growth seems to have recovered. In 1993-94, 94-95, and 95-96, the industrial growth has been 6, 9.4 and 12% respectively.

The composition of industry since independence has undergone significant transformation. A very diversified industrial base has been created, At the time of independence, the consumer goods industry accounted for almost half of all industrial production. Now, consumer goods industry accounts for only about 20%. On the other hand, capital goods, which constituted less than 4%, now account for around 24% of the industrial production. Similarly, the share of basic goods industries, increased from around 20% in 1950-51, to almost 40% now. From hardware to software; from potato chips to microchips, is the spread of production. A national consensus exists that we should raise our rate of industrial growth and quality of industrial products through intense technological upgrading and competition between firms within and outside.

The small-scale sector is an important component of the industrial sector. The government has given protection to the small scale industry and a number of advantages were given to this sector, including reservation of a large number of products. The small sector now contributes over 40% of the gross turnover in the manufacturing sector, 45% of manufacturing exports and 34% of total exports and provides employment for 15. 3 million workers. However, it is now felt that reservations for a small scale sector should be abolished completely, so as to encourage other sectors of industry.

India Key Industry

Steel

The iron and steel industry in India is over 122 years old. However, a concerted effort to increase the steel output was made only in the early years of planning. Three integrated steel plants were set up at Bhilai, Durgapur and Rourkela. Later two more steel plants, at Bokaro and Vishakhapattanam, were set up. Private sector plants, of which the Tata Iron and Steel Company (TISCO) is the biggest, have been allowed to raise their capacity.

TISCO and a large number of mini steel plants in the country contribute about 40 per cent of the steel production in the country. The Government has given a push to sponge iron plants to meet the secondary sector's requirement of steel scrap.

Engineering and Machine Tools

Among the Third-World countries, India is a major exporter of heavy and light engineering goods, producing a wide range of items. The bulk of capital goods required for power projects, fertilizer, cement, steel and petrochemical plants and mining equipment are made in India. The country also makes construction machinery, equipment for irrigation projects, diesel engines, tractors, transport vehicles, cotton textile and sugar mill machinery. The engineering industry has shown its capacity to manufacture large-size plants and equipment for various sectors like power, fertilizer, and cement. Lately, air pollution control equipments are also being made in the country. The heavy electrical industry meets the entire domestic demand. Electronics

The electronics industry in India has made rapid strides in recent years. The country produces electronics items worth over Rs. 200 billion annually. The Software Technology Park scheme for attracting investments has proved successful. The relative low cost of production in India makes items made in India competitive in the world market.

Some of the major items manufactured in India are computers, communication equipment, broadcasting and strategic electronics, television sets, microwave ovens, and washing machines.

The compound growth of the computer industry has been 50 per cent during the last five years. With the availability of trained technical manpower, computers have been identified as a major thrust area. Special emphasis has been given to software export. The Indian software industry has developed skill and expertise in areas like design and implementation of management information and decision support systems, banking, insurance and financial applications, artificial intelligence and fifth generation systems.

Recognition for the Indian computer software industry has been global. Indian software enterprises have completed projects for reputed international organisations in 43 countries. Textiles

Textiles, the largest industry in the country employing about 20 million people, account for one-third of India's total exports. During 2000-01, textile exports were estimated at Rs. 49,831 crore, which is more than the export during 1999-2000.which was Rs. 40,178 crore. In recent years, several controls have been removed and in October 1996, a new Long-Term Quota policy was announced to boost exports.

Public Sector

The public sector contributed to the initial development of infrastructure and diversification of industrial base. It is now being exposed to competition. Part equity of some units is being disinvested. But many core and strategic areas, important for economy and self-reliance, will remain in the public sector.

Bhakra Dam

Bhakra Nangal Dam is a concrete gravity dam across the Sutlej River, near the border between Punjab and Himachal Pradesh in northern India. The dam, located in the village of Bhakra in the Bilaspur region of Himachal Pradesh, is Asia's largest at 225.55 m (740 ft.) high. It is the highest gravity dam in the world. The length of the dam (measured from the road above it) is 518.25 m; it is 304.84 m broad. Its reservoir, known as the "Gobind Sagar", stores up to 9340 million cu m of water, enough to drain the whole of Chandigarh, parts of Haryana, Punjab and Delhi. The 90 km long reservoir created by the Bhakra Nangal Dam is spread over an area of 168.35 km^2. In terms of storage of water, it is the second largest dam in India, the first being Indira Sagar dam in Madhya Pradesh with capacity of 12.22 billion cu m.

Described as 'New Temple of Resurgent India' by Jawahar Lal Nehru, the first prime minister of India, the dam attracts tourists from all over India.

History

The Bhakra-Nangal multipurpose project was among the earliest river valley development schemes undertaken by independent India, although the project was conceived long before India became a free nation. Preliminary works commenced in 1946. Construction of the dam started in 1948, Jawahar Lal Nehru poured the first bucket of concrete into the foundations of Bhakra on 17 November 1955 and the dam was completed by the end of 1963. Successive stages were completed by the early 1970s.

Initially, the construction of the dam was started by Sir Louis Dane, the Lieutenant Governor of Punjab. But the project got delayed and was restarted by the reoriented and phased soon after Independence. In October, 1963 at the ceremony to mark the dedication of the Bhakra –Nangal Project to the Nation, Prime Minister Jawaharlal Nehru said-"This dam has been built with the unrelenting toil of man for the benefit of mankind and therefore is worthy of worship. May you call it a Temple or a Gurdwara or a Mosque, it inspires our admiration and reverence".

Features

The dam, at 741 ft. (226 m), is one of the highest gravity dams in the world (compared to USA's largest Hoover Dam at 732 ft.). The 166 km^2 Gobindsagar Reservoir, named after Guru Gobind Singh, is created by this dam.

Statistics

It is the largest dam in India :

- Type of Dam: Concrete Straight Gravity
- Height: 740 ft. (225.55 m)
- Height (above river bed): 550 ft. (170 m)
- Length at top: 1,700 ft. (520 m)
- Width at top: 30 ft. (9.1 m)

- Length at bottom: 325 ft. (99 m)
- Width at base: 625 ft. (191 m)
- Elevation at top of dam: 1700 ft. (above sea level)
- Steel used: 100000 tons.

Usage

The dam was part of the larger multipurpose Bhakra Nangal Project whose aims were to prevent floods in the Sutlej-Beas river valley, to provide irrigation to adjoining states and to provide hydro-electricity. It also became a tourist spot for the tourists during later years because of it huge size and uniqueness.

Irrigation

The dam was constructed with an aim to provide irrigation to the Punjab and Himachal Pradesh. Another reason behind the construction of the dam was to prevent damage due to monsoon floods. The dam provides irrigation to 10 million acres (40,000 km^2) of fields in Punjab, Himachal Pradesh, Haryana, Delhi and Rajasthan.

Electricity Production

Bhakra Nangal dam houses hydroelectric power generators, which are situated on both the sides of the dam. Nangal hydel Channel and Anandpur Sahib Channel are used for power generation and irrigation purposes.

It also has 4 flood gates which are fully functional during the period of floods and also has 2 power-stations situated on the either side of the dam, which receives water through huge pipes which are directly connected from the dam's reservoir to each power-plant. Each of the power plants comprise of 5 generators, and a power station.

Two power houses with a total capacity of 1000 MW flank the dam, on either side of the river. A smaller subsidiary dam, called the Nangal Dam is located downriver from the Bhakra Dam.

Although the Bhakra Dam is situated in the Indian state of Punjab, 80/90% of the electricity produced is given to Delhi leaving only 10/20% to Punjab which faces a lack of electricity itself.

AND the total power produces by the Bhakra dam is 1209 MW.

Hirakud Dam

Hirakud Dam is built across the Mahanadi River, about 15 km from Sambalpur in the state of Orissa in India. Built in 1956, the dam is the world's largest earthen dam. Behind the dam extends a lake, Hirakud Reservoir, 55 km long. Hirakud Dam is one of the longest dams in the world, about 16 mi (26 km) in length. It was the first major multipurpose river valley project started after India's independence.

Construction History

Before the devastating floods of 1937, Sir M. Visveswararya proposed a detailed investigation for storage reservoirs in the Mahanadi basin to tackle the problem of floods in the Mahanadi delta. In 1945, under the chairmanship of Dr. B. R. Ambedkar, the then Member of Labour, it was decided to investigate the potential benefits of controlling the Mahanadi for multipurpose use. The Central Waterways, Irrigation and Navigation Commission took up the work.

On 15 March 1946, Sir Howthrone Lewis, then the Governor of Orissa, laid the foundation stone of the Hirakud Dam. A project report was submitted to the government in June 1947. Pandit Jawaharlal Nehru laid the first batch of concrete on 12 April 1948. The dam was completed in 1953 and was formally inaugurated by Prime Minister Jawaharlal Nehru on 13 January 1957. The total cost of the project was Rs. 100.02 crores (in 1957). Power generation along with agricultural irrigation started in 1956, achieving full potential in 1966.

Details

Total length of Dam :15,748 Feet or 4800 Meter

Concrete Dam :3,937 Feet or 1200 Meter

Earth Dam :11,811 Feet or 3600 Meter

Left Dyke :32,274 Feet or 9837 Meter

Right Dyke :35,299 Feet or 10759 Meter

Maximum Height of Massonary Dam :200 Feet or 61 Meter

Maximum Height of Earth Dam :195 Feet or 59.5 Meter

Sluice Gates Total :64 Nos.

Sluice Gates (Left) :40 Nos.

Sluice Gates (Right) :24 Nos.

Crest Gates :34 Nos.

Crest Gates (Left) :21 Nos.

Crest Gates (Right) :13 Nos.

Crest Gate Size :15.54 Meter * 16.1 Meter

Top Dam Level :RL 195.680 Meter (RL 642Feet)

Full Reservoir Level :Rl 192.024 Meter (RL 630 Feet)

Dead Storage Level :Rl 179.830 Meter (Rl 590 Feet)

Seal of Sluice Gate : 510 feet (160 m) RL

Gross Storage : 5,830,000 acre feet (7.19×10^9 m^3)

Live Storage : 4,360,000 acre feet (5.38×10^9 m^3)

Catchment Area : 83,400 km^2

Total Power Capacity :275.5 MW.

Structure

The Hirakud Dam is a composite structure of earth, concrete and masonry. Ten km north of Sambalpur, it is the longest major earthen dam in the world, measuring 24 km including dykės, and stands across the river Mahanadi. The main dam has an overall length of 4.8 km spanning between two hills; the Lamdungri on the left and the Chandili Dunguri on the right. The dam is flanked by 21 km earthen dykes on both the left and right sides, closing the low saddles beyond the adjoining hills. The dam and dykes together measure 25.8 km. It also forms the biggest artificial lake in Asia, with a reservoir holding 743 km^2 at full capacity, with a shoreline of over 640 km. There are two observation towers on the dam one at each side. One is "Gandhi Minar" and the other one is "Nehru Minar". Both the observation towers present breathtaking views of the lake.

Purpose and Benefits

In the upper drainage basin of the Mahanadi River, centred on the Chhattisgarh Plain, periodic droughts contrast with the situation in the lower delta region where floods may damage crops. The dam was constructed to help alleviate these problems by creating a reservoir and controlling river flow through the drainage system. The dam regulates the flow of the Mahanadi River and produces hydroelectricity through several hydroelectric plants. The dam helps control floods in the Mahanadi delta and irrigates 7,500,000 hectares of land. Hydroelectricity is also generated. The Hirakud Dam regulates 83,400 km^2 (32,200 mi^2) of Mahanadi's drainage. The reservoir has a storage capacity of 5.818 km^3 with gross of 8.136 km^3.

It drains an area of 133,090 km^2, more than twice the area of Sri Lanka. The amount of earth, concrete and masonry materials used to build the dam is sufficient to make a road 8 metres wide and pave it from Kanyakumari to Kashmir and from Amritsar to Dibrugarh in Assam. With successful irrigation provided by the dam, Sambalpur is called the rice bowl of Orissa. Here photography is strictly prohibited.

The project provides 1,556 km^2 of kharif and 1,084 km^2 of rabi irrigation in industries of Sambalpur, Bargarh, Bolangir, and Subarnpur. The water released by the power plant irrigates another 4360 km^2 of CCA in Mahanadi delta. The dam can generate up to 307.5 MW of electrical power through its two power plants at Burla, on the dam's right bank and Chiplima, 22 km downstream from the dam. In addition, the project provides flood protection to 9500 km^2 of delta area in district of Cuttack and Puri. Source: Dilip Kumar Padhi VU2DPI

Chiplima has gained prominence as the second hydroelectric project of the Hirakud Dam. A natural fall of 80 to 120 feet (25 to 40 m) in the river Mahanadi is used to generate electricity. The place is mostly inhabited by fisherman, whose deity Ghantlei is very popular in the neighbouring area. The State Livestock Breeding Farm and Agricultural Farm are located here.

People Affected by the Dam Construction

Main Purpose of Hirakud dam was to check the massive flood that was effecting a large part of coastal Orissa. But construction of the dam greatly affected the native of western part of Orissa. Nearly 1.5 lakh people got affected by the Hirakud project. Nearly 22,000 family were displaced under the Hirakud dam project, but are yet to be rehabilitated and receive their due compensation by the Orissa government. In the original estimate, an amount of Rs 12 crores was provided for payment of compensation to the affected people. After revision, the amount was reduced to Rs 9.5 crores and the total compensation paid to the people was, in reality, only Rs 3.32 crores. A large number of families were evacuated from their hearth and homes without compensation from 1956 onwards. INKNLK;M;

Cattle Island

Cattle Island exists in one of the extreme points of Hirakud Reservoir, a natural wonder. It is near Kumarbandh village of Belpahar-Banharpali range which is about 90 km from Sambalpur. By motor launch from Hirakud Dam, it is closer by 10 km via the river. The island is a submerged hill, and prior to the construction of Hirakud Dam it was a developed village. During the resettlement period, villagers left some of their cows and bulls behind; when the dam construction was over, the cattle settled on the hilltop. With the passage of time the nearby area filled up with the reservoir water, turning the hilltop into an island.

Being away from mankind, the cattle are now wild, very swift and not easily caught. Living on a hilltop with dense forest, they are larger than tame cattle, almost all of which are white in colour. Nearby residents attempt to hunt these animals from time to time, but these hunts are rarely successful.

Though descended from tame cattle, these animals provide a contrasting picture of this breed of animal returning to life in the wild. *'The dam with the channel provides an ideal environment for the wildlife. Nowadays due to mining and deforestetaion this nature's beauty is about to be lost. On one edge of the dam lies a chain of 12 mountains with deep forest and even rare wildlife of leopard, Chittah and various species of deer.*

Small Scale Industries

Small Scale Industries may sound small but actually plays a very important part in the overall growth of an economy. Small Scale Industries can be characterized by the unique feature of labour intensiveness. The total number of people employed in this industry has been calculated to be near about one crore and ninety lakhs in India, the main proponents of Small scale industries.

The importance of this industry increases manifold due to the immense employment generating potential. The countries which are characterized by acute unemployment problem especially put emphasis on the model of Small Scale Industries. It has been observed that India along with the countries in the Indian continent have gone long strides in this field.

Advantages Associated with Small Scale Industries

This industry is especially specialized in the production of consumer commodities.

Small scale industries can be characterized with the special feature of adopting the labour intensive approach for commodity production. As these industries lack capital, so they utilize the labour power for the production of goods. The main advantage of such a process lies in the absorption of the surplus amount of labour in the economy who were not being absorbed by the large and capital intensive industries. This, in turn, helps the system in scaling down the extent of unemployment as well as poverty.

Large-Scale Industries

Woollen Manufactures: These may be described under three different heads, viz., wool spinning, woollen textile and woollen hosiery.

(i) Wool Spinning. –The worsted, shoddy and indigenous woollen yarns are the most important basic raw materials for woollen textile and hosiery, which are manufactured on a large scale in the district. Prior to 1949, the supplies of yarn had to be obtained altogether from the spinning mills outside the State, which were situated in Calcutta and Bombay, except the one at Kharar. This created practical difficulties for the hosiery manufacturers as the supplies from the spinning mills were irregular, particularly during the season when the stocks invariably ran short and the prices rose to unjustified levels. Quite often it was not possible for the industrialists to get the yarn of requisite count and quality at the appropriate time. This naturally prompted some of the more enterprising and bigger units to install spinning plants within the city itself.

The first worsted wool spinning mill was established at Ludhiana in 1949. It gave impetus to several others with the result that by 1956 the number rose to six. In 1965-66 nineteen textile mills in the large-scale sector were engaged in the spinning of worsted yarn and manufacturing woollen textiles. The total number of authorised spindles installed with these units was 23,526. Powerlooms numbered 159 and handlooms 316. Their investment in this industry amounted to Rs 472 lakhs and provided employment to 3,160 workers. The capacity is partially utilised due to limited import of wool tops. Shoody and indigenous wools are also now being used as raw materials. The production during 1965-66 was valued at Rs 424.27 lakhs. Besides these, there exist 14 small-scale unauthorized spinning mills.

These units work throughout the year and engaged in the production of hosiery yarn, knitting yarn and yearn required for woollen textiles. Previously, the yarn was produced only from wool tops imported from abroad. But, due to the limited supply of wool tops and import restrictions thereon, indigenous wool is also now being used for spinning yarn. Even imported shoddy wool is being used for course woollen textiles and hosiery.

A big Government undertaking on cooperative basis for combing, viz., All-India Wool Combers Cooperative Society, Ltd., has been set up at Dhandari Kalan, a few miles from Ludhiana.

(ii) Woollen Textile. – Woollen Textile industry was started in the district in 1949. At Ludhiana, 14 big and 6 small units are engaged in the manufacture of woollen textiles, viz., worsted cloth, woollen cloth, tweeds and blankets. The industry has a bright future. Its products are also exported to Hongkong and Afghanistan. Worsted, woollen and shoddy yarn constitute the raw material.

About Rs. 5 crores are believed to have been invested in the industry.

(iii) Woollen Hosiery. – It item has been dealt with in detail in subsequent pages.

Cycles and Cycle-Parts: In the industrial boom which occurred in the wake of independence, manufacture of cycles and cycle-parts is by far the most important of the industries developed in the district. Although the industry has shown phenomenal development in the post-independence period, its beginnings can be traced as far back as 1936, or even earlier, when certain repair shops took up the manufacture of accessories like stands, carriers and axles as spares. Reduced imports from abroad during the course of the World War II (1939-45) provided an opportunity for the industry to grow both in volume and diversity. The next phase of expansion came in 1957, when the Government of India restricted the imports and fixed assemblage quota of full cycles as between small-scale units and large scale establishments. Manufacture of cycle-parts and assembling of complete cycles is now a leading engineering trade in Ludhiana though some units also exist in other towns of the district, such as Jagraon.

The All India combers Cooperative Society, Ltd., Dhandari Kalan, was registered on January 31, 1961, mainly to establish a Wool Combing Plant in the cooperative sector. The promoters of the scheme included the spinners, hosiery manufacturers, weavers and workers, etc. As a result of the Chinese aggression in 1962, the State Government decided to contribute to the share capital of the society on matching basis, in order to accelerate the pace of the project, which had assumed great importance as a defence oriented industry. The total membership of the society as on March 31, 1966, was 451, which included most of the big industrialists of Ludhiana and Amritsar, connected with the woollen industry.

The subscribed capital of the society as on March 31, 1966, was Rs 11,98,200 out of which a sum of Rs 9,44,670 was fully paid.

The Society has constructed the administrative block and the factory building and imported a part of the machinery (Nobel Combs) from U.K. It has also been granted an important licence for the import of the requisite machinery for the working of the Noble Combs from Japan. The capacity of the Noble Comb's is about 1.2 million Ibs. wool tops annum, on two shift basis.

The various items of raw materials and components required by the industry are: Free Cutting Steel, Steel of various types, Steel pipes, M.S. Sheets (10 to 24 gauges) M.S. Strips, M.S. rounds and bars, M.S.wires and seamless tubes, etc. The other anciliaries are tyres, brake rubber, pedal rubber, oils component parts like chains, rims, BB. Shells, steel balls, etc., and consumable stores, such as nickle anodes, copper electroplating and mopping materials, coal, paints, etc. Steel balls land rims are imported from other States. With the exception of cold roller sheets and seamless welding tubes, all other verities of iron and steel are produced in India.

Labour required for the industry, both skilled and unskilled, is available locally. It has been one of the main reasons for the localization of the industry at Ludhiana. The Ramgarhia community, who are born technicians and possess a mechanical bent of mind, have a natural aptitude for engineering industries. Over the years the workers have become specialised in their particular fields. The Government Testing and Finishing Centre, Ludhiana, renders cheap services in heat-treatment, electroplating, enamellings and testing to the industry. The Small Industries Service Institute set up by the Government of India at Ludhiana, is also playing an important role in disseminating the use of latest methods of producing various parts, up-to-date machinery, etc.

It is estimated that in 1947 the district had 25 units in the line, producing goods worth about Rs. 10 lakhs. In 1966-67, there were 558 small-scale units manufacturing cycle parts besides 9 small-scale units manufacturing cycle parts besides 9 small-scale and 2 large-scale units assembling complete bicycles. The industry provided employment to over 6,000 persons during the year amounted to Rs. 896 lakhs. Cycles and cycle-parts manufacturing units are also having a good demand of their products in the foreign markets, especially from the Middle East countries.

Goods worth Rs. 15.45 lakhs were exported to foreign countries during 1965-66. A notable feature of the Industry during the year was that a Ludhiana firm in the large scale sector gave collaboration to the Ceylon Government for establishing cycle manufacturing units there.

Sewing-Machines and Parts: The manufacture of sewing-machine parts and assembling of sewing-machines is another important industry of the district. Its origin in the Punjab can be traced back to 1925, when a unit took up the manufacture of sewing-machine components at Bassi Pathanan (district Patiala). These components were initially manufactured in the crude manner and no crude and self-improvised machinery, and were mainly supplied to certain repair shops for replacements, etc. The industry greatly developed greatly developed during the World War II (1939-45) when, on the inevitable stoppage of imports, acute shortage of sewing-machine parts was felt. People had to pay high prices for sewing-machine parts needed for replacement in the imported sewing-machine.

The situation induced some people to start manufacture of these parts. The requisite equipment and machine-tools for the manufacture of the parts were not available; but the enterprising spirit of the people overcame the difficulties. It was not long before the industry was centralized in Ludhiana, which had all the needed skill and favourable circumstances for the development of a small-scale industry of this kind. The industry made good progress because the indigenous parts were much cheaper as compared to the imported ones. The quality of the locally made parts also improved steadily.

On the partition displaced person as had their own workshops for the manufacture of sewing –machine parts in Lahore and other places in West Pakistan, resumed this activity in a small way at Ludhiana. In 1953, only eleven spare-parts were allowed to be imported. The industry progressed very much as there was shortage of sewing machines since World War 11. In 1964, Government imposed further restriction on the import of spare-parts.

Nearly Rs.25 lakhs are invested in 3 factories in the Large-scale and Rs.2 lakhs in 325 factories in the small-scale sectors. At present out of the total of 106 spare-parts required for assembling a sewing-machine, 100 spare parts are manufactured locally and the rest are imported from other district/States. In 1966-67, there were 4 large-scale and 18 small-scale assembling units, and 1 large scale and 194 small scale units manufacturing sewing-machine parts. The total production during the year was 63,723 machines valued at Rs. 81 lakhs. The exports during the same year valued at Rs.6 lakhs. The principal raw materials required for the manufacture of sewing machines and parts are steels of various kinds, casting, oil and nickel and chrome salt nickel, anodes, peerless polish, coal, etc.

Steel Re-rolling,-This industry was started in the district about the year 1940 when two concerns were established. In 1956, there were 3 re-rolling mills-two at Ludhiana and one at Khanna. In the large –scale sector, one unit went in to production during 1965-66 and produced goods worth Rs. 13.84 lakhs. In the small scale sector, the number of units increased from 3 in 1964-65 to 12 in 1965-66 with production valued at Rs.3.79 lakhs. In 1966-67 there were 12 units in Ludhiana, 3 in large-scale and 9 in small-scale sector and 1 in large scale sector in Khanna and 2 in small scale sector. About Rs. 25 lakhs were invested in the industry.

The annual outturn was worth about Rs. 10 lakhs. Round, square and flat bars, hoops and strip angles are manufactured. These products are used in cycle, automobile and building industries. The raw material includes scrap iron and billets and steam coal.

Machine-Tools. Till 1947, Ludhiana could hardly boast of any well-developed small machine tool industry. In 1947, there was one such unit in Ludhiana with a complement of 30 workers and an estimated production of Rs.0.5 lakhs. The number of units rose to 9 in 1951,39 in 1955,44 in 1956 and 255 small-scale and 4 large-scale in 1966-67. The estimated production in 1966-67 was valued at Rs.291 lakhs, providing employment to 3,809 workers. Goods worth Rs.3 lakhs were exported.

During the following two decades, the concentration of various industries and the availability of skilled labour have been the city a centre for the manufacture of various machine-tools like lathes, drilling-machines, milling-machines, planners, shapers, presses drills, grinders, hacksaw, power-presses, slotting-machines, circular saws, wood-working lathes, band sawing-machines, small tools with accessories for different machine tools, etc. The raw materials used are iron, steel and hard coke.

Automobile Parts: The Automobile (chassis and suspension) industry is also gaining importance in the district. Its origin can be traced to the World War II (1939-45) when nuts and bolts began to the locally. As time passed, the number of items manufactured increased. The real start of the industry was made after the partition when some local Ramgarhias took it up as comparatively more profitable of the engineering industries. About Rs. 1.25 crores are invested in the industry: 150 registered units and 100 unregistered units are in the field and all are located at Ludhiana. Out of these, one unit is in the large-scale sector.

The major items manufactured in respect of chassis and suspension comprise: hub bolts, U bolts, centre bolts, spring leaves, hangar shackle, engine pullies, hubs and hub-drums, king pin and spring pins. The industry has shown rapid development. In 1956, there were 30 units engaged in it at Ludhiana. In 1965-66, there was I large-scale unit and 148 small-scale units, providing employment to 1,826 workers. The production during the year was of the value of Rs. 19.08 lakhs and Rs. 112 lakhs in the large and small-scale sectors, respectively. The main raw materials are iron and steel, pig iron, gun metal, constructional alloy steel, etc.

Diesel-Oil Engine and Parts: The origin of the industry in the district can be traced to impetus of World War II when in 1941-42 Ludhiana entered the field. To begin with, small spare-parts needed for the repair of diesel engines were manufacture of major spare-parts was also started from 1945-46. Complete diesel engines came to be manufactured form 1948 onwards. In 1966-67 there were 10 units with annual production of Rs. 17 lakhs.

Scooters: One unit is engaged in the production of scooters at Ludhiana since 1962. It is working in collaboration with a Japanese motor company in respect of technical know-how. About Rs. 8 lakhs have been invested in the industry. In the beginning, the yearly out-turn was 1,500 sectors. But, due to certain technical difficulties, the production was reduced to 800 to 1,000 in 1965. In 1967-68, however, the production was raised to 7,500 scooters.

Hosiery Needles: The industry was started for the first time in the country in 1960 when a unit was established at Ludhiana with Japanese technical Know-how. From 1962-63, an automatic plant has been installed. About twenty types of needles, used in knitting machines, are manufactured. The industry faces competition from Chandigarh. Its annual production in 1966-67 was of the vale of Rs. 2,10 lakhs. The raw materials comprise high carbon strips and wire, both of which are imported from Japan.

Card Clothing: There is only one unit at Ludhiana engaged in card clothing since 1960, with a capital investment of about Rs. 10 lakhs. Its yearly out-turn is about Rs. 20 lakhs. Card clothing is Key industries for all textile mills. It provides employment to some 45 persons. The raw materials for the card clothing are foundation cloth, steel wire and end clips and plates (imported from Japan and Belgium). Stepping fillets-a kind of hard brush for clearing and clothing-are also manufactured.

Nylon and Staple Spinning: Only one unit is engaged in the production of nylon in the district at Ludhiana. It started production in April, 1964. The yearly output is worth about Rs. 7 lakhs.

Gas (Oxygen): The production of oxygen gas, used for welding purposes as well as in hospitals, started in the district towards the end of the year 1963, when the first factory was established at Ludhiana. The gas was thus made available at the place at comparatively cheap rates. Another concern also came up by the end of 1964. Rs. 18 lakhs have been invested in the industry. Previously the Ludhiana industry had to face difficulty in getting the materials from Delhi. The total capacity of both the units is 163 cubic metres per hours. The annual production in 1966-67 was worth Rs. 9.30 lakhs.

Measuring Tapes: The industry was started at Ludhiana in

1950 by the only concern which has since greatly expanded and is single largest tape producing unit in Asia. The technical know-how is indigenous. The installed machinery valued at Rs. 10 lakhs is both imported and improvised. Local made machines and parts have also been adapted for the purpose. Earlier only metallic woven measuring tapes were produced, but now glass fibre tapes, steel tapes and steel rules are also manufactured. There has been a remarkable improvement in the get-up of the tape in regard to shape and final finish. Besides there are 4 units in the small-scale sector. The annual production of industry in 1977-67 was worth Rs. 23 lakhs.

The industry meets the entire home demand, which was previously met through imports. The tapes are also exported to Middle East, South-East Asian countries and U.K. etc. The industry is thus a great foreign exchange earner.

It is a type of steel wire brush spread on 2" wide foundation cloth. This is used in cylinder, doffer and tops used in cotton and woollen textiles. This issued for carding in Cotton and Woollen Textile Mills. The special type of Brush is fitted I a cylinder in the doffer and tops machines. It functions as a spiral and spiral the material into fine fibres as a result of rotation.

Flour Mills: There are 2 roller flour mills at Ludhiana in the large scale sector. These produce flour, *maida, suji, dal, chokar, etc.* One of these was started in 1931 and the other in 1937. The mills have a total capacity of grinding 6,400 tons of wheat per month, but, due to shortage of food-grains, these are required to grind only imported wheat.

Hosiery: Ludhiana has been accepted as the home of hosiery industry, which has been established there for over a century. Ludhiana knitters control almost all markets with in the country and cater for about 90 per cent of the total demand. They have also entered the overseas marked to which the hosiery products have started flowing for the last about a decade and a half in ever increasing volume. Within the country, the industry meets the needs of both the civil population and the requirements of the Defence, Police and other Government Departments. Ludhiana hosiery products are very popular in several foreign countries like Ceylon, Burma, Africa, Thailand the Middle East and the Far East.

The industry races its origin to the thirties of the 19th century when, as a result of severe famine in Kashmir, several Kashmiri families left their homes in distress and settled down in Ludhiana and its environs. With their traditional skill and artistic talent they soon made the town a centre of knitting socks on wooden or steel rods. Thus they laid the foundation of a craft, which initially formed a useful spare-time job for the ladies only, but in course of time developed in to an important industry through the agency of the local traders who commercialized the artifact of the womenfolk. They usually knitted topless socks. After some years the knitting of complete socks was introduced here mainly through the enterprise of Jullundur girl, who was married to a businessman at Ludhiana. The girl had learnt the art from the wives of Gorkha military officials stationed at Jullundur. Thereafter, the socks and banians of a fines quality began to be knitted here.

It was near about 1894 that this primitive organisation of hosiery knitting by the women folk was given up and machine knitting was introduced at Ludhiana. This gave the local industry a revolutionary turn. The success of the first hosiery machine installed at Ludhiana in that year led to a number of firms installing these machines.

During the World War-I (1914-18), like many other industries, the hosiery industry also received its share of war boom, and the manufactures who had till then confined their attention to foot-wear alone, extended their activities to produce woollen sweaters and pullovers. Soon Ludhiana developed a brisk trade in this type of goods. Thus, it emerged as the home of Indian hosiery and was poised for a big leap forward. The introduction of Raschel loom from Germany brought about a radical change in the technique of production. It facilitated cheaper production on a mass scale.

During the depression following the World War-I (1914-18) the industry passed through a period of crisis as the prices of hosiery goods fell by 25 to 30 per cent due to competition from Japan. The local hosiery manufactures boldly faced this crisis by reducing the margin of profit and increasing their efficiency. The then Government of India also afforded adequate protection to hosiery industry through the Tariff Amendment Act of 1934, against Japanese dumping, which was further amended in 1936 to cover all braches of the hosiery industry.

The stoppage of imports chiefly from Japan and the tremendous demand for hosiery good by the Defence Department during the

World War-II (1939-45), helped the industry towards unprecedented expansion. But, the shortage of yarns and the scarcity of hosiery machine needles, for which the industry was dependent upon foreign supplies, did not allow the manufacturers to take full advantage of the position. To overcome this difficulty, the yarns and needles were supplied by the purchasing agency of the defence equipment. In spite of all these favourable circumstances the condition of the industry during the period was not satisfactory.

In spite of some major set-backs during the last 20 years-partition of the country, shortage of foreign exchange, Chinese aggression, Indo-Pak conflict, credit squeeze, re-organisation of Punjab, political agitations and the severe recession through which all the industries are presently passing-the woollen hosiery industry of Ludhiana has made remarkable progress. With the small hand-driven machines installed in the dark corners of small houses in the obscure little lanes of Ludhiana, the industry has been turning out production worth crores of rupees and catering to the entire needs of the country, both for civil and defence requirements. In 1966-67, there were 2,000 units in the industry with a total annual installed capacity of about Rs. 25 crores and an actual production of Rs. 12 crores, and an actual production of Rs. 12 crores, almost equally divided under three broad sections, viz:

(i) Home Market,

(ii) Defence requirements, and

(iii) Exports.

All the 2,00 units in the industry are not well-equipped, not more than about 50 per cent, i.e., 1,000 units, could be termed as effective.

The potentiality of the industry as a big foreign exchange earner has been realised in recent years. A beginning in the export field was made about 15 years back when some enterprising industrialists of Ludhiana visited foreign countries to explore markets for woollen hosiery. Despite tough competition, both in quality and price, from advanced countries, the industrialists succeeded in procuring orders in small lots, more or less as 'trial orders'. Till five years back the export of goods had grown around Rs. 50 Lakhs per annum.

The big leap in exports was accomplished four years ago when the East European countries felt interested in Indian woollen hosiery. Although still working with out-moded machines, this small-scale industry has now started exporting woollen hosiery in large quantities. The exports in 1966 were worth 4.55 crores of rupees and during 1967 these touched Rs. 4 crores. During the last three years, the major buyers were East European markets.

During the last three years, the major buyers were European markets. Goods worth about Rs. 50 Lakhs were also sold in the general currency areas, principally in the Middle East countries. During the current years, the industry has orders in hand worth Rs. 5 crores, of which about Rs. 3 crores are from East European Markets, and the remainder from the Middle East and African countries.

With successful fulfillment of the orders in hand, the industry expects to procure contracts for an additional value of at least Rs. One crore, which will make it possible for the industry to achieve a target of exports worth Rs. 6 crores in 1968. The war in the Middle East year has assisted the industry in exploring new avenues for its products, where from the orders have increased to about Rs. 50 Lakhs two years back. The main markets for the products of the industry are U.S.S.R., Czechoslovakia, Poland, Hungary, Bahrein, Burma, Kenya, Kuwait, Aden, Sudan, Libya, Honkong, Zambia, Tanzania, etc. The industry expects to touch the annual exports of atleast Rs. 8 crores in the next three years.

16. Power looms. – Started a few years before the World War II, the power loom industry made great strides in the post-Independence period. It switched on to the production of staple fabrics as mill made cotton yarn became un-available. The main raw materials for the industry, viz., staple yarn, art-silk, cotton-yarn of medium counts and woollen yarn, are produced mostly in other States. Some finer varieties are imported from abroad.

Mostly the powerlooms are of indigenous make. The industry includes both self-sale units and fabricators. Their number, which was only 50 in 1947, rose to 165 in 1954-55 and to 570 in 1966-67. The total investment in the industry was estimated at Rs. 75 lakhs in 1947 and Rs. 365 lakhs in 1961.

The total value of the production was estimated at Rs. 92 lakhs in 1947 and Rs. 430 lakhs in 1961. It rose to Rs. 722.60 lakhs in 1964-65, but fell to Rs. 497 lakhs in 1966-67.

Most of the powerlooms are working on staple and art silk

yarn. The main products are tehmats, linen and other varities of staple fabrics, ninon and shantoon, woollen shawls and corduroy.

Small Scale Industries

The small scale industries sector has progressively acquired a prominent place in the development activities of the country. Consequent upon the revision of the definition of the small-scale industry, the size and scope of the small scale industries sector has been considerably widened, thus enabling a large number of industrial units to avail themselves of increased assistance and facilities. The socioeconomic significance of the role of small-scale industries in relation to the economic development of the country has been more fully realised in the post-independence period. It is reflected in the two Industrial Policy Resolutions of the Government of India adopted in 1948 and 1956 as well as in the progressive allocations made for the development of this vital sector in the Five-Year Plans.

The total number of small scale units in Ludhiana district during 1965-66 was about 4,200 which rose to over 4,300 during 1966-67. The total production, which was worth about Rs. 26 crores during 1965-66, also rose to Rs. 27,50 crores during 12966-67. The increase in the new units during 1966-67 was the largest in the woollen hosiery; which rose from 1,887 in 1965-66 to 2,000 in 1966-67. The machine tool industry witnessed an increase in 11 units from 244 in 1965-66 to 255 in 1966-67. In the field of production the maximum increase was shown by the hosiery and machine tools sectors. The woollen hosiery production rose from Rs. 7 crores in 1965-66 to Rs. 8 crores in 1966-67 while the machine tools production registered an increase of Rs. 60 lakhs bringing total production to Rs. 2.5 cores.

Agricultural Implements: The incentive given by the Government for the development of agriculture in general and the selection of Ludhiana district for intensive agricultural programme in particular has given good stimulus to the manufacture of agricultural implements at Ludhiana. The industry has also shown good progress. In 1956 there were 15 units – 4 at Ludhiana and 11 at Samrala, engaged in the manufacture of agricultural implements. The production during the year was valued at Rs. 1.34 lakhs. In 1966-67, the number of units increased to 68 and produced goods worth Rs. 23.6 lakhs.

Dyeing: The dyeing industry made a start almost simultaneously with the setting up of the textile industry at Ludhiana. It caters to the needs of hosiery, power-looms and handloom industries. In 1960 the Ministry of Industry, Government of India, had defined small scale industries as industrial units with a capital investment of not more than Rs. 5 lakhs, capital investment for the purpose of the definition meant investment in fixed assets like land, buildings, machinery and equipment.

In view of the changed conditions and, in accordance with the recommendations of the Small Scale Industries Board, the Ministry of Industry, Government of India, has further amended the definition of small scale industries as:-

"Small Scale Industries will include all industrial units with a capital investment of not more than Rs. 7.50 lakhs irrespective of the number of persons employed. Capital investment of this purpose will mean investment in plant and machinery only."

In calculating the value of plant and machinery, the original price paid by the owner, irrespective of whether the plant and machinery, are new or second-hand, will be taken into account.

Previously, dyeing of wool in the district was done on a very small scale. The investment of the different units was meager and they were hardly in a position to install modern equipment. This position continued up to 1954-55 when there were 46 such units. In course of time, in addition to these hundreds of small units, eight bigger units came into existence in 1966-67. With the installation of modern equipment, the output has considerably improved in quantity and quality.

The units are split into the following three sectors:-

(i) units engaged in staple dyeing;

(ii) units engaged in wool dyeing; and

(iii) units engaged in wool dyeing for military contractors.

The raw materials for this industry are dyes-English and Indian, acids, bleaching power, soda ash and wood. Except for wood and acids, all the items are obtained from other states.

These units more or less work on fabrication basis and dye yarn of others. There are different grades of dyeing; fast to soap, fast to bhattim etc. Staple yarn dyeing is mostly indirect, i.e., kachha or fast soap. Wool dyeing for military contractors is fast to bhatti, whereas for civil consumption it is kachha or pucca. Staple dyeing is done mostly for handloom units.

Washing and Finishing: Washing and finishing is ancilliary to textile industry. On the setting up of textile units at Ludhiana, this industry has developed simultaneously. In 1956, there were 16 units located at Ludhiana, out of which two were registered under the Indian Factories Act. The number of units rose to 3 big and 20 small in 1965-66.

The machines used by these units comprise hydro-extractor for squeezing, dry-cleaning plant, tables, brass-press, wooden or stainless vats for bleaching tubs, etc.

The raw materials required for the three different processes of the industry are:

Wet washing	:	Soap, Soda and sulphuric acid.
Bleaching	:	Sodium hydro sulphite or potassium permanganate and sodium bisulphate.
Dry Cleaning	:	Petrol and turpentine oil (for woollen cloth).

Ludhiana badly needs a dyeing and finishing plant for hosiery industry. A plant will be installed at a cost of Rs. 50 lakhs. The State Government will purchase shares of Rs. 10 lakhs and the remaining will be owned by the private sector. It would increase the export potential of hosiery goods.

Calico Printing: The industry developed in Ludhiana alongside the development of textile industry. Mill made designed and printed cloth, however, caused a set back to calico printing. Although it is on the decline, yet some of the units are catering to the varied needs of the public. The industry is perennial but its peak season is summer months. In 1956, there were 12 units functioning in urban areas of the district. The number of units rose to 32 in 1965-66.

The tools consist of wooden blocks and addas, like tables with small legs and a stove. These are available locally except wooden blocks which are sometimes got prepared from other places.

The raw materials used are dyes, gum, acids, caustic soda and fuel, all of which are available locally.

The industry generally works on fabrication basis for printing chaddars kheses, etc., for the general public. The charges depend on the number of colours used.

The calico printing done at Ludhiana is popular with the public in general and sometimes people prefer to get some of their requirements printed instead of purchasing mill-made printed goods.

Nuts and Bolts: The products of this industry comprise two main types as under:

(i) Nuts and Bolts (hardware). – This industry was started in 1958. One big and two small units are engaged in the manufacture of nuts and bolts, panel pins, tinmen, rivets, nails, special type of screws and bolts, etc. This industry is auxiliary to Government projects and other industries. Besides, 100 units were in small scale sector, engaged in the manufacture of miscellaneous types of nuts and bolts, in 1966-67.

(ii) Nuts and Bolts (patta kabal). _ These comprise three main types, viz., oval plate belt, original potent plate and button plate, which are further sub-divided into several types.

The industry originated during the World War I (1914-18). Taking advantage of the heavy reduction in imports and the prevailing high prices for these articles, a number of small units sprang up in and around Ludhiana. The product turned out by these factories was of somewhat crude type, yet it could find market because of acute scarcity of this essential component of industrial machinery.

The industry entered a new phase after the partition in 1947 when it began to expand on a big scale.

In the district, there are 16 units engaged in the manufacturing of patta-kabla. Out of these one is in the large-scale category. About Rs. 4 lakhs are invested in the industry. The annual out-turn is Rs. 4 lakhs. The products of large-scale unit are certified to be of the standard prescribed by the National Physical Laboratory, Delhi.

The raw materials used are iron, steel and stainless steel, indigenous as well as imported.

Electrical Goods: The industry was started in 1955 on a small-scale. Initially only starters for electric motors were manufactured. In course of time, iron clad switches, of different ranges up to 200 AMPS 500 Volts, began to be manufactured.

Rs. 10 lakhs have been invested in the industry. 4o units were engaged in 1966-67 in the manufacture of electrical goods worth Rs. 20.05 lakhs.

At present, the industry is on small scale. But, with the increasing electrification of rural areas and the installation of tubewells, it has a fairly bright chance of entering into the large scale phase.

Cotton Ginning and Oilseed Crushing: Khanna was a well known cotton mandi in the beginning of the present century. Gradually the people of the area switched over to sowing of groundnut. Before the installation of oil/ginning mills in Khanna, cotton and groundnut were exported to other areas. The export entailed a lot of trouble due to unwieldy volume/bulk of the cotton/groundnut. The first ginning and oil mill was established at Khanna in 1905. It had daily oil capacity of 9 tons and 7,632 bales of ginned cotton. During the World War II (1939-45) two more oil mills were started in 1939 and 1941. Since 1958 six oil/ginning mills were opened. Thus by 1967 there were 9 oil mills, out of which 4 were also engaged in cotton ginning. Rs. 78 lakhs were invested in the industry with the annual out-turn extraction of 3,38,886 quintals of oil and 52,632 ginned cotton bales with daily capacity of 220 tons and 240 bales, respectively. There are also two cotton ginning mills of sizable capacity at Jagraon.

Amongst these mills one is a solvent oil mill at Khanna. It also manufactures cattle feed, fertilizers and poultry feed from by-products, viz., deoiled cake. This unit also manufactures vegetable oil biscuits. The Mill also produced soap from certain by-products. This unit further extracts oil from rice bran.

In the district oilseed-crushing, flour-milling dal-milling and cotton-ginning is a composite industry. There were 12 units of cotton-ginning and 28 units engaged in oilseeds crushing. The annual production was 60,000 bales in 1968. Besides, groundnut, the oilseed industry crushes mustard, cotton seeds, linseed (alsi), etc. The groundnut-crushing is confined to Khanna. Its by-products are oil-cakes, etc.

Surgical Instruments: The manufacture of surgical instruments at Ludhiana is, like many other industries, a product of the partition of 1947. The only unit engaged in the manufacture of surgical instruments at the place was originally shifted from Sialkot where surgical instruments were manufactured by the well-known ironsmiths of kotli Loharan, who were the famous manufacturers of the guns and arms under the Lahore Darbar. The industry was rehabilitated at Ludhiana through the enterprise of the dealer, who migrated from West Pakistan. He was fortunate to find a handful of refugee workers from Sialkot and readily engaged them in this industry.

The Unit was first established in 1949. Till 1966-67 there were 2 units, one on very small scale with annual production worth about Rs. 2.5 lakhs. The industry, however, does not admit of rapid scope of expansion.

Different kinds of surgical instruments used in government as well as private hospital are manufactured. These include ophthalmic instruments, special purpose needless and canulae, electric-medical appliances, table-lamps (anglepoise type), etc. Eye-operating instruments are a speciality of one unit throughout the country. That concern has been approved by the All India Institute of Medical Sciences. The industry foreign exchange earner and saver. The main raw materials required by the industry are mild steel, carbon steel, stainless steel, brass, etc.

Plastic Goods: The industry developed in the district along with the cycle industry as it meets the requirements of some plastic cycle parts. Out of the two units engaged in it the first was established in 1952. The industry manufactures cycle-handle grips reflectors polythene tubular film, plastic bags and plastic cane etc. In 1966-67 there were 15 units with annual production for Rs. 9.75 lakhs.

Paints and Varnishes: The only concern in the district for manufacturing paints and varnishes is located at Ludhiana. Started on a very small-scale in 1955, it has made marked progress and has taken up the preparation of synthetic enamels, stoving enamels, black Japan, stoving varnishes, stiff paints and primus. About Rs. 2 lakhs have been invested in the industry with annual production of Rs. 3.15 lakhs in 1966-67.

Umbrella Ribs: First started at Ludhiana in 1957 on a small scale, the industry became well-established by 1961. high carbon steel wire is used in the manufacture of umbrella ribs. Nearly Rs. 3 lakhs have been invested in the industry. In 1966-67 annual out-turn was Rs. 3.15 lakhs.

Radio Assembling: This industry sprang up in the district after Independence in 1947 when three units started assembling radio-sets. On an average all of them assembled nearly 500 sets in a year. The number of units gradually rose to ten. In 1966-67 the number of units assembling radios and transistors was 44.17. Only four parts of the radios and eleven of the transistors are said to be imported while the rest are manufactured in the country.

Rubber Goods: Started in 1956, this industry manufactures saddle tops, rubber-paddle rods, rubber solution (rough), V-shaped chappals, motor spare-parts (rubber), etc. It is sustained by cycle and motor industry. Rs. 1.50 lakhs have been invested in the industry. In 1966-67 there were 9 units with annual production worth Rs. 3.45 lakhs.

Stationery Articles: The main articles manufactured in the district include pencils, pins and table stationery as detailed below:

(i) Pencils. – Only one unit is engaged in the district at Ludhiana since 1949. Started on a small scale to begin with, it developed in course of time and by 1960 automatic machines were installed. All types of pencils, viz., writing, drawing, checking, artist, copying and even cosmetic, are manufactured at Ludhiana. For the manufacture of superior types of pencils, cedar wood is imported from U.S.A. Stamping foil is also imported. Due to import restrictions, major portion of the product, consisting of cheap pencils, is manufactured constituent, is obtained from Ahmadabad (Gujarat).

(ii) Pins. – The industry was started in 1961. There are two pin manufacturing concerns in Ludhiana, Pins, gem-clips (triangular) over-clips and stapple (used in stappling machines) are manufactured. The total production per year is worth Rs. 1.50 lakhs. The total production per year is worth Rs. 1.50 lakhs. Mild steel wire constitutes its main raw material.

(iii) Table Stationery. – The only unit engaged in the industry in the district at Ludhiana was started in 1959. It manufactures office punching machines – small and heavy, stamping machines, stamp-stands, blotters, table-files, paper-trays, waste-paper baskets, pen-trays, letter-racks, call bells, commercial office file clips, etc.

Snap Buttons: The industry was started in Ludhiana at 1959 when only one unit had gone into production. Afterwards two more units came up, of which only one could survive. Manufacture of both parts of snap-button, viz., male and female, as also their tin-plating, is done locally. Rs. I lakh have been invested in the industry. In 1966-67 the annual production was worth Rs. 4.75 lakhs.

The raw materials used are brass strips and phosphor-bronze wire.

Spray Pumps: There is only one unit in the district at Ludhiana, engaged in this industry. Established in 1959, it has the capacity of manufacturing goods worth about fifteen lakh rupees which can fully meet the requirements of the State as a whole. It manufacturers spray dusting machines — — both power and hand-operated, used for anti-malarial operations and civil defence purposes.

Steel Furniture: In 1966-67, three units were engaged in the manufacture of steel furniture and produced goods worth Rs. 6.10 lakhs during the year. The main items produced are steel almirahs, sofa-cum-bed, sofa fix-tubulars, cash-boxes, safes and a few items of office furniture.

Washing Soap: Soap making is an old indigenous industry of the district. The principal centre is Ludhiana, others being Khanna, Raikot and Jagraon.

The important raw materials needed by the industry are caustic soda, oils, soapstone or sodium silicate.

In 1966-67, 94 units engaged in this industry, with production amounting to Rs. 29 lakhs.

Zip Fasteners: The only unit of its kind in the country engaged in the manufacture of invisible zip fasteners is located at Ludhiana.18 It was started in 1963 with the American machinery and technical know-how. The articles manufactured are invisible-zip fasteners. Its production in 1966-67 was of the value of Rs. 2.05 lakhs.

Chemicals: There is no chemical industry as such in the district. However, an agency of the D.C.M. (Delhi Cloth & General Mills) at Ludhiana deals in soda caustic, bleaching powder, all kinds of acids, etc. After packing the goods in sizeable packs, this firm supplies them to retailers and consumers.

Casting/Forging: Casting industry was started at Ludhiana about the year 1922 when two or three small units, having small crucible furnaces, one of them having small cupola furnace, were set up. During the early stages, the Industry was confined to casting of hosiery machine parts and oil-engine small parts for repair purposes. The above strength of casting units continued for some two decades whereafter the industry began to expand and by the time of the partition of 1947 the number of units had gone up to about 15. At the time, toka (fodder cutter) and oil engine main parts also began to be manufactured. After the partition, the number of units increased in 1966-67 to 140 with annual production of Rs. 39.25 lakhs and the industry concentrated itself at Ludhiana.

The industry produces oil engines, machine tools, sewing-machines, hosiery-machines, re-rolling mills, centrifugal pumps and other miscellaneous agricultural implements which have been discussed under respective heads. The forging industry has also been discussed under the heading nuts and bolts.

Oil Expellers and Parts: The post-partition period also saw the brewing of another industry, viz., the manufacture of oil expellers and their parts. In 1954-55, the number of units was 8, besides one composite unit which had also undertaken the manufacture of spare-parts, employing 77 workers in all. The only unit of its kind in India, his is the second in Asia, the first being in Japan which started production in 1960.

Hosiery Machines: As an important ancilliary to the well-developed industry, the credit for starting the manufacture of hosiery machines goes to a Ludhiana (Nandpur) firm which launched the enterprise in 1921. It started with the manufacture of simple circular socks-machines. Shortly afterwards, about 6 to 7 units entered the field and round and dialdar machines also began to be manufactures. About the year 1938-39, was started the manufacture of Raschal machines which revolutionized the industry. By 1950-51, flat interlock and sinker machines also began to be manufactured. Flat machine was sub-standard in the beginning; but attained perfection about the year 1958-59. Now all types of machines used in the industry are manufactured in the district. With the exception of one unit working in Nandpur, the industry is, however, concentrated in Ludhiana proper. The district can boast of a well-developed hosiery manufacturing industry with several concerns manufacturing quite elaborate structures with reputable precision. Major portion of the demand for machines is being met locally.

There were 20 units engaged in the hosiery machine manufacturing industry in 1954-55. In 1956, the number rose to 28 which continued as such till 1965-66.

Lathes of different sizes, drilling machines, milling machines, shapers and grinders are some of the machines used by this industry.

Iron and steel are the chief raw material of the industry. The machines manufactured are: "Check Petti, Jay Jacquard Machine, Circular Non-Sinker Body Machine, Sinker Body Machine, Interlock, Raschal Machine 96" wide, cold Calendering Machine, Steam Calendering Machine, Battle Bobbin Winder, Circular Hand Knittin, Circular Plain Rib, Circular Half Jacquard, automatic sock machines, flats and over-look, etc.

Textile Machinery (Spare-parts): There is only one unit in the district at Ludhiana engaged in the manufacture of textile machinery spare parts in the district, such as reel and pin, winders, reeling machine, powerloom spare parts, and steam and cold calender.

Conduit Pipes: This industry was started in the district as late as 1959. In 1966-67, there were 6 units engaged in the manufacture of conduit pipes and produced goods worth Rs. 5.22 lakhs and provided employment to 55 workers. The number of units decreased in the said year due to inter-State competition.

Village Industries

A village industry means any industry which forms the normal occupation, whether, whole-time, of any class of the rural population. According to the Planning Commission, village industries are those small industries which are, in the main, an integral part of the village economy. The small-scale industries located in village areas, thus, come under the village industries category. The employment provided by the village industries is mainly seasonal, and the seasons vary from industry to industry as well as from area to area.

The manufacture of power looms is restricted under the orders of the Textile Commissioner, Government of India. The first effort in the direction of developing village industries and of reviving the old industries started with the *Swadeshi* movement launched by Mahatma Gandhi.

Handloom Weaving.-It is an age-old industry carried on by hereditary weavers. The period prior to and following the World War II helped the industry to regain some importance because of the shortage of cloth. Though of late textile mills and powerlooms have dealt a stunning below to the handloom industry, it is receiving due protection from the State. Some varieties of cloth have been earmarked for manufacture only by the handloom. Weavers are helped to convert throw shuttle looms into fly-shuttle looms. A cess has been imposed on mill-made cloth, the proceeds of which are utilized towards rebate to customers.

The main raw materials are hand and mill spun yarn, staple and woollen yarn. Hand spun yarn is available in plenty from village folk in the district. All other varieties of yarn, excepting worsted yarn to some extent, are secured form other States.

Handloom weaving is carried on in all towns of the district. In villages it continues as an important industry. The goods produced by handloom are khadi, woollen mufflers, shawls, tie-cloth, khes and staple cloth.

Leather and Hides Tanning: Hides, skins and bark of kikkar tree form the main raw materials for the industry.

The industry mainly depends upon the death rate of cattle. The hides and skins of dead animals are first flayed and then treated with kikkar bark which forms the locality available tanning material.

The hereditary Chamars (tanners), who are mostly engaged in this occupation, lack up-to-date technical know-how and hence do not use modern type of equipment. They remove the leather with crude knives and spoil it. The tanners, too, are not acquainted with modern technique of tanning and thereby reduce the value of leather. Tanning is, however, practiced by few only, the general practices is to sell away hides.

In 1966-67, 450 units were engaged in this industry which produced goods worth Rs. 35.75 lakhs.

The cottage units, engaged in the industry, have been mostly organised into cooperative societies. Some of these cooperative societies are working as production-cum-sales organisations. These model tanneries have been set up with the assistance from the Khadi Board.

Jagraon is the main urban centre for the industry in the district. The cottage units there have been organised into cooperative societies.

The leather produced by these cottage establishments is mostly used as sole leather or for making country (desi) shoes

Shoes and Leather Goods Manufactures. – Shoe making is also an ancient industry among the traditional shoe-makers. Based on style, leather foot wear is commonly classified into western type and desi type. These types of footwear are manufactures of all leather, upper leather and sloe of other material, etc., in the district. The raw material for western type of shoes and chrome used as upper, mostly in the manufacture of desi type, are imposed fro other States. 1135 units were engaged in this industry in 1966-67 with yearly out-turn of Rs. 9.30 lakhs.

Kohlu (Village Oil Presses). – With the introduction of power driven oil-crashers, the use of kohlus has greatly decreased. Now, there exist only a few kohlus in rural areas. 10 units were engaged in 1966-67 in the industry with annual out-turn of Rs. 1.15 lakhs.

Ban and Rope Making. – It is the industry of the villages in the bet area, lying near the bank of the river Satluj, where bhabar grass-the basic raw material for the industry – is available in appreciable quantities. Besides bhabar grass, the locally produced moonj is also used for ban making. Improved types of machines, hand-driven and power-fitted, are now used for ban making. These are provided by Government besides loans for purchase of raw material, etc., in the form of loan and subsidy, etc. There were 70 units engaged in ban and rope making in 1966-67 with annual production of Rs. 105 lakhs.

Gur and Khandsari. – The indigenous production of sugar consisted of gur and Khandsari. Machhiwara was famous in olden days for the manufacture of *khandsari* by means of Khanchi system, whereby the raw material, rab, was allowed to settle for a number of days in Khanchi tanks lined with green fibrous material (cellulose) found in the nalas; and the upper layer of the sediments was separated after the drainage of the residual (seera) through a hole at the bottom of the tank. The sediment thus collected was strongly rubbed by feet-pressing and white khandsari, stated to be most useful from health point of view, was available for marketing.

With the partition of the country in 1947, the Muslim artisans shifted to Pakistan, and the sugarcane crop having failed for a number of years afterwards, the khandsari industry could not be revived on previous scale for lack of skill and shortage of sugarcane.

Sugar industry in the modern sense meaning white sugar industry, is new in India Indigenous production of sugar usually consisted of brown sugar popularly known as gur. Although gur is simply unrefined sugar its nutritive value is far greater than that of the white sugar. White sugar was also being manufactured under the khandsari process

In the absence of any sugar mill in the district, these is not much allurement to the cultivators to grow sugarcane. They produce gur, etc., on small scale, mostly for their personal use. The surplus is sold in the market. The popularity of white sugar has, therefore, not much affected the production of gur and khadsari, which are imported even from places outside the district. 26 units engaged in gur and khadsari in 1966-67 produced goods worth Rs. 4.80. Lakhs.

Handicrafts.-Punjab is justly pound of its rich and remarkable heritage if industrial arts and crafts. The Land of Five Rivers is rightly renowned for its notable contribution to the art of embroidery, especially the unique phulkari work, which until recently used to be common in rural areas, fine and soft embroidered shawls and artistic multi-design and colourful bedspreads and kheses are some of the well known handicrafts of the district. Traditional pottery wares, dolls, toys, bastetry and artistic bamboo articles are also characteristic crafts of this area.

These cottage industries not only provide gainful primary or subsidiary occupation to a large number of people in the rural and urban areas, but also serve as medium of self-expression. Long period of foreign rule and the impact of the western mode of life and import of cheap foreign good were largely responsible for the progressive deterioration of most of the traditional handicrafts.

The partition dealt a severe blow to the large numbers of skilled craftsmen who had to leave the district and also gave a severe set-back to the mixed economy. The mass migration of Muslims adversely affected industrial arts and crafts. The people and the Government had thus to grapple with a very difficult situation. The innate fortitude and mettle of the people and the willing help by the Government arrested the decadence in economy.

The placing of our handicrafts on a sound and stable economic footing is a very difficult problem. Their diversity and wide diffusion through the countryside complicated the organisational problem. In a country like India, with a very low per capita income, the economy of handicrafts is bound to have weak foundations. In the present day economic set-up, whatever the degree of skill and competence, it is difficult for an individual craftsman to stand in isolation and survive in the face of strong competitive pressures. The remedy lies in creating a proper association or organisation of craftsman.

The best organisation in which lay hope of survival for this loosely organised sector is the cooperative pattern. This pattern has already proved its worth in handloom cooperatives. Industrial cooperative in other fields are also gaining ground. The cooperative idea has come to stay and it is hoped that the organisational weakness from which handicrafts suffer will be largely met as cooperatives in this field gain in strength and stability. The policy of the State Government has been to encourage the formation of the cooperatives of artisans and craftsman. Upto June 30, 1966, 25 handicrafts cooperative societies for women and 4 for men with a membership of 267 and 43 workers, respectively, were organised in the district. The inadequacy of finances for day-to-day working is another serious hurdle. The credit institution for the supply of capital requirements of this sector are ill-developed. As far as possible, requirements are being met under the provisions of the State Aid to Industries Act, 1935.

The State Government is also channelising its fund for credit to industrial cooperatives, including handicrafts cooperatives, through cooperative financing institutions. Separate industrial cooperative banks have been set up for this purpose. These banks provide credit facilities to handicrafts workers in the cooperative field on easy terms.

Role of Industrial Cooperatives

The role of cooperatives in the sphere of industrial development has been recognised. An average industrial worker, particularly in rural areas, does not possess sufficient capital for installing improved type of machinery. Apart from this, he requires raw material and working capital for running his unit. After production of goods, their sale at such prices as can bring adequate return to the worker, is equally essential. In short, credit, raw material and marketing of finished gods are three important requirements of an industrial worker.

The best solution of these difficulties seems to be organisation of cooperatives of industrial workers. It provides two distinct advantages: requisite facilities by the Government and the pooling of capital and skill.

The industrial cooperative movement has made considerable progress in the district. The industrial cooperatives governing hosiery goods are the most organised and 90 per cent of the production of hosiery cooperatives in the country is from Ludhiana. The other cooperative of note cover cycle-parts, sewing-machine parts, etc. The following table indicates the industrial cooperative societies working in the district up to June, 1966:-

S. N.	*Name of Industry*		*No. of Societies*
1.	Handloom Weaving	..	97
2.	Small-scale Industries-		
	(a) Leather goods	..	26
	(b) Engineering Industries	..	89
	(c) Wood work	..	14
	(d) Miscellaneous (brick kilns, hosiery, etc.)	..	111
3.	Khadi and Village Industries-		
	(a) Non-edible Oils and Soap Industries	..	12
	(b) Pottery	..	1
	© Gur and Khandsari	..	6
	(d) Ghani oil	..	13
	(e) Cobblers	..	102
	(f) Leather tanning and flaying of skins	..	19
	(g) Others	..	3
	(h) Handicrafts	..	4

The value of the goods produced by these societies, during the years ending June, 1965 and 1966, is given below:

Industrial Cooperatives	Year ending June, 1965 Rs.	Year ending June, 1966 Rs.
I. Handloom Weaving	1,34,630	79,018
II. Khadi and Village Industries	1,08,420	56,820
III. Small-scale Industries (including handicrafts)	2,72,215	18,36,550

The District Cooperatives Industrial Union, which looks after the sale of manufactures goods and supply of raw materials to various cooperative societies in the district, was registered on October 5, 1950. It has its sale depot at Ludhiana. The affairs of the Union are looked after by a Board of Directors of ten members. It has a membership of 152 societies including 18 individuals.

The administrative control of the industrial cooperative was transferred to the Industries Department in September, 1963, prior to which these cooperatives were under the Cooperative Department. The Deputy Registrar, Industrial Cooperatives, Ludhiana, attends to the field work throughout the State. He has under him Industrial Assistant Registrars, Cooperative Societies, Jullundur, Ludhiana, Amritsar and at the State headquarters.

The development of industrial cooperatives in the district is looked after by the Industrial Assistant Registrar, Cooperative Societies, Ludhiana, who is assisted by 5 Inspectors, 16 Sub-Inspectors (including 2 Handloom Sub-Inspectors), Statistical Assistant, and other miscellaneous staff.

Details regarding the loans and subsidies advanced to the cooperative societies, during the years 1964-65 and 1965-66, are given below:

Particulars	*1964-65*		*1965-66*	
	Loans Rs.	*Subsidy Rs.*	*Loan Rs.*	*Subsidy Rs.*
Weaver's society	53,814	2,282	51,660	900
Small-scale Industries Societies	2,99,543	36,540	2,38,957	22,095
Khadi Societies	48,778	—	86,516	—
Handicrafts Societies	—	—	—	—

A weavers colony is under construction near the Model Town, Ludhiana.

Manufactures Association

The registered manufactures associations functioning in the district in 1965 were s under:

S. N.	Name of Association	Date of Registration
1	Home Hosiery Manufactures Union, Ludhiana	September 4, 1941
2	Northern India Hosiery Manufacturing Corporation, Ludhiana	July 28, 1950
3	Bharat Hosiery Manufacturing Corporation, Ludhiana	May 24, 1951
4	Shawl Manufacturing Association, Ludhiana	July 20, 1961
5	Hosiery Industry Welfare Board, Ludhiana	September 18, 1961
6	Ludhiana Machine Tools Makers Guild, Ludhiana	October 24, 1961
7	Cottage Hosiery Manufacturing Corporation Ludhiana	July 2, 1962
8	Ludhiana Foundry and Engineers Association, Ludhiana	July 18, 1962
9	Ludhiana Knitting Wool Processor's Merchants Society, Ludhiana	August 21, 1962
10	Ludhiana Hosiery Small-scale Union Ludhiana	October 16, 1962
11	Hand Knitting Wool Processers Welfare Society, Ludhiana	October 19, 1962
12	Hosiery Industry Federation, Ludhiana	November 14, 1962
13	Interlock Cloth and Banyan Manufacturing Association, Ludhiana	January 28, 1963
14	Ludhiana Cycle Parts Suppliers Association, Ludhiana	April 1, 1963
15	Ludhiana Electroplaters' Association, Ludhiana	July 30, 1963
16	Banyan Manufactures Association, Ludhiana	August 16, 1963

Industrial Labour

The industrial labour in the district is mostly drawn from the local population or from the neighbouring villages. They live in all localities including slum areas and industrial colonies. Besides, a good number return to the neighbouring villages. The industrial expansion in the district has provided an incentive to the agricultural labour to switch labour to switch over to industry.

The industrial Training Institute, Institute of Textile Chemistry and Knitting Technology, and Industrial Schools now increasingly meet the demand for skilled labour and thereby greatly help the development of industries in the district.

Labour and Employees Organisations.-The following is the list of registered industrial workers unions as it stood in 1965:-

S. N.	Name of Union	Date of Registration
1	Hosiery Workers Union, Ludhiana	February 21,1952
2	District Textile Workers Union, Ludhiana	June 10,1955
3	Hosiery Workmen Association, Ludhiana	February 6, 1959
4	Ludhiana Iron and Steel Workers Union, Ludhiana	September 29,1959
5	District Iron and Steel Workers Union, Ludhiana	November 10, 1959
6	General Labour Union, Ludhiana	May 28,1960
7	Hosiery Mazdoor Union, Ludhiana	July 27, 1962
8	Pearl Woollen Mills Workers Union, Ludhiana	August 21, 1962
9	Chakki Mazdoor Union, Ludhiana	November 3, 1962
10	Cycle Mazdoor Union, Ludhiana	April 11, 1963
11	Metal Mazdoor Snagh Union, Ludhiana	June 1, 1933
12	Dyeing and Finishing Workers Union, Ludhiana	June 12, 1963
13	Ludhiana Textile Mazdoor Union, Ludhiana	October 5, 1963
14	Woollen Mills Workers Association, Ludhiana	November 4,1963
15	Supreme Karamchari Union, Ludhiana	November 8, 1963

Contd...

16	National Saw Mills Mazdoor Union, Ludhiana	December 26, 1963
17	District Engineering Workers Union, Ludhiana	January 20, 1964
18	Hosiery Mazdoor Sangh Union, Ludhiana	February 12, 1964
19	Press Workers Union, Ludhiana	August 12, 1964
20	Krishna Roller and Flour Mills Workers Union, Ludhiana	May 13, 1964

(Source:-Labour Commissioner, Punjab, Chandigarh)

SSI in India

In 1947 after gaining independence, India initiated a path of industrialization to achieve economic prosperity. India focused on developing the manufacturing base. Much of the countries development was done through the five year plans. Industries like iron and steel, oil refineries, cement and fertilizer were brought under the gamut of public sector enterprises. The decision makers then encouraged the development of small scale industries. They perceived that Indian small scale industries would play a vital role in the economic progress of the country and had immense potential for employment generation. Developing small scale sector would also result in decentralized industrial expansion, better distribution of wealth and to encourage investment and entrepreunial talent.

The government has initiated several policies for the growth and development of small scale industries. They included reservation of certain items to be manufactured only by the small scale sector. Other measures include credit marketing, technology, and entrepreneurship development, fiscal, financial and infrastructural support. In 1999, the government established the Ministry of Small Scale Industries and Agro and Rural industries to make policy decisions for the development and well being of the small scale industries.

Initially the small scale sector was characterized as traditional labour intensive units with outdated machineries and inefficient production techniques. But in the recent past the condition of the small scale units has improved. Today they have installed modern machines, applied better management techniques and are much more productive than before.

SSI-Location

Small Scale Industries are located throughout the country, though predominantly in the rural areas. The small scale industries in the rural areas are skill based, wherein the skill for manufacturing is passed on from one generation to another. Some of the goods manufactured in these units are textile handicrafts, woodcarving, stone carving, metal ware etc. Small scale industrial factories are also present in urban areas and usually they account for the maximum volume of production for that particular good in the country. For e.g. Ludhiana in the state of Punjab is the main centre in the country for producing woollen hosiery, sewing machine parts, bicycles and its parts, similarly Tiruppur in Tamil Nadu accounts for small scale firms that are involved in spinning, weaving and dying of cotton garments.

Post Liberalization

Post liberalization economic conditions has created immense growth prospect for the small scale industries. The government has also supported the small scale industries by the way of implementing policies like investment ceiling for the SSI sector and priority lending. The formation of WTO in 1995 resulted in a major challenge to the well being of the SSI. The protection given to the SSI in the form of reservation and quantitative restrictions has been withdrawn. More than 160 items reserved under the SSI category have been de reserved. It has been found that if the SSI upgrades the technology, adopt better management practices, reengineer the factories to improve productivity and provide qualitative product, they would be competitive in the post WTO scenario. The advancement in computer and telecommunication technology, increase in e commerce, opening up of markets due to WTO, mergers and acquisitions, improved infrastructure and outsourcing noncore area of business have all contributed to the growth of SSi.

50 years of Industrial Development: 1947-1997:

Punjab's industrial development can be broken up into five periods:

- The post-1947 phase
- The development of small-scale units

- Large and Medium scale industry
- The high-tech phase
- The diversification of industries

Post-Partition:

Pre-partition Punjab had very little industry and the industries that existed were a few woollen mills in Amritsar and Dhariwal, some old iron foundries in Batala and Mandi Gobindgarh and a couple of sugar mills. The economy of the state was totally dominated by agriculture and but processing of agricultural products was virtually unknown.

The Development of Small Scale Units

During the '50s and '60s, there was an explosion in the number of small scale units. Growth centred around Ludhiana, Jalandhar, Amritsar, Goraya. Most of these units produced bicycles, sewing machines, agricultural implements, medical instruments, hosiery, machine tools and sports goods or parts for these goods. This phase saw the emergence of a few units to process agricultural produce such as sugar mills at Batala and Bhogpur. Small scale industrial units number more than 0.2 million in Punjab today; they employ more than 0.9 million workers and constitute a vital and dynamic segment of industry. The growth of the small scale sector was encouraged by government policies in the Five-Year Plans and the establishment of the Punjab Financial Corporation in 1953.

Large & Medium Scale Industry:

Unavailability of major raw material such as Iron or Coal, was a definite hindrance for the establishment of large and medium scale units in Punjab. Punjab Government stepped in to help make large & medium scale production profitable in Punjab. The establishment of the Punjab State Industrial Development Corporation in the '60s was intended to fill the gap in the development of the state. Acting as an entrepreneur, the PSIDC, on its own promoted projects and also set up larger units in the joint sector. These objects reached their fruition in the '70s and '80s and included Punjab Tractors Ltd (PTL), Punjab Wireless (PUNWIRE), Punjab Alkalies Ltd, Punjab Communication Ltd. (PCL) are some of them.

The High-Tech Phase

The '70s witnessed the foundation of electronics production. The Punjab government set up an Electronics Township called ELTOP on a 290-acre site in Mohali, near Chandigarh. This township has emerged as one of the fastest growing centres for electronics production in the country. Projects set up in the township cover microelectronic devices, computers, computer peripherals, communications, electronic typewriters, nickel cadmium batteries, uninterrupted power supply systems, colour picture TV tubes, medical electronics, X-ray equipment, EPABX systems, many with technical collaboration with companies like Granger of USA, OKI and NEC of Japan, and ARE of Italy. The only facility in the country for the design and fabrication of very large scale integrated circuits, the Semiconductor Complex (SCL) is also located in this township.

Punjab Leads in manufacture of machines and hand tools, printing and paper machinery, auto parts and electrical switchgears. Punjab produces around 75% of bicycle and bicycle parts, sewing machines, Woollen and other Hosiery items, Shoddy blanket and jacket clothes and sports goods.

About Kssidc

Profile of the Company

The growth of Small Scale Industries in our country since independence is rightly regarded as one of the most significant features of planned economic development. The very concept of small-scale industries, as we know, was not in vogue on the eve of independence. Rural and Cottage industries, which constituted the "indigenous sector" of our industries, were wide spread throughout the length and breadth of our country. Various programmes to sustain, modernise and further develop this group of industries were initiated soon after the independence and the modern small-scale industry scheme has gradually emerged out of this programme. The Small Scale Industries have provided opportunities for self employment to educated young men and experienced technicians from the middle level of society and contributed full to the growth of industrial entrepreneurship in our country. To day small-scale industries is regarded as power tool for balanced regional economic development. These achievements are primarily due to the dynamic enterprising spirit of the small-scale industrialists themselves. A positive programme for assistance of small-scale industries was initiated towards the end of 1954 on the basis of a suggestion made by the international planning team sponsored by the Ford Foundation at the request of Govt. of India. Further, on the basis of the recommendations of the central small scale industries advisory board the state level organisations to assist the small scale industries for procurement of scarce raw materials establishment of industrial estates, etc., have been set up in all states. KSSIDC, is one of such Corporations, established on 29th April 1960. The registered office of the Company started functioning at Bangalore in the State of Karnataka. The Company framed comprehensive and well-defined Memorandum of Association and Articles of Association. Which permit the Corporation to take up any activity aimed at the rapid development of small-scale industry, subject to the guidelines issued by the Government from time to time and also as per Govt.

4

Land Reform after Independence

The Agrarian Reforms Since Independence

During the last years of the colonial era, numerous congresses and commissions called for agrarian reforms and worked out appropriate suggestions. If, prior to independence, the demand for agrarian reforms was part of the strategy of the leading parties to gain power, independence fostered not only a favourable climate for such measures, but helped the new governments to legitimize their power. Not only the motivation, but the measures, too, were very similar in India and in Pakistan. However, each time, they were enforced more rapidly and strictly in India, whereas Pakistan showed more regard for the landowning strata.

Agrarian Reform in India

Agrarian Reform in India had been adopted to reallocate the agricultural resources among all the people directly connected with agriculture. After independence, the Government of India started the process of building equity in rural population and improvement of the employment rate and productivity. So for this reason the Government had started agrarian reform.

Reasons Behind Agrarian reform:

- Since India had been under several rulers for a long time, i.e right from the beginning of the middle age, that's why it's rural economic policies kept changing. The main focus of those policies was to earn more money by exploiting the poor farmers.

- In the British period the scenario had not changed much. The British Government introduced the "Zamindari" system where the authority of land had been captured by some big and rich landowners called Zamindar. Moreover they created an intermediate class to collect tax easily.
- This class had no direct relationship with agriculture or land. Those Zamindars could acquire land from the British Government almost free of cost. So the economic security of the poor peasants lost completely. After independence, the Government's main focus was to remove those intermediate classes and secure a proper land management system. Since India is a large country, the redistribution process was a big challenge for the Government.

Objectives:

According to agrarian reform land was declared as a property of State Government. So agrarian reform varied from state to state.

But the main objectives of agrarian reform in India were:

- Setting proper land management,
- Abolition of Intermediaries
- Preventing fragmentation of lands,
- Tenancy reform.

The land policies of different states faced several controversies. In some state the reform measures were biased in favour of the big land owners who could wield their political influence. However, agrarian reform in India had set a healthy socioeconomic structure in the rural areas.

Agrarian reform measures since independence had been determined by more than hundred laws of the Indian constitution. India is a democratic country and so every state had different laws. So, construction of a general idea of agrarian reform measures in India was tough. Agrarian reform measures in India since independence had similarity with that of Pakistan.

- Interpretations of Agrarian Reform Measures:

Agrarian reform measures can be interpreted commonly through two measures.

- Land Management Reform Measures: The purpose of agrarian reforms can be fulfilled by land management reform measures. The marketing system for both producing the inputs and as well as selling the outputs is important to improve the income of common farmers. Political power of the big landlords should be minimized to improve land management.

- Land Ownership Reform Measures: It includes five things:
  - o Redistribution of Land: This involves requisition of lands, redistribution of land and finally the financial redistribution.
  - o Collectivization of Land,
  - o Individualization of Land.

Improving Ceilings for Landholdings

Ceilings for Landholdings was imposed as one of the measures of agrarian reform in India after independence to redistribute land and land properties. The main aim of these ceilings was the demolition of the large amount of land properties that had been captured by the big landowners.

— Reasons behind the ceiling:

- Before independence, the British government created a "Zamindari" system through which the Zamindars, i.e the big land owners, had the power to exploit the poor farmers. They could also forcefully acquire the land of the farmer. There was no limit of this land occupation as well.
- Even the intermediaries between landholders and Government, developed by the British, also captured the land of the cultivators.. Therefore, the farmers were hardly interested to invest.
- So, after independence, the ceiling for landholdings was absolutely necessary for tenancy reform and proper redistribution of land.

— Rules of the Ceilings for Landholdings:

- At first, the limit was set only for those landholdings or land properties which would be captured in future. But later, a fixed upper limit was set for the amount of landholdings. If the size of land exceeded the prescribed limit then that would be taken by the

Government and redistributed to the small and marginal farmers.

- The landholders were given the choice to decide which part of the land they would give if the amount of land exceeded the ceiling limit. So the obvious result was that most of the acquired land were infertile and wastelands. So later on, the choice was transferred to the government and the limit was set in terms of land utility.

— Effects:

- The ceilings for landholdings abolished the concept of big land property and helped the tenancy reforms.
- By the imposition of ceilings, land were redistributed in an equitable manner and no big landowners could capture the lands unlimitedly. This also helped to develop a good land management system.

Abolition of the 'Intermediaries'

In 1951, as the first agrarian reform measure, the intermediaries, the numerous revenue collectors who often did not have a definite function, lost their rights. Considerable problems cropped up because of the large number of very different cases. This measure did not aim at abolishing the ownership of large amounts of land, but only of specific rights. Among those who were affected were numerous small zamindars who earned low incomes from a few acres of land. Often, this was their only source of income, and they had come legally into possession of it, either through purchase or inheritance.

Illegal methods my also have played a role when the titles were acquired, but some jagirs were conferred in return for important services. For all the above as well as constitutional reasons, the government took over these rights in return for quite high compensations whose rates increased inversely to the amount of income earned from the land. The compensation was paid in instalments without binding conditions for its use and burdened the government in India with Rs. 6.3 billion and in Pakistan with Rs. 360 million.

An exceptional situation arose in the former jagirs which had often been very badly administered. Not only was the government forced to make considerable investments in health services, schools, etc. to bring these regions the same level as the rest of the country, but ithbad to take over the jagirdars' staff as well as pay their pensions. An additional burden resulted from the fact that many jagirdar families were not in a position to make a new start in life. After having spent the sum they had received as compensation, they became destitute, and it became necessary to draw up special rehabilitation programmes.

Since the measures aimed at abolishing specific legal conditions, land which belonged to the same people under other legal conditions was not affected by this measure. Nor was land expropriated that was self-cultivated. To provide them with a basis for existence, those who until then had not cultivated any land themselves, were granted the right to dismiss tenants of land up to three times the size of an average family farm before expropriation was enforced. The term "self cultivation" was not clearly defined and gave rise to many manipulations.

The zamindars began to let hired labourers cultivate land they tad leased to tenants until then and even persuaded illiterate tenants to give up their rights. This abuse took on such proportions that special laws had to be passed to cancel the voluntary waives made during the last years. In spite of this, the number of protected tenants decreased considerably.Despite all these problems, by the mid fifties, the intermediaries had been abolished in the two countries. The farmers in these regions more than 20 million in India alone had come into direct contact with the government whose tax revenues increased considerably. However, the above described higher burdens largely counterbalanced this increase. For the farmers, this meant freedom from the arbitrariness of the zamindars and of the numerous "abwabs," but the tax burden remained the same with the only difference being that the government was now the recipient.

At any rate, the legal status of the "occupancy tenants" was now clearer. However, only those who were well off could avail themselves of the possibility of purchasing land rights since most of the actual tenants lacked the necessary funds to that end. The larger cultivators could thus enlarge their farms and became the new lessors in the village. These measures did not affect in any way the large number of subtenants who had leased land from occupancy tenants.

Land Reform

As the basis of all economic activity, land can either serve as an essential asset for a country to achieve economic growth and social equity, or it could be used as a tool in the hands of a few to control a country's economic independence and subvert its social processes. The introduction of land as private property destroyed the community ownership systems of tribal societies, and makes a few powerful, rather than sharing the wealth from the land.

During British colonization, land ownership and land use patterns were changed to make it easier for the British to buy land at low prices for mines, plantations etc. The British did not introduce this system to India, but they popularised it. With the introduction of the land tax under the Permanent Settlement Act 1793, the British popularized the 'zamindari' system (where landowners collect tax from the peasants) at the cost of the 'jajmani' system (where everybody shares the land).

When the British ruled India, there existed 17 provinces and a large number of princely states. After independence, the princely states were offered to join the nation, or remain independent. Old states were dissolved and new states created on the lines of shared linguistic and ethnic demographics. For example, the separation of Kerala and the Telugu-speaking regions of Madras State enabled the creation of an exclusively Tamil-speaking state of Tamil Nadu, in southern India.

At independence, ownership and control of land was highly concentrated in a few landlords whose main intention was to get maximum rent from their tenants. Under this arrangement, the tenant farmer had little economic motivation to develop farmland for increased production (because they would not make any money out of it). At the same time, the landlord wasn't particularly concerned about improving the economic condition of the farmers (because the landowner would lose money). As a result, agricultural productivity suffered and the tenants' situation deteriorated.

In the years immediately following India's independence, land ownership was recognised as crucially important. India was extremely poor, and in order to try and abolish poverty, progress was needed on two fronts: high productivity and sharing equally. Land reforms were to be an important pillar for a strong and prosperous country. A lot of money was dedicated to this, with a degree of success in certain regions and states: the abolition of intermediaries, protection to tenants, and a restriction on how much land could be owned by any individual. This improved the situation for many middle class people, but has not benefited the poor who actually work on the land. Sixty years down the line, a number of problems are still far from resolved.

Most studies indicate that inequalities have increased, rather than decreased. The number of people who do not own any land has gone up and the top ten percent of the population monopolizes more land now than in 1951. Meanwhile, the issue of land reforms has over the years, either unconsciously faded from public mind or deliberately been glossed over.

Rich landowners often have powerful political friends, whereas the powerless poor often cannot get their voices heard. As a result, we are today at a juncture where land, mostly for the urban, educated elite, has become more a matter for housing, investment and building infrastructure. The idea of land as a basis of livelihood – for subsistence, survival, social justice and human dignity has largely been lost, so the poor become even poorer.

So what can be done?

Under the Indian Constitution, land reform is the responsibility of individual states so while the federal government provides broad policy guidelines, the nature of land reform legislation, the support for land reform and the degree of success in implementing it have varied considerably from state to state.

Indian officialdom acknowledges its failure to implement land reforms. Dr. K. Venkatasubramanian, member of India's Planning Commission, says "In India everyone was talking about land reforms but this vital area has taken a back seat with nothing being done."

He lists some of the key factors behind the mismanagement of land reform:

- land reforms have excluded the farmers themselves, who till the soil, and have only benefited the middle classes
- tenants have been kicked off the ground that they have been working on, leaving them completely helpless
- land-grabbing (i.e.-stealing and taking over tracts of land) by the unscrupulous

- fair rents are not uniform across the country, and are not even implemented in some states because of the acute land hunger existing in the country
- ownership rights could not be conferred on a large body of tenants (a collective of individual farmers, who would share the land) because of the high rates of compensation that need to be paid to the tenants, according to legislation

Today, land reform in rural India is at the crossroads. Despite the injustice of the current system, the campaigns of people who seek land reform are getting weaker. There are those who argue that 'ceilings' on land ownership (i.e. a restriction on how much land one person can own) are a bad idea, and that it would be more profitable for the Indian economy if people could own as much land as they wanted, and could afford, which would develop India's 'agrobusiness' (i.e. large-scale farming of goods for export). The implication of this would spell disaster for the poor.

Increasingly, there is a demand for re-examination of the land reform issue, through campaigners for social justice and social economics. It is also being argued that liberalization of land ownership would not only increase the availability of land in the lease market but would also increase the poor people's access to land.

There are land reform projects, which seek to:

1) raise awareness of the issue of land ownership, especially amongst the poor, who do not own land
2) monitor specific projects (being funded by international financial institutions) to assess how it affects the communities involved
3) monitor economic trends that might affect land and agriculture
4) consider alternative systems, whereby poor people, if they were able to own land, might be more productive if they were directly benefiting
5) take indirect action and recommend alternative landownership policies to politicians.

While talking on this issue is easy, action is difficult. To redress the imbalance and introduce a fairer system is very hard because those who have power, wealth, land and status do not want to give it up, even if it means a fairer world. Also, loopholes in legislation have meant that people can avoid their responsibilities. Furthermore, bureaucracy and political stalling (the landowners often have powerful political friends, remember!) present even more obstacles to reform. This is particularly serious in India, where 58% of the population relies on farming for their livelihood. Only 2% of these farmers own more than 10 hectares of land.

Though not all of the social problems in India come down to the failure of land reforms, poverty, violence and extremism are linked to lack of access to land. Ten years of economic liberalization have not made any significant difference to the extremely poor people in India: they lack education, awareness and are overwhelmingly from the bottom of India's caste hierarchy (i.e. Dalits). Poverty-stricken farmers from rural areas flock to the large cities in India, in desperate search of a livelihood. But they don't find it, and end up living in slums, exposing themselves and their families to disease, malnutrition and crime.

Land reforms alone will not rid India of its vast number of the abject poor. Education and awareness among those at the bottom of the social ladder (mostly Dalits) in the countryside is crucial. In order to pull people out of poverty, a national consensus on the caste system and a real end to the ritual discrimination of low-castes is vital. Credit reform to enable the poor to get out of the clutches of the money lenders will also help, and projects such as Microcredit are starting to help in these areas. But without the effective implementation of land reform, it is difficult to see how the lot of the rural poor can be changed. In the final analysis, land reform is not a sufficient but a necessary condition for putting a stop to poverty once and for

Land Policy Issues in India

Land problems in India continue to attract equal attention from policy-makers and academics. The renewed interest in land issues stems from the perceived impact of liberalization and opening up the economy. Tenancy, land ceiling and land administration are being revisited with a new perspective. Among the issues under renewed focus, legalizing tenancy, revising the ceiling limits, quality of land, meeting the challenge of miniscule holdings that are a consequence of marginalization and land administration are dominating the debate. This paper looks at these issues. It sets a background to the emergence of land policy in India from pre-Independence and, after tracing it through various phases, maps out the impacts and emerging challenges. After an analysis of the development of land policy over various planning periods, the issues at stake during the 1990s are reviewed. Finally a case is made for a new land-policy framework that includes reforms to the maintenance of land records, deals with concealed tenancy and nonviable land holdings, and the problem of land quality. These issues have assumed greater importance in the current economic transition in rural areas.

Introduction

Land policy in India has been a major topic of government policy discussions since the time prior to Independence from British rule. The peasants of the country strongly backed the independence movement and the "Land to the Tiller" policy of the Congress Party because of the prevailing agrarian conditions. The agrarian structure during British administration emerged with a strong historical background. The land-revenue system implemented by Todar Mal during Akbar's regime can be traced as the possible beginning of systematic efforts to manage the land. This method incorporated measurement, classification and fixation of rent as its main components.

Under the various pre-British regimes, land revenues collected by the state confirmed its right to land produce, and that it was the sole owner of the land. British rulers took a cue from this system and allowed the existence of noncultivating intermediaries. The existence of these parasitic intermediaries served as an economic instrument to extract high revenues (Dutt, 1947) as well as sustaining the political hold on the country. Thus at the time of Independence the agrarian structure was characterized by parasitic, rent-seeking intermediaries, different land revenue and ownership systems across regions, small numbers of land holders holding a large share of the land, a high density of tenant cultivators, many of whom had insecure tenancy, and exploitative production relations (Appu, 1996).

Immediately after Independence a Committee, under the Chairmanship of the late Shri J. C. Kumarappa (a senior Congress leader), was appointed to look into the problem of land. The Kumarappa Committee's report recommended comprehensive agrarian reform measures. India's land policy in the decades immediately following its independence was dominated by legislative efforts to address the problems identified by the Kumarappa Committee. A substantial volume of legislation was adopted, much of it flawed and little of it seriously implemented.

Several important issues confronted the policy-makers.

1. Land was concentrated in the hands of a few and there was a proliferation of intermediaries who had no vested interest in self-cultivation. Leasing out land was a common practice.
2. The tenancy contracts were expropriative in nature and tenant exploitation was ubiquitous.
3. Land records were in extremely bad shape giving rise to a mass of litigation. It is ironic that the Supreme Court of India in 1989 commented that the revenue records are not legal documents of title (Wadhwa, 1989). This is a sad commentary on the land records of the country.

It is against this background that land policy has been shaped in India. While land-reform legislation remained active, land policies in more recent decades have focused less on land reform and more on land development and administration.

Land policy in India has undergone broadly four phases since Independence:

1. The first and longest phase (1950-72) consisted of land reforms that included three major efforts: abolition of the intermediaries, tenancy reform, and the redistribution of land using land ceilings. The abolition of intermediaries was relatively successful, but tenancy reform and land ceilings met with less success.
2. The second phase (1972-85) shifted attention to bringing uncultivated land under cultivation.
3. The third phase (1985-95) increased attention towards water and soil conservation through the Watershed Development, Drought-Prone Area Development (DPAP) and Desert-Area Development Programmes (DADP). A central government Waste land Development Agency was established to focus on wasteland and degraded land. Some of the land policy from this phase continued beyond its final year.

4. The fourth and current phase of policy (1995 onwards) centres on debates about the necessity to continue with land legislation and efforts to improve land revenue administration and, in particular, clarity in land records.

This paper is an attempt to discuss the critical issues pertaining to land policy in India beginning with the emergence of a post-Independence policy in a historical context, and from a viewpoint of differential provincial policies. Naturally, land reforms predominate the discussion here. Land reforms have been one of the important land policy initiatives in India that have brought a fundamental change in the entire approach towards development. The paper discusses the impact of land reforms and the changing phases of land administration. The focus is on the role and development process of land policy in India in the context of overall changes in India's development policies.

It also addresses the political and economic aspects of the policy initiatives, beginning with the various land-reform efforts and finally analysing the recent land development and administration policies. The paper incorporates a discussion on the closely related goals of land policy, i.e. poverty elimination, conflict management, sustainable economic growth and good environmental management. In the final analysis, the paper highlights current issues pertaining to the relationships among land policy, poverty and the development initiatives.

Emergence of Land Policy in India

Given India's vastness, diversity and various political, economic and social influences from a history of various rulers and foreign conquerors, it is not surprising that land tenurial and administration practices varied significantly throughout the subcontinent at the time of Independence. One common factor was that land policies had been driven by the rulers' efforts to extract land revenue or tax from those working on the land. Throughout much of the country, the rulers appointed Zamindars, or tax collectors, who were contracted to collect land revenue for a given large territory and pay fixed sums to the government (but often extracted as much as they could from the landholders and pocketed the difference).

Though tenurial conditions varied significantly from region to region, the numerous tenures could be classified under two broad categories-the Zamindari and Rayatwari systems. The Zamindari system was characterized by one or more layers of proprietary rights between the state and the actual landholder. In the Rayatwari (or peasant proprietorship) system, no intermediaries existed in design but emerged in the process.

The British rulers continued with existing land-revenue policies and procedures with a few but significant modifications. Perhaps most importantly, the British made the tax-collecting Zamindars into proprietors of the estates over which they had tax collection duties. This change was aimed at accomplishing two objectives: simplifying the land-revenue collection process and creating a rural elite with a vested interest in British rule. Unfortunately, it converted the erstwhile landowners into insecure tenants.

Over time, many Zamindars assigned their land-revenue collection duties to one or more layers of intermediaries who were also given interests in the land. The historical emergence and perpetuation of intermediaries served the purpose of land revenue administration and political control of the successive rulers, but their numbers swelled. The large patches of land held by them were let to tenants at exorbitantly high rents. That created a disincentive among the tenant cultivators to develop the land, and consequently impacted upon production. Thus, the Colonial Government, out of its interest to administer the country effectively, did not make any substantial changes in the land-revenue system but promoted the class of non-cultivating intermediaries.

At the time of Independence, India faced a major challenge of setting right the agrarian structure as promised during the independence struggle. Thorner and Thorner (1961), in an analysis of the agrarian structure of India, vividly describe the pre-Independence structure as a complex of legal, economic and social relations-a multilayered structure that pulled down the production efficiency in the agricultural sector.

A brief review of the literature also reveals a myriad of agrarian relations in India, varying from peasant proprietorship to a pure landlord-serf relationship. The first task placed before the first Indian parliament was to address land policy. Because India has a densely populated agrarian economy, almost all other developmental initiatives also involved land as a central and a complex issue, as it clearly represented social status and not just the means of production. While recognizing the need to bring about land reforms in the country, the Constitution of India provided under Article 39 that: (1) the ownership and control of the material resources of the country should be so distributed as best to serve the common good; and (2) the operation of the economic system should not result in a concentration of wealth or a means to production to the common detriment.

The Constitution of India also made land a state (provincial) subject. So, only state (provincial) legislatures have the power to enact and implement land-reform laws. However, the central government played a significant advisory and financial role in land policy based on its constitutional role in social and economic planning (a role held concurrently with the states). The Government of India established a National Planning Commission immediately after Independence to fulfil this role of social and economic planning.

The Planning Commission has prepared a series of Five-Year Plans since 1951. Land policy has been one of the important components incorporated in all the plans. The policy statements are sometimes quite explicit in the plan documents, but are more often implicitly stated. Land reform policy was spelt out in the First Five-Year Plan.

The plan aimed to reduce disparities in income and wealth, to eliminate exploitation and to provide security to tenants, as well as to achieve social transformation through equality of status and an opportunity for different sections of the population to participate in development initiatives.

The focus and emphasis on land policy has changed during the last 50 years, but the core issues continued to revolve around a just distribution of land resources. Land reforms predominated the land policy issues during the first three decades after Independence. Initially land reforms and community development came more or less together and these interventions were meant to provide a means of production to the millions of poor, who either lacked resources or did not have know-how to use them.

Among the first phase reforms were:

(1) the abolition of intermediaries, aiming to eliminate the land rights of intermediaries who held large share of the land resources;

(2) tenancy reforms based on the hypothesis "tenant efficiency" and expecting an increase in capital growth.

In addition to these economic goals, the tenancy reforms were taken as an intervention to provide tenants with more secure and profitable land rights. Efforts to establish ceilings on the size of land holdings followed. These were intended to reduce the concentration of wealth in the hands of few and provide a means of living to others. The second important intervention that was superimposed on the ongoing process of land reforms came in the form of the area-development programmes like the Drought-Prone Area Programme and Desert Development Programme.

Both programmes focused on building land resources in ecologically fragile regions and providing employment opportunities to their inhabitants. Another similar intervention came from the policy's emphasis on soil and water conservation through a massive Watershed Development Programme highlighting the qualitative aspect of land. A Wasteland Development Programme to restore biodiversity and manage the environment in drought-prone areas came next in the form of the National Wasteland Development Board. Until the Watershed Development Programme, land reforms dominated the land policy scenario. There is now a fresh debate about the next phase of land reforms.

Tenancy Reforms: What Succeeded and what Failed?

In the earlier phases of land reforms the emphasis was on food production, extending technology and abolishing regressive institutions; poverty as an issue was not explicitly addressed. Raj Krishna (1961) grouped land-reform measures into four groups: liberative, distributive, organizational and developmental. These groups help to clarify the role of land policy as a process of overall development.

The liberative measures aimed at the emancipation of the actual tillers of the land from the yoke of the landlord. This was to be achieved by conferring the land title or occupancy rights of the tenant. Fixing of rent was undertaken in a few states, e.g. West Bengal's "Operation Barga", where tenancy was recorded. The distributive measures were meant to achieve this by delivering material resources to the poor as promised by the Constitution of India, especially those who required land as a productive resource.

This was to be achieved by redistributing landownership from large landholders to the landless, specifically from socially weaker sections. The tenancy reforms and ceiling on land holding represented liberative and distributive measures according to Raj Krishna's categorization. Organizational reforms aimed at selecting and implementing a particular form of agricultural production practice, with the help of technological change, were introduced in the mid-1960s. These three policies operating together put pressure on land resources, prompting a need for developmental reform. Developmental reforms encompassed other issues interconnected with land policy, which impacted the overall development of the agricultural sector.

All four components taken together form a part of the overall distributive and development initiatives that were taken immediately after Independence. Even though Raj Krishna wrote this chapter almost at the beginning of the first phase of land reforms, the description aptly gives a clear theoretical view of the reforms that followed in the next two decades.

Immediately after Independence four important components of land reform were thought of as major policy interventions in building the land policy. These included: (1) the abolition of intermediaries; (2) tenancy reforms; (3) fixing ceilings on land holdings; and (4) consolidation of landholdings. These were taken in phases because of the need to establish a political will for their wider acceptance. By 1960, the whole process of legal enactment of the abolition of intermediaries was completed. This was the most successful component of the landreform process.

The major planks of tenancy reform included security of tenure, termination of tenancy, resumption for personal cultivation by the landlord, regulation of rent and confirmation of ownership rights. Various state laws were enacted between 1960 and 1972. These differed across the states and territories.

Owing to the diverse and complicated nature of social and agrarian structure in the countryside, no uniform guidelines could be formulated for the whole country. However, some broad guidelines were given in addition to the directives in the successive plan documents. The consensus on the policy of tenancy reforms favoured neither complete expropriation of landlordism nor the interests of the tenants. In the national guidelines the following measures were communicated to the state governments for incorporation in the state legislation:

- security of the tenancy to be conferred on the actual cultivator;
- fair rent to be fixed between 20 and 25 percent of the gross produce;
- landowners may be permitted to cultivate land for their personal use;
- the surrender of the tenancy rights with mutual consent;
- in respect of some of the area, the landlord-tenant relationship to be ended and the tenant cultivator be brought directly into contact with the state;
- disabled persons, defence personnel and other such exemptions to be allowed to lease their land;
- the term "personal cultivation" should be clearly defined if landlords are allowed to remove tenants in order to resume cultivation;
- tenancy records should be corrected and oral tenancies should be abolished.

Because land is subject to state control in India and the relationship between production and land tenure varies from state to state, the national policy recommendations resulted in differing tenancy reform laws in each state.

Tenancy is completely prohibited in some states but completely free in others. Punjab and Haryana have not prohibited tenancy whereas Karnataka has a nearcomplete ban on tenancy. Some states have conferred ownership rights on tenant cultivators except for sharecroppers, whereas West Bengal chose to provide owner-like rights only to the sharecroppers. Some states, such as Maharashtra and Orissa, chose to provide different tenancy reform regimes for different areas within the state.

Many states allowed tenancy only for certain limited groups of people, often broadly termed "disabled" (referring to physical disability). Orissa law considers a landowner owning less than 3 acres of land as a disabled person. In Rajasthan a student pursuing studies in an educational institution and less than 25 years old is also a disabled person. In Uttar Pradesh, such a student is included if his father is dead. In Uttar Pradesh all minors, women and unmarried daughters are not treated as disabled, unless their husband or father is dead. In Bihar a public servant whose salary is below the given norm is treated as disabled.

Among the various exceptions given under the tenancy acts, provisions allowing the landlords to remove tenants in order to resume personal cultivation assumed greater importance as the dominant landlords took advantage of this clause. The clause was entered with a view to induce the landlord to undertake personal cultivation and also to control absentee landlordism. Tenancy acts in almost all the states allowed the landlord to return land, if required, for personal cultivation, but the terms and definitions differed.

Most tenancy reform laws also contained provisions concerning the ability of tenants to surrender the land back to the landlord voluntarily. These provisions were used by landlords to weaken the impact of the laws. In most states the surrender of land falls under the jurisdiction of the revenue authorities. The authorities allowed such surrender after verification of the voluntary element in the process. The strong relationship between landlords and revenue officials often allowed the landlords to skirt the law's intention (Deshpande, 1998).

Punjab, Kerala, Karnataka, Gujarat, Tripura and Andhra Pradesh (Telangana area) did not provide for any surrender by the tenant to the landlord, but some did allow for surrender to the state. Tenants in some states were also given the right to purchase the land. For example, in Maharashtra, where tenancy is not prohibited, the tenant acquires the right to purchase the land after one year from the date of tenancy.

Table: Variations in Tenancy Laws Across Major Indian States

State	*Specific Features*
Andhra Pradesh	In Andhra region leasing is permitted but regulated. In Telangana region leasing out land by large holders is prohibited. Smallholdings below three family holdings are allowed to lease out land for a period of five years. Exemptions are provided.
Assam	There are no restrictions on leasing out of land.

Contd...

Bihar	Leasing out is prohibited except for persons with disability. Public servants with a salary not exceeding Rs250 are included under exempt category.
Gujarat	Leasing is prohibited and unauthorized leasing is punishable offence with a fine up to Rs1 000.
Karnataka	Leasing is generally prohibited. Soldiers and seamen are exempted. Recent amendments allow further limited exemptions, most granted on a case-by-case basis. Violations result in land vesting in the state.
Maharashtra	No ban on tenancy, but the tenant acquires the right to purchase the land within one year of the commencement of tenancy.
Madhya Pradesh	Abolished the past leases but not the future leases. Past leases are divided into two categories called Bhumiswami tenant without payment and other tenant with payment. They cultivate on terms and conditions agreed between parties. Other land owners can lease out their lands for one year during consecutive period of three years.
Orissa	Prohibited all future leases. Past leases continue after surrendering half of the leased land to the landlord or rayat.
Punjab and Haryana	There is no ban on leasing and the tenants do not acquire any rights on land.
Rajasthan	The landowners (Khatedar) can lease out for a non-renewable period of five years. Ghair Khatedar tenants can sublease for a period of one year.
Tamil Nadu	Leasing is permitted but the law stipulates that every contract should be in written form and in triplicate. A copy of the document shall be deposited with the revenue officials
Uttar Pradesh	Lease for any period is prohibited. Exemptions allowed for widows, unmarried women, military persons, students and physically disabled.

Contd...

West Bengal	Fixed-rent leasing is prohibited, but sharecropping is allowed and subject to protection. A person lawfully cultivating others' land is presumed to be a sharecropper and is given permanent and heritable rights with a fixed level of rent (25% if sharecropper provides inputs and 50% if landlord shares in inputs). On resumption the sharecropper has to be left with 1 ha of land and the landowner can resume on a maximum of 3 ha.

The types of tenancy contracts have also changed since 1971-72. There are fluctuations in cash rents and rents in terms of fixed produce over years and across states, but rents in terms of share of produce show a consistent decline. The picture has different shades across regions/states.

The regulation of rent levels was an important aspect of the tenancy reform legislations. The prevailing rent levels differed across the states in the country. The national policy recommended that fair rent payable by a tenant shall be subject to mutual agreement but should be limited to 20-25 percent of the produce. Individual states recalculated this for the purpose of their legislations, some using land revenue as a basis and others using the gross value of produce.

Most states using the gross value of produce set the maximum rent levels in the range of 25-33 percent. Therefore, the variations in the tenancy contracts across states is not unexpected, nor are changes to these contracts over the decades.

The most controversial and debated provision of the tenancy reforms has been the complete or near-complete ban on tenancy in many states. In some states where tenancy is legally allowed, the tenancy reform laws also provided for the termination of tenancy under various circumstances:

(1) the tenant has failed to pay rent for the year within the time stipulated in the law;

(2) the tenant has been using land for purposes other than agriculture;

(3) the land has been made unfit for cultivation;

(4) the tenant has not been personally cultivating the land; and

(5) the term of the lease period has elapsed or the landlord has returned the land to personal cultivation (Deshpande, 1998).

It must be noted that even where tenancy is technically allowed, provisions that give long-term and protected rights to tenants can have the same impact as a ban as they prevent landowners from leasing out their land. The National Commission on Agriculture has asserted that under India's present ratio of agricultural land per capita, tenancy as such cannot and should not be totally banned.

Experience and field studies have shown that prohibition on tenancy is not entirely effective. Tenancy continues to exist and some observers note that the ban on tenancy negatively impacts the landless and land-poor (Shah and Sah, 2002). It is interesting that all these restrictions have given rise to a refractory tenancy market. Concealed tenancy and reverse tenancy proliferated as new forms (Nadkarni, 1976, 2002).

The enactment of tenancy legislation in 1962-77 appears to have resulted in a sharp decrease in tenancy. National sample surveys (NSS) also record a dramatic fall in the area under tenancy from 23.34 percent during 1952-53 to 10.7 percent in 1961-62, down to 7.2 percent in 1982. This settled down to 8 percent by 1991 as revealed by the 48th NSS round.

Three important points need to be noted here. First, at least part of the decrease in tenancy resulted from landlords evicting their tenants either in anticipation of the laws or using loopholes in the laws. One estimate is that tenancy reform laws led to evictions resulting in the rural poor losing access to about 30 percent of the operated area in India (Appu, 1996). Second, the NSS almost certainly underestimate tenancy: both landowners and tenants are often afraid to reveal tenancy relationships because of the existing legal restrictions.

The question of concealed tenancy has been debated and it is recorded that anywhere between 15 and 25 percent of tenancies in the country are illegal and concealed. NSS data show that informal leasing of land is dominated by smaller and marginal farmers. More than 80 percent of the leased-in land is held by this group. Because the tenancy agreement is oral and sharecroppers are weak both economically and politically, they are rarely adequately recompensed.

Sharecroppers only have a tenuous hold on the land they cultivate and invariably have to hand over the land to the owner at any time they demand. Third, the tenancy laws helped tenants to acquire ownership or owner-like rights in about 4 percent of the operated area. These benefits were concentrated in a small number of states including Kerala, West Bengal, Karnataka, Assam, Gujarat, Jammu and Kashmir, and Maharashtra.

The agricultural land-lease market has changed substantially in the last 30 years. Five components assume significance in this process.

1. The period of lease that used to be lifelong has been reduced, and in most states the period of lease (in many cases concealed tenancies) is now less than three years.
2. Earlier there used to be little or no supervision by the landlord of the leased land. This has increased as a result of the fear of tenant occupancy and the landlord-tenant relations have become stronger in terms of resource-sharing and cost-sharing.
3. The share of the landowner in investment used to be negligible but that has increased substantially as a consequence of technological advances.
4. The rent that used to be fixed by the landlord has been regulated in a few states, but rarely effectively (West Bengal is an exception). In a few other states where tenancy is undercover, the landlord fixes the rent and this can be 50-85 percent of the net produce.
5. During the early years of Independence tenants were exploited and therefore rarely identified themselves with the land they cultivated.

However, now the tenants identify themselves with the land. Thus, the tenant cultivator's production efficiency is likely to have increased. This should be true where tenancy has been recorded in the legal and protected framework of the landlease market. But it is important here to take cognizance of two situations:

(a) illegal tenancy in a region with a total ban on tenancy and

(b) informal tenancy in a region where tenancy is legally permitted but for various reasons the tenancy contract is not recorded. In these two cases the allocation and technical efficiency of the tenant is likely to be low and needs attention.

Ceilings on Holdings: Revisited

Land distribution at the time of Independence was extremely skewed. Fifty-three percent of the land was held by 7 percent of the landowners, whereas 28 percent of landowners with submarginal and marginal holdings owned about 6 percent. The land distribution across the states was also quite skewed as can be seen from the Lorenz ratios of 1952-53.

Central policy-makers felt that ceilings on landholdings were essential because of three economic compulsions:

(1) there was strong evidence indicating an inverse size-productivity relationship, hinting that the aggregate production efficiency is hampered when land is held in large holdings;

(2) there was some evidence that large holders of land left large areas fallow thereby perpetuating uneconomic land use;

(3) a large proportion of the population were land-based poor who wanted land as an economic resource for their livelihood. It was thought that surplus land could be distributed to such poor people.

The general position in favour of land ceilings was based largely on providing social justice and equity and not on the grounds of increasing production and developing agriculture.

Legislation providing for ceilings on agricultural holdings was enacted in two phases, 1955-72 and 1972-present. The second phase was more radical in its content and to a large extent was based on the ineffectiveness of the first phase. The implementation process revealed several loopholes which landlords effectively exploited. Among the major loopholes that existed in the ceiling acts of various states included an ambiguity in various definitions, retrospective transfers, large numbers of exemptions, and the basis of fixing ceiling limits. High ceiling limits exempted a large number of landlords.

The national guidelines for this phase were prepared during a Chief Ministers' Conference in July 1972. Consequent to the formation of the national guidelines, all the states modified or enacted their own laws. Among various factors that featured in the debate were the definitions of family, transfers, standard holdings, ceiling limits and exempted categories. The National Commission on Agriculture has asserted that any attempt to lower the ceiling limits might further create uncertainty in the minds of the middle and large farmers that may undermine agricultural production.

Many of the matters were intended to simplify the process but in effect complicated the implementation. Ironically, legislation was passed by those who were likely to be affected by it. Mearns (1999) writes: "Various exemptions and loopholes left by individual states allowed landlords to retain control over land holdings, most infamously through benami (nameless entity) transactions, whereby village recordkeepers (patwaris) could be bribed to register holdings in the names of deceased or fictitious persons".

Many analysts of the Indian land-market situation have noted that the process of marginalization is sharply increasing in the country, proliferating the number of holdings considered economically unviable. Moreover, demographic pressures are reducing the size of holdings in the top brackets and leading to marginalization of holdings in the smaller brackets. A recent study on the causes of farmers' suicides in Karnataka noted that the land size has been fast declining making many holdings inefficiently small to sustain a farm family (Deshpande, 2002).

India's First Five-Year Plan suggested the concept of an economically viable holding, which was then about 2 acres for self-cultivation. The Maharashtra law defined the economic holding as four permanently irrigated acres. Presently, more than 60 percent of the holdings fall under the definition of marginal and submarginal land holding (less than 1 ha). It must be emphasized that during 1961-62 this proportion was only 47 percent.

The entire emphasis of placing ceilings on landholdings was to detect surplus land that was above economic holding size, acquire that land and redistribute it among the landless who require an economic base. However, redistribution failed in most states. Acquiring surplus land was not effective and as the acquisition was meagre the redistribution was also insignificant. This failure was mainly a consequence of the associated political process and the village-level politicization of the issues. The relationship between the bureaucrats and politicians substantially fuelled this. A government document states: "It is widely recognized that the chief reason for the poor implementation of land reforms has been the lack of political will. It would not be surprising to expect so, if we appreciate the realities of the rural situation and development of Indian politics" (quoted in Rao, 1990).

Even the microlevel studies noted that the functioning of land tribunals (local level bodies established to implement the land reforms) was not transparent and doubts were raised about the functioning of unofficial members (Thimmaiah and Aziz, 1983). The surplus land distributed does not form even 2 percent of the total net operated area, and even this small share was concentrated in only six states (West Bengal, Maharashtra, Andhra Pradesh, Assam, Jammu and Kashmir, and Rajasthan).

Despite the limited success in the redistribution of surplus agricultural land, ceiling laws have succeeded in keeping a check on concentration of land in the hands of a few. A large number of experts now agree that the further lowering of ceilings and further implementation of ceiling laws is no longer a feasible option of engendering social equity. Marginalization of the size of holdings, with the proliferation of miniscule holdings, has emerged as a new challenge.

Consolidation of Holdings

Of all land-reform components, the consolidation of holdings has received least attention because of the timing of its attempted implementation and political process through which it went. During the early 1970s it was observed that many landowners held several fragmented parcels scattered across the revenue villages.

This was an easy escape from the Land Ceiling Act and therefore it was felt that landholding of an individual holder should be consolidated. The economic efficiency was also an associated argument. Legislation on consolidation was adopted in some states in order to reduce inefficiency in operations and cultivation. For the most part, these laws and associated consolidation programmes have failed to achieve their goals because of a lack of political will and administrative difficulties.

The legislation was difficult to formulate and did not consider the reality of the caste system within the farming communities, and the local processes of politicization. Except in Punjab, Haryana and Uttar Pradesh, consolidation programmes have not made any impact. Although legislative provisions for consolidation have been adopted in 15 states, these laws included too many get-out clauses. For example, Madhya Pradesh and West Bengal provide only for voluntary consolidation; it is more or less similar in Gujarat, Himachal Pradesh and Maharashtra. Given its importance and the extremely unsatisfactory results of this programme, it is essential to evaluate the effectiveness of the legislation and to rethink an institutional solution.

Table: Lorenz Ratios for Operational and Ownership Holdings Across States

State	*Operational holdings*			*Ownership holdings*		
	1953-54	*1971-72*	*1991-92*	*1953-54*	*1971-72*	*1991-92*
Andhra Pradesh	0.64	0.60	0.58	0.80	0.73	0.71
Assam	0.46	0.42	0.49	0.74	0.62	0.56
Bihar	0.57	0.55	0.64	0.70	0.62	0.69
Gujarat	0.58	0.54	0.59	0.72	0.69	0.71
Haryana	0.52	0.44	0.68	0.76	0.68	0.68
Karnataka	0.58	0.53	0.61	0.72	0.66	0.66
Kerala	0.64	0.61	0.64	0.79	0.67	0.67
Madhya Pradesh	0.56	0.53	0.56	0.71	0.62	0.65
Maharashtra	0.58	0.53	0.60	0.74	0.68	0.71
Orissa	0.58	0.50	0.51	0.68	0.63	0.66
Punjab	0.52	0.44	0.73	0.76	0.78	0.76
Rajasthan	0.57	0.62	0.61	0.69	0.61	0.65
Tamil Nadu	0.61	0.51	0.65	0.79	0.74	0.77
Uttar Pradesh	0.51	0.49	0.57	0.64	0.63	0.63
West Bengal	0.56	0.48	0.58	0.73	0.66	0.67
All-India	0.62	0.59	0.64	0.75	0.71	0.71

Sources for data: (i) Reports on Landholdings (3 &4); 8th Round 1953-54, NSS Report No. 36 and 66. (ii) Report on Some Aspects of Landholdings; 26th Round 1971-72, NSS Report No. 215. (iii) Report on Some Aspects of Household Ownership Landholdings (1); 48th Round, 1991-92, Report No. 399.

Demographic and economic pressures naturally cause fragmentation of land and marginalization of holdings can be seen as an important outcome of this. There are different views on the process and economic impact of the fragmentation of holdings. As can be seen from the data (NSS, 1992; Mearns, 1999), the number of parcels per holding has been declining: 5.7 in 1961-1962; 4 in 1982; 2 in 1992. Thus, theoretically there is little justification for consolidation in the usual manner.

But the numbers of holdings smaller than 1 ha and especially those smaller than 0.5 ha have been increasing over the decades. This process causes concern. One successful approach has been taken by a few groups of small and marginal farmers in Karnataka and Maharashtra. These farmers came together to cultivate a particular crop (strawberries, tomatoes, gherkins or rose onions) on a contract basis with a price for the produce agreed in advance with the contractor. They could therefore overcome the viability threshold to cultivate such investment-intensive crops. This experiment provides an institutional alternative to consolidation of holdings.

Political and Economic Aspects of Land Ownership

In India, land has always been associated with social status and has historically remained in the control of certain social groups. Social stratification is strong in India and is based on the caste system. The main caste groups are Brahmin, Vaishya, Kshatriya and Shudra, and each main group consists of hundreds of subcastes. Some groups are not included in this classification, especially the tribals and other groups with limited access to productive resources.

The caste groups are associated with specific occupations and work; hence, they can be categorized into land-associated castes and other castes. The land-associated castes are usually the traditional cultivators.

The social structure in terms of caste itself was geared to the mandatory segregation of groups associated with cultivation, trade, teaching along with priesthood and other services. This segregation of social structure was associated not only with the political base, but also with the landownership pattern in the country. The power relationship derived advantage from this social segregation, and the emergence of political power in the country can be easily associated with caste groups. Although land reforms became a prominent post-Independence policy initiative (in order to keep the commitment made by many of the leaders of the independence movement), the landassociated caste groups wielded significant political power after Independence, so the very interests of those responsible for lawmaking were tied with the implementation of the law.

Naturally, as a result the landreform laws were either not thoroughly implemented or were manipulated with the help of administering institutions (Deshpande, 1998).

In the course of the last five decades all social groups have confronted the process of shrinking holding sizes, but the politically weak felt it more acutely. It must be noted here that the Scheduled Castes and Scheduled Tribes are the groups that have the highest concentration of poor in India. It can be observed that the share of landholdings belonging to Scheduled Castes is declining at a sharper rate than the general trend. Marginalization is a clear phenomenon in this group.

Furthermore, their participation in the land-lease market is also marginal and concentrated on small fragments of land. Only 82 000 ha were leased by the cultivators belonging to the Scheduled Castes in 1990-91, which is about 0.62 percent of their total operated area. Of this, more than 34 percent comes under the marginal farmers' group.

The tenancy contracts are generally constructed in terms of share of produce or fixed money rent. The number of holdings under the group defined as marginal farmers is increasing and that under the group large holdings is declining.

The number of marginal farmers with less than 1 ha belonging to Scheduled Castes, however, is increasing much faster than those in other social groups. Moreover, the number of small farmers (those owning 1-2 ha) belonging to Scheduled Castes is declining, while the number of small farmers belonging to other social groups is increasing.

This is clearly reflected in the average size of holding, which is decreasing more rapidly for Scheduled Caste households than for other social groups. The sharp decline in the land base of the Scheduled Caste is quite alarming, and has happened even in the presence of legislation, which makes the land transfers from Scheduled Castes to other castes difficult.

Table: Distribution of Ownership Holding among Weaker Sections

Size class	*Scheduled Caste*		*Scheduled Tribe*		*Others*	
	1982	*1992*	*1982*	*1992*	*1982*	*1992*
Marginal (less than 1 ha)	26.6	30.2	12.0	18.7	10.9	14.9
Small (1 to 2 ha)	22.71	22.2	18.8	22.7	15.6	17.5
Medium (2 to 4 ha)	24.0	20.4	29.2	27.7	22.6	24.7
Large (above 4 ha)	26.8	27.2	40.0	30.9	50.9	42.9
Total	100.0	100.0	100.0	100.0	100.0	100.0

Source: NSS, Land Holding Survey 37th round No. 330 1982 & 48th round No. 399 1992, Central Statistical Organisation, Delhi.

Land: Poverty and Policy Issues

In the context of globalization, it is clear that the small and marginal farmers are handicapped when it comes to participation in domestic and foreign markets. Their competitiveness is hampered by the crops they produce, by market imperfections and by a lack of access to available information. Other factors that inhibit India's farmers in competitive world markets include the small size of landholdings and low throughput of production.

It is difficult for the small and marginal farmers to grow the commodities that are in demand in the world market, mainly because of the high cost of cultivation of these goods and their limited knowledge of them. In order to overcome this problem it is important to encourage entrepreneur groups (as suggested earlier), which can take the risk of competing to grow the crops with a domestic and international demand.

Although there is no direct correlation between land-policy initiatives and agricultural growth, the available evidence may not be significant enough to suggest a relationship. However, oppressive land relations were certainly barriers to growth, and land reforms have created preconditions favourable for growth. Because the majority of India's population depend upon land for their livelihood, poverty issues are also closely associated with land policy.

Besley and Burgess (2000) gave robust evidence of a link between poverty reduction owing to tenancy reforms and abolition of intermediaries. They also inferred that land reforms also benefited the landless. A reconciliation of this with the process of the marginalization of landholdings in rural India is, however, an analytically challenging task. The dilemma is this: reform measures have helped in poverty reduction, but the average size of a poor landowner's holdings has decreased. Further evidence in this context is V.M. Rao's pertinent observation:

> *"This identification is based on three premises about the role of land reforms and common lands in the emerging development strategy. First, they have to serve as a link helping integration of growth policies with poverty alleviation programmes. Such integration is necessary to focus the development strategy as a whole-and not merely the individual schemes and programmes-on the rural labourers and poor. Second, at the ground level, land reforms and improved access to common lands need to be part of a package of measures specifically designed to the requirement of different subgroups of rural labourers and poor. Third, the ultimate goal of land reforms and other structural reforms is to promote the emergence of a viable and modernized peasantry consisting of small farmers and providing as much room as possible for the landless to enter the peasant sector." (Rao, 1990)*

Therefore, even though a direct relationship between land policy and poverty cannot be established, an influence can be inferred.

The poor in rural India are located mostly among the landless agricultural labourers, and marginal and smallholder farmers. NSS data (Rao, 1992) indicate that landlessness is the best predictor for poverty in India. In a cross-section analysis of the states in India, the empirical data suggest that marginalization is fast increasing. Trends differ across various regions and social groups, but it is clear that the landbased poor are becoming poorer because of marginalization. India's land policy interventions during the last five decades can be assessed based on their impact on various parameters, including alleviation of poverty, conflict management and equity, sustainable economic development, environmental impact, and production efficiency.

The land policy interventions have had varying impacts across the states, depending in large part on the agrarian situation and the extent to which a given policy was implemented.

Poverty alleviation could be significantly impacted by the first three phases of land reform, but the DPAP and DADP have made little inroad. Similar results are seen in respect of conflict management and equity, but a significant change was recorded in this area because of the computerization of land records. DADP, DPAP and Wasteland Development Programmes could impact environmental management significantly. Similarly, these could influence sustainable growth in some pockets.

The major contributor to sustainable growth came, however, from the abolition of intermediaries and the ceiling on land holdings, which together have put a pressure on economic use of resources. While production efficiency is not a direct derivative of land policy, its components can help. The abolition of intermediaries, land ceilings and the consolidation of holdings (wherever it could be done) have certainly contributed.

The Watershed Development Programme has been one of the important land policy interventions in the recent past and has impacted poverty alleviation, conflict management and environmental management significantly. However, its influence on production efficiency was not very significant (Deshpande and Narayanamoorthy, 1999). Land quality issues dominated policymaking during the 1980s and continued thereafter. Initially, the soil and water conservation programmes were undertaken in a few selected states to merge into the wider National Watershed Development Programme for Rainfed Agriculture. This stemmed from a mid-term appraisal of the Seventh Plan and continued thereafter. Even though the main focus of the programme was to conserve soil and water resources, increases in income and productivity were an essential component.

The programme went through a phased implementation, various models of which operate throughout the country :

1. A state-implemented programme with the help of existing line departments, focusing more on technical parameters.
2. A state-non-governmental organization (NGO) partnership, largely implemented by the latter. This model allows a good institutional set up and focuses on people's livelihoods. Its flexibility is also one of its constraints.
3. Experiments outside of the ambit of state agencies, funded and implemented by NGOs.

The watershed development initiatives have had an impact on the quality of land as well as on the income of the beneficiaries. However, their impact on a sustainable environmental system is not very significant or at least not well documented (Deshpande and Narayanamoorthy, 1999). The DDP has been effective in certain pockets but the wasteland development initiatives have yet to make a significant mark. Bearing in mind the longer gestation period of these interventions, it would be misleading to consider tangible benefits alone. Other positive benefits of such programmes may be considerable.

A systematic forest policy in India dates back to 1855 when Dietrich Brandis, a German botanist, was appointed as the first Inspector General of Forests in India. The purpose was to bring the commercial exploitation of forests under state control. The first Forest Act came into being in 1865; this gave power to the state to declare any land cover with trees as government forest by notification. The profitability and growing commercial potential of the forest caused a further amendement to in the Forest Act of 1878.

The Indian Forest Act was passed in 1927; it tried to make the law uniform in different regions of the country. However, Provincial laws were coexisting with the Central law. The 1927 Forest Act was the baseline for independent India's forest policy. Until 1988, forest was considered as the sole property of the state, and state had all the rights to manage and appropriate the revenue generated from forests. However, with the emergence of the concept of joint forest management (JFM) and community forest management (CFM), management and revenue-sharing with the local people (often through Panchayat or similar parallel political institutions) was considered by many states as a method of involving people and giving them rights on the forest resources.

The main emphasis of the 1988 Forest Policy was to halve forest degradation, retaining as well as enhancing the quality of land use in this sector. The policy also aims to create a partnership between forest dwellers and forest development authorities.

Women in India have traditionally been deprived of property rights. The Hindu Succession Act of 1956 provided property rights to the daughters, widow or mother of a dying property owner. Women's property rights still meet with strong social opposition and even now the rights are not easily transferred. Gender equity in land rights is promoted on the basis of welfare, efficiency, equity and empowerment (Mearns, 1999). The Eighth Plan (1990-95) called for providing gender rights and asked the states to make provision in the Land Ceiling Act.

Current Phase

Independent departments at federal and state government levels handle land and agricultural administration. In one way, this helps to monitor land outside agricultural use separately from agricultural land, but the lack of integration creates uneasy administrative regimes. Moreover, there are several different departments responsible for various aspects of land administration, land data, and land legislation. Unfortunately, these do not work with perfect coordination, which gives rise to various problems. The spread of administrative regimes makes land-policy decision-making and implementation difficult.

The Department of Land Resources in the Central Ministry of Rural Development has the primary central government responsibility for addressing issues related to land administration, particularly of degraded land. This department oversees a range of programmes that set the national framework. The Department of Land Resources also works as an advisory and coordinating body for the implementation of land reform, and helps in arriving at a consensus among states on the changing emphasis in land reform.

For example, recently the Department of Land Resources convened a national workshop focused on tenancy reform, which drew together a group of experts to review the current situation in land policy. The question of opening of the leasing market was debated and there was a general consensus that the leasing of land should be liberalized. However, no firm decisions were made in the workshop. Subsequently, however, the National Agricultural Policy focused for the first time on the policy of leasing and suggested a liberalization of leasing legislation, an increase in land ceilings, and allowing for contract farming.

The Department of Land Resources at the central level also issues guidelines for strengthening land revenue administration and updating land records. It has recently initiated a large-scale programme for computerizing land records. The department has also initiated various activities focused on wasteland (droughtprone areas, desert development, integrated wasteland development, technology development, extension and training, investment promotion and support for NGOs/voluntary organizations for such activities).

It is now accepted in India that the recording of land rights, and their periodic updating, is an essential prerequisite for an effective land policy. During the Seventh Plan Period (1997-98) a Centrally Sponsored Scheme on Computerization of Land Records (CLR) was introduced with 100 percent financial assistance from the Central Government for pilot projects in a few selected districts (Gulbarga in Karnataka, Rangareddy in Andhra Pradesh, Sonitpur in Assam, Singhbhum in Bihar, Gandhinagar in Gujarat, Morena in Madhya Pradesh, Wardha in Maharashtra, Mayurbhanj in Orissa, and Dungarpur in Rajasthan).

These pilots were undertaken with a view to removing problems inherent in the manual maintenance and updating of land records, and to ensure the issue of timely and accurate copies of Records of Rights to landowners by the local land revenue officials. The main objectives of the scheme were to:

(1) computerize ownership and plot-wise details for issue of timely and accurate copy of the Records of Rights to the landowners;

(2) achieve low-cost, easily reproducible storage media for reliable and long-term preservation of land records;

(3) provide fast and efficient retrieval of textual and graphical information;

(4) create a Land Information System (LIS) and database for the agricultural census.

By the end of the Eighth Plan (1997), 323 districts in the country were to be brought under the computerization of land records scheme. During the first year of the Ninth Plan (1997-98), 177 new project districts were covered. The available feedback from our fieldwork and other sources clearly indicate that the scheme has been slow to progress. Many bottlenecks are also emerging in the process, including:

(1) delayed transfer of funds to the final implementing authority in the field by the state governments;

(2) a delay in the development of appropriate software tailored for the specific requirements of different states;

(3) a lack of adequate training facilities to the revenue staff who handle computers in the field areas; and

(4) unavailability of private vendors to enter data.

In addition to these, an administrative system for the computerization has not been clearly set up. It is operated under the state-government revenue departments, sometimes with only partially trained staff. Therefore, a quantum change in this process is needed.

Proper land records continue to be a major problem even after five decades of land policy interventions. Computerization alone may not solve the problem and land surveys involve heavy costs. The body appointed by the Planning Commission recommended the Torrens System for land records in order to provide clear title to land. The Government of Maharashtra has taken steps to introduce the Torrens System on a pilot basis.

The scheme provides for the conversion of the present presumptive titles to land into conclusive titles, which requires the updating and publication of the Records of Rights. The scheme is being implemented in two districts and the pilot process may come out with a fool-proof scheme.

Towards the Next Phase

In recent years, the government's land policy interventions have focused on the correction and computerization of land records, improving the land survey process, and improving land quality through the reclamation of degraded wasteland and forests. Land reform implementation is almost thinning out as a priority. In fact, the important policy discussions now centre on whether certain land-reform interventions should be reversed; particularly whether the land ceilings should be increased and whether tenancy restrictions should be liberalized. Marginalization of land holdings and land administration are also of major concern.

Policy discussions concerning rolling back land ceiling laws have assumed prominence. It is argued that the current ceiling limits hinder investment in agriculture and diversification to high-tech agriculture. It is questioned that there are no limits on investment in other sectors, yet agriculturalists face a restriction on increasing the size of holding. Added to this the average size of holding is sliding down in successive censuses because of nationalization of the smaller holdings.

Putting a bottom ceiling on the smallest size is worth considering given the present political and administrative climate in the country; rolling back the land ceiling limits seems to be a difficult political option. It is argued that economies of scale could be achieved by allowing larger holdings and that large farms would also attract greater investment in the agriculture sector. This is necessary before it is possible to generate an exportable surplus and to participate effectively in the world market. Pooling small farms together to form formal or informal groups of producers for purposes of marketing may be a way to achieve this goal. This was successfully attempted in Karnataka, growing rose onions and gherkins for export.

The second policy option being actively discussed in a countrywide debate is the desirability of liberalizing the current restrictions (sometimes prohibitions) on agricultural tenancy. The argument that liberalizing tenancy restrictions will have a pro-poor impact has gained ground. It is felt that a majority of the beneficiaries from tenancy liberalization will be small and marginal farmers. Presently, most concealed tenancies give no protection for the tenant or the landlord. Moreover, informal (or concealed) tenants cannot gain access to capital from banks and financial institutions.

A recent study of a spate of farmers' suicides in Karnataka found that many of them were informal tenants who borrowed from moneylenders and could not pay back because of high interest rates (Deshpande, 2002). Legalizing tenancy will also help to bring the small and marginal tenants within the ambit of institutional credit. If legal status is conferred on the tenant, this may not leave room for imperfections in the tenancy market usually caused by concealed tenancy and unilateral fixation of land rent. It is also expected that opening the lease market will attract much-needed private investment in agriculture. It may be possible to prevent possible imperfections by restricting the upper limit and allowing leasing of land up to that limit.

The limit should also serve as a threshold to allow only those who have ownership of land below such a limit. Similarly, the tenant as well as the owner should have a guarantee of protection of their interests. Interestingly, the National Commission on Agriculture referred in 1976 to the need for new amendments in tenancy reform to overcome the problems of concealed tenancy as well as reverse tenancy. Leasing in land belonging to the disempowered people should be regulated, with a proper intervening authority to help protect them from unscrupulous dealings

Conspectus

Land policy in post-Independence India has evolved through different phases. These include: two phases of land reform; attention to issues pertaining to quality of land through the Drought-Prone Area and Desert Development Programmes, Wasteland Development and Watershed Development Programmes designed to reclaim environmentally degraded land. These policy interventions have had varying impacts on poverty and the overall development process.

It is difficult empirically to segregate the influence of the changes in land policy on poverty, environmental management, sustainability and production, but available studies indicate that land-reform measures have had a significant impact on equity and poverty. The measures dealing with the quality of land have a partial to significant impact on environmental parameters. In addition to these, other land-policy instruments were used for the purpose of transforming development policy effectively.

In the previous section we have indicated the key areas for the purpose of action and major policy interventions required. The key areas for future land policy action include legalizing the tenancy market, contract farming, and watershed and wasteland development to assume greater significance. Such interventions involve important implementation issues relating to the political economic aspects of the reform measures and reform of the institutions. Future research should be directed towards establishing the institutional framework to fit these issues into a broader policy-making process.

Abolition of the Intermediaries

Abolition of the intermediaries was started as the first agrarian reform measure to redistribute the agricultural resources equitably.

- Reasons Behind the Abolition of Intermediaries:
    - Before independence the Indian rural economy and polity had been dominated by some big landowners. They could acquire lands by paying a very small amount of money to the British government.
    - In addition to that, an intermediate class was also developed by the British government to simplify their tax collecting system. The people of this class had no direct connection with land and agriculture, but they could capture land easily and this had no limit. So the small and marginal farmers were exploited and forced to transfer land to the big landlords. As a result of this, rate of employment decreased and so was the productivity.
    - The sharecroppers had been exploited by both the intermediaries and the big landlords. So they lost their interest to work completely.
    - After independence when the Government of India started agrarian reform, the main issue was the abolition of intermediaries. Otherwise redistribution of lands would have been extremely difficult for the Government.
- Process of the abolition: The government took the land from the intermediaries. The small landowners were compensated by the government for giving their land. The amount of this compensation was inversely proportional to the amount of revenue earned from the land.
- Effects:
    - Government expenditure in the agricultural sector has escalated due to the compensations that have to be given for the loss of land brought about buy the imposition of ceilings.
    - Many intermediaries were not in a position to start a new way of income. So the government had to arrange pension scheme for them which was again a huge burden.
    - Despite the bad effects, due to the abolition of the

intermediate classes not only more than twenty million farmers in India had been connected directly with the government but also the tax revenue from the rural area increased.

- The increase in tax revenue compensated the huge burden of the government mentioned above.
- The financial security of the farmers improved and as a result of that, productivity and rate of employment also increased. But this measure had no effect on the numerous sub tenants of India.

Land Reforms in India

One of the most ticklish questions in Indian economy has been the nature and relevance of land reforms. Advocated and implemented for decades as a major instrument of state-mediated and progressive socioeconomic change, the very utility of land reforms has increasingly been questioned in the post-1991 reform era. Comprehensive land reforms were among the first priorities of the Government of India immediately after Independence. For this the manifold imbalances of the colonial legacy of two centuries had to be dismantled, and a new beginning made.

It was a semi-feudal system that was inherited from British rule. A handful of intermediaries rack-rented a large mass of hapless tenantry. A widespread system of subletting, often several rungs deep, worsened the situation by reducing the holdings to uneconomic proportions. In this system, neither the intermediaries had any interest nor the tenants any incentive or resources for introducing land improvements or for using HYVs or other costly inputs likely to yield higher returns.

With the twin objectives of achieving social equity and ensuring economic growth, the land reforms programme was built around three major issues:

1. Abolition of intermediaries.
2. Settlement and regulation of tenancy.
3. Regulation of size of holdings.

The central thesis behind the abolition of intermediaries, underlined by the first as well as the Second Five Year Plan, was that owners themselves should operate and manage farm business, and so the tenant-landlord nexus should be put to an end. The intermediary's privileges were conceived as having an adverse impact on agricultural productivity as well as denying the tiller of the soil his rightful place in the economy. 'Between 1947 and 1954 ... a law for the abolition of the *zamindari* system was adopted [passed] by the state legislature and then ratified by the President of India. However, these acts of agrarian reform did not affect landownership in the *ryotwari* areas where system was in existence, i.e. 57 per cent of the country's occupied land. Tenancy reforms were launched to confirm the rights of occupancy by tenants, regulate rents on leased land and to secure their possession of tenanted land. It was argued, especially in the context of the spread of modern technology, that the tenants lacking a security of tenure and paying excessive rents suffer a relative decline in inputs compared to the owners. To this end the following recommendations were made by the Chief Ministers' Conference in 1967:

1. The rate of interest should not be more, preferably less, than 1/4 or 1/5 of the gross produce.
2. Records of tenancy should be prepared and maintained.
3. Tenants in cultivating position of land should be given complete security of tenancy by: i) staying all evictions; ii) suspending rights of resumption where such rights had been given to landowners; and iii) regulating voluntary surrenders in such a way landowners do not get an advantage by persuading tenants to surrender their tenancy. The third major land reform plank was regulating the size of land holdings through ceiling as well as consolidation to correct the extremely skewed distribution of agricultural land.

It was designed to

(i) to meet land hunger of working cultivators,

(ii) to reduce the disparities in agricultural income, ownership, and use of land, and

(iii) to increase rural employment in the sector.

At the same time, consolidation of holdings was also advocated to group together the numerous tiny and scattered holdings of poor cultivators in order to form bigger tracts, susceptible to more efficient management. Cooperative farming on these would increase productivity and employment through economies of scale.

The large, economical units of consolidated land, it was opined, would mitigate the problem of poor yield and enhance productivity through economies of scale and also increase employment.

Of all these laws only the abolition of intermediaries was achieved successfully. The bulk of the *zamindars'* lands were alienated: 87% in Uttar Pradesh and 84% in Bihar for instance; and the landlord class lost close to 60% of the land it had owned previously. However, it was achieved at a great cost to the Exchequer as the compensation to the intermediaries came to be some 7,000 million rupees. The source from which these compensation payments were drawn was the land-revenue paid to the state by the ex-tenant farmers now farming on the land alienated from former *zamindars'* estates. In most cases the tenant farmers continued to pay the same land-rent as before, but now to the state direct.

As to the implementation of the two other sets of reforms, namely tenancy and regulation of land holdings, legal, administrative, and other factors became principal bottlenecks. In most cases and for a long time, the factual evidence and administrative machinery for enforcement of the laws just did not exist. For instance, land policy in the First Five Year Plan was formulated without sufficient knowledge about the size and distribution of agrarian land holdings. It was in the 8th round of the National Sample Survey in 1954 that a considerable volume of data was collected for the first time; this too was submitted to the Union Government only in 1960, a full six years later.

On tenancy reforms, from a lifetime of study, P. S. Appu has concluded that the laws have not put an end to absentee ownership of land, nor has it led to the disappearance of tenancies. Being a state subject, there have been striking differences in the track records between the various States in the formulation and enforcement of the reform measures. It was not before the Operation Barga in 1978, for instance, that tenancy reforms met with any noticeable success in West Bengal, and then overtook the rest of the country in a most spectacular manner.

If political will is taken as the main reason behind the success of tenancy reforms there, the absence of such a will must be held responsible for its failure elsewhere. Taking the country as a whole, by 1992, ownership rights over 14.4 million acres of land have been conferred on some 11 million tenants. That constitutes, however, no more than 4% of operated area. The seven States of Assam, Gujarat, Himachal Pradesh, Karnataka, Kerala, Maharashtra, and West Bengal account for 97% of the beneficiaries. Practically no benefits accrued to the tenants in the other states.

An ambitious movement to achieve redistribution of land, called Bhoodan, was launched by a prominent Gandhian Vinoba Bhave in the early fifties. 'The essential feature of this movement was the voluntary requisition of land which was subsequently redistributed among peasants who owned little or no land at all.' Launched in the Telangana region to counter the militant peasant struggle there, the Bhoodan movement made some notable headway in Bihar and Uttar Pradesh, where, by 1955, the landlords voluntarily relinquished over 4.3 million acres.

However, most of this land 'proved unfit for cultivation' whenever it was not disputed property. The second phase of the movement was Gramdan, the giving away of the whole villages, which would belong to the village community as a whole. The movement was virtually non-existent beyond a handful of tribal pockets where private property in land did not matter in any case.

It is in the field of redistribution and consolidation of land holdings that the reforms have met with the least success, mainly because they met with a most determined resistance from the very substantial and politically influential landed interests, quite unlike the handful of politically isolated intermediaries. It was not before mid-1960s that ceiling laws could be passed in the majority of states. Even then enough loopholes remained which enabled landlords to circumvent legislation 'while in the remainder they had still to pass through the various readings in the legislatures'. Even after the law, 'the landlords succeeded with little difficulty in circumventing the new laws making full use of the numerous loopholes in them.'

For instance, the law allowed division among the members of a joint family, by taking recourse to which the total holdings of landlord family remained several times over the legal limit. 'As experience was to show, after the "ceiling" acts had been applied in Andhra Pradesh and Bengal, hardly any surpluses were revealed.' By 1992, only about two million hectares of surplus land, amounting to less than 2% of the operated area on a pan-Indian scale with very wide regional differences, could be distributed to some 4.76

million beneficiaries. As the land reforms reach an impasse, a series of considerations have raised serious doubts about their continuing relevance as to whether they are really the best way for achieving growth with general well-being and whether they are in harmony with the ongoing liberalisation of Indian economy. Demographic and economic forces have proved more effective than legislation in bringing about a redistribution of land in favour of medium and, and even more, marginal farmers. The latter, it is said, now dominate the agrarian landscape in most of India outside Panjab and Haryana. Inequality among landowners is no longer a key issue, as landholdings are not very skewed any more, except in certain small pockets.

On the other hand, widespread poverty and hunger remain. In particular, the plight of the landless or near landless, whose number has steadily grown over the decades and is estimated to constitute almost half the agricultural population, requires urgent attention. Above all, agricultural growth has, in general, been sluggish in India, and the Green Revolution has failed to spread beyond a handful of states led by Panjab and Haryana, which are now in fact producing food surpluses to feed the rest of them.

Many critics such as V. M. Dandekar argue that the ceiling and tenancy laws not only do not have much relevance in this sorry state of affairs but also must share part of the blame at least for perpetuating them. The most critical long-term impact of the ceiling law has been, as pointed out by Hanumantha Rao, that it killed the land market, and thereby the scope for investment in land, by preventing an increasing concentration in landholding through depeasantisation. 'The same is true', Dandekar says, 'of the present tenancy laws which have practically abolished lease market in land'.

Among the alternative policy prescriptions that have been put forward, those of Dandekar constitute the most radical departure from the prevailing policies. Dandekar advocates exposing agriculture to the full play of market forces through either an outright abolition or gradual relaxation of the ceiling and tenancy laws. His is essentially a plea for unrestrained growth through modernisation of agriculture that will bring benefit to all, if differentially. From a similar perspective, another prescription is to encourage corporate sector to enter agriculture for commercial production of high-value and processed agricultural products, and earn thereby valuable foreign exchange. The corporations should set up agro-processing units in the rural areas and help in diversifying agriculture, encourage contract farming, and also develop infrastructural support in the area of their operation.

Once the market forces are fully unleashed and business people from outside begin to invest in the agricultural sector, it would also become necessary to impose agricultural income tax and agricultural holding tax. These taxes then could be used, among other things, to build up infrastructure and provide employment in the countryside.

Such prescriptions however cannot be assessed in terms of their economic soundness alone. One must also take into account their implications for employment as well as recognise the social, political, and cultural milieu in which they have to operate.

Expert opinion is divided on the question of employment. Some fear that modern technology being generally labour saving and capital intensive, its introduction will aggravate further the unemployment problem. In support, studies by S. K. Ray and others are cited showing that the employment elasticity of output in agriculture has fallen sharply in the post-new technology agriculture. However it does not necessarily imply an aggravation of the problem; it just means that a growth in productivity does not lead to *a proportionate increase* in employment.

On the contrary, data show a threefold increase in the number of agricultural labourers in Panjab between 1961 and 1981, the increase in demand having to be met by large-scale migrations from eastern UP and Bihar. Fears of increasing unemployment due to mechanization have not materialised so far. The victims of tractorization, it has been well said, were bullocks, not labour.

In the end, the social and political costs of the policy prescriptions will need to be carefully examined. By all reckonings, while poverty and hunger may become a thing of the past, the distribution of income would tend to be more skewed. This may become a cause of serious concern through the social friction that it would intensify. Ultimately, the success or even the initiative for such policy measures would depend on the extent to which our decision-makers believe them to be compatible with the politics of competitive populism.

5

Land Reform in India: Issues and Challenges

The Land Question in India: A Brief Historical Review

As the basis of all economic activity, land can either serve as an essential asset for a country to achieve economic growth and social equity, or it can be used as a tool in the hands of a few to hijack a country's economic independence and subvert its social processes. During the two centuries of British colonization, India experienced the latter reality. During colonialism, India's traditional land-use and landownership patterns were changed to ease the acquisition of land at low prices by British entrepreneurs for mines, plantations, and other enterprises.

The introduction of the institution of private property delegitimized the community ownership systems of tribal societies. Moreover, with the introduction of the land tax under the Permanent Settlement Act 1793, the British popularized the zamindari system at the cost of the jajmani relationship that the landless shared with the landowning class.

By no means a just system, the latter was an example of what has been described by Scott (1976) as a moral economy, and at the least it ensured the material security of those without land. Owing to these developments in a changing social and economic landscape, India at independence inherited a semifeudal agrarian system. The ownership and control of land was highly concentrated in the hands of a small group of landlords and intermediaries, whose main intention was to extract maximum rent, either in cash or in kind, from tenants.

Under this arrangement, the sharecropper or the tenant farmer had little economic motivation to develop farmland for increased production; with no security of tenure and a high rent, a tenant farmer was naturally less likely to invest in land improvements, or use high-yielding crop varieties or other expensive investments that might yield higher returns. At the same time, the landlord was not particularly concerned about improving the economic condition of the cultivators. Consequently, agricultural productivity and the oppression of tenants resulted in a progressive deterioration of their well-being.

In the years immediately following India's independence, a conscious process of nation building considered the problems of land with a pressing urgency. In fact, the national objective of poverty abolition envisaged simultaneous progress on two fronts: high productivity and equitable distribution.

Accordingly, land reforms were visualized as an important pillar of a strong and prosperous country. India's first several five-year plans allocated substantial budgetary amounts for the implementation of land reforms. A degree of success was even registered in certain regions and states, especially with regard to issues such as the abolition of intermediaries, protection to tenants, rationalization of different tenure systems, and the imposition of ceilings on landholdings. Fifty-four years down the line, however, a number of problems remain far from resolved.

Most studies indicate that inequalities have increased, rather than decreased. The number of landless labourers has risen, while the wealthiest 10 percent of the population monopolizes more land now than in 1951. Moreover, the discussion of land reforms since World War II and up through the most recent decade either faded from the public mind or was deliberately glossed over by both the national government of India and a majority of international development agencies. Vested interests of the landed elite and their powerful connection with the political-bureaucratic system have blocked meaningful land reforms and/or their earnest implementation.

The oppressed have either been co-opted with some benefits, or further subjugated as the new focus on liberalization, privatization, and globalization (LPG) has altered government priorities and public perceptions. As a result, we are today at a juncture where land—mostly for the urban, educated elite, who are also the powerful decision makers—has become more a matter of housing, investment, and infrastructure building; land as a basis of livelihood—for subsistence, survival, social justice, and human dignity—has largely been lost.

International Financial Institutions (IFIs) and Issues Related to Land in India.

Any reform is as difficult an economic exercise as it is a political undertaking, since it involves a realignment of economic and political power. Those who are 74 land and agrarian reform: historical perspectives likely to experience losses under reform naturally resist reallocation of power, property, and status. The landholding class, therefore, is unlikely to willingly vote itself out of possession, nor should it be expected that they would be uniformly inflamed by altruistic passions to voluntarily undertake the exercise.

Hence, one cannot underestimate the complexity of the task at hand. However, the political will of the landowning class is as much a challenge to the redistributive process as are the existing legal and structural dimensions of the current landholding regime. A brief review of the legal history that has accompanied India's land struggles is therefore a necessary detour for continuing this discussion in all its complexity.

Loopholes in land tenure legislation have facilitated the evasion of some of the provisions in land ceiling reforms by those large landholders who have wanted to maintain the *status quo*. At the same time, tardy implementation at the bureaucratic level and a political hijacking of the land reform agenda, by both the state and private interests, have traditionally posed impediments in the path of effective land reforms. Even in regional states throughout India that have attempted reforms, the process has often halted midway with the co-optation of the beneficiaries by those working to resist any further reforms.

For instance, with the abolition of intermediary interests, some middle-income farmers have gained economic leverage through the expansion of agricultural export. The most affluent of these tenants have acquired a higher social status as the rise in agricultural productivity, land values, and incomes from cultivation have added to their economic strength. These classes have since become opposed to any erosion in their newly acquired financial or social status.

Land-related problems such as tenancy rights and access to land for subsistence farming continue to challenge India. The importance of the land issue may be inferred from the fact that, notwithstanding the decline in the share of agriculture in the GDP, more than half of India's population (nearly 58 percent) is dependent on agriculture for livelihood. Yet more than half of this population (nearly 63 percent) own smallholdings of less than 1 hectare, with large parcels of 10 hectares of land or more in the hands of less than 2 percent. The absolute landless and the nearly landless (those owning up to 0.2 hectares of land) account for as much as 43 percent of total peasant households (Mearns 1999).

The reality represented by these statistics, however, did not seem to worry the governments of the late 1970s and 1980s. It was only in the 1990s, with the initiation of the economic restructuring process, that the issue of land reform resurfaced, albeit in a different garb and with a different objective and motivation. Whereas the government-led land reforms had been imbued with some effort to attain equity, social justice, and dignity, the new land reform agenda is solely market driven, and aimed at increasing GDP regardless of any externalities or costs associated with the process. Promoted and guided by various international financial institutions (IFIs) such as the World Bank and the International Monetary Fund (IMF), government emphasis on land reform since the 1990s reflects and seeks to fulfil the macroeconomic objectives of these multilateral economic institutions.

While the return of land reform to the government's list of priorities is a welcome development, the manner in which it is being undertaken—its objectives, and, consequently, its impact on people, especially those already marginalized and now being further deprived of a stake in the system—raises a number of questions and prompts one to look for alternatives. The remainder of this chapter, therefore, will devote its energies to identifying and monitoring the implementation of certain specific IFI-sponsored programs in particular states with a view to examining their short-term and long-term impact on the lives and livelihoods of local residents. It is hoped this shall enable an informed critique of the IFI-led land reform programs and serve as a lesson for peoples elsewhere in India and in other regions of the globe.

Market-Led Land Reform: The Current Emphasis on Land Administration, Titling, and Registration

In their analyses of India's land reform program, most international financial institutions have highlighted the basic problems that rural poor people face is accessing land and security of tenure, and they advocate redress of this situation through the structural reform of property rights, to create land markets as part of a broader strategy of fostering economic growth and reducing rural poverty (Mearns 1999).

A large emphasis has, therefore, been placed on the need to establish the basic legal and institutional framework that would facilitate a market takeoff in land and resource exchange. The goals of the new legal framework include efforts to improve property rights as a means to protect environmental and cultural resources, facilitate productivity-enhancing exchanges of land in rental and sales markets, link land to financial markets, use land to generate revenue for local governments, and improve land access for the poor and traditionally disenfranchised.

The neoliberal package endorsed by the IFIs includes a number of reforms 76 land and agrarian reform: historical perspectives that will transform the current system of land tenure into a market-oriented system of exchange. This tranformation includes a number of incremental steps that begin with titling and cadastral surveys (mapping). The latter are then formally tied to the establishment of state land registries, the creation of new landholding legislation, the concomitant establishment of a land administration department within the state, and finally the removal of restrictions on land leasing.

A similar plan had already been put forward as early as 1975, when a land reform policy paper published by the World Bank described land registration and titling as the main instruments for increasing an individual's tenure security and linked titling and registration to the establishment of flourishing land markets. The process of land tenure formalization provided the major tools—land titles and cadastral mapping—that were to enable the use of land as collateral for credit.

While none can argue against the need for straightening land records and providing secure land titles and registration, the motivation for the exercise must delve deeper than the mere creation of land markets for private profit. The belief that land markets alone would take off and address the historical inequality that was their foundation has been challenged by the reality of India's ongoing crisis in food security.

The shift in agriculture that has taken place since the first period of World Bank–endorsed privatization schemes in the 1970s points to an important historical and economic trend that has complicated the more recent attempts at marketization and poverty reduction in the twenty-first century. Industrialization, and the limits placed on national development programs to that end, exacerbate already existing inequalities in land distribution. The shift in Indian agricultural policy toward export and the increased embrace of neoliberal economic model casts much doubt on the purported benefits of the current World Bank land reform agenda in India.

The Commercialization/Industrialization of Agriculture

The influence of industrialization on national and international economic systems has reshaped the manner in which agriculture is conducted and for what purpose. From a family, or, at the most, a community affair, agriculture has been "professionalized" into an industry in which a farmer produces for the global market. Indeed, modern farming methods and techniques have transformed agriculture into a science of food production and a system of commodity distribution.

This shift in agricultural production goals has been promoted most fervently since the 1980s, by policy makers and politicians, who conceptualize agriculture more as an industry that must be conducted to maximize profits, and less as a way of life with social and ecological ramifications. The trend has been justified by the substantial increases in agricultural output, which, it is argued, has substantially eased India's national food-security concerns. Undoubtedly, Indian granaries are overflowing. And yet, the individual in the typical Indian village is starving to death, and a "failed" farmer resorts to suicide. Surely, the disparity between these two realities calls for a closer examination of the issues involved.

Commercialization of agriculture first gained a foothold in India in the 1960s, with the green revolution in Punjab, when the World Bank, along with the US Agency for International

Development (USAID), promoted agricultural productivity through importation of fertilizers, seeds, pesticides, and farm machinery. The Bank provided the credit necessary to replace the low-cost, lowinput agriculture in existence with an agricultural system that was both capital-and chemical-intensive.

The Indian government decided that the potential of the new technology far outweighed the risks and, accordingly, devalued the Indian rupee for the five-year plan period (1966–1971) to generate the purchase of approximately US$2.8 billion in green revolution–related technology, a jump of more than six times the total amount allocated to agriculture by the state during the preceding plan period (Shiva 1991). Most of the foreign exchange was spent on imports of fertilizer, seeds, pesticides, and farm machinery.

While subsidizing these imports, the World Bank also exerted pressure on the Indian government to obtain favourable conditions for foreign investment in India's fertilizer industry, for import liberalization, and for the elimination of most domestic controls on prices for basic agricultural products, e.g., grains and milk. The Bank advocated the replacement of diverse varieties of food crops with monocultures grown from imported varieties of seeds. In 1969, the Terai Seed Corporation (TSC) was started with a US$13 million World Bank loan.

This was followed by two National Seeds Project (NSP) loans. This program led to the homogenization and corporatization of India's agricultural system. The Bank provided the NSP US$41 million between 1974 and 1978. The projects were intended to develop state institutions and to create a new infrastructure for increasing the production of green revolution seed varieties. In 1988, the World Bank gave India's seed sector a fourth loan to make it more "market responsive." The US$150 million loan aimed to privatize the seed industry and open India to multinational seed corporations.

After the loan, India announced a New Seed Policy that allowed multinational corporations to penetrate fully a market that previously had not been directly accessible; Sandoz, Continental, Monsanto, Cargill, Pioneer, Hoechst, and Ciba Geigy now are among the multinational corporations with major investments in India's seed sector.

While the revolution did ease India's grain situation and transformed the country from a food importer to an exporter, it also enabled the rich farming community to politicize subsidies, facilitate concentration of inputs, and increase dependence on greater use of capital inputs such as credit, technology, seeds, and fertilizers. Moreover, the green revolution had increased Indian food production by only 5.4 percent, while the new agricultural practices resulted in the loss of nearly 8.5 million hectares, or 6 percent, of the crop base to waterlogging, salinity, or excess alkalinity (World Resources Institute 1994).

Furthermore, although the amount of wheat production doubled over a period of twenty years, and rice production increased by 50 percent, greater emphasis has been placed on production of commercial crops such as sugarcane and cotton at the expense of crops like chickpeas and millet, traditionally grown by the poor for themselves. These changes in practice have steadily eroded the self-sufficiency of the small farmer in food grains.

Yet in the face of such statistics successive Indian governments remain stuck on the same model of agrarian reforms, and they are generously encouraged by the IFIs. Agriculture is the World Bank's largest portfolio in any country. One hundred and thirty agricultural projects have received US$10.2 billion in World Bank financing in India since the 1950s. These projects have generally taken the forms of providing support for the fertilizer industry, exploiting groundwater through electric or gas-generated pumps, introducing highyield seed varieties, and setting up banking institutions to finance capitalist agriculture.

Water Sector Restructuring as Part of Agrarian Reform

Most supporters of land reform view the process as more than the mere redistribution of land to the landless. Rather, they place an equal importance on the availability of other inputs that can help turn the piece of land into a productive asset. In an agricultural country such as India, where two-thirds of the agricultural production is dependent on irrigation and irrigation accounts for 83 percent of consumptive water use (World Bank 1999a), irrigation schemes that can enhance agricultural productivity assume special importance. However, such projects launched by the government have often become entangled in a range of controversial issues. Questions have been raised about their actual merit, about cost versus benefit—especially in view of the numbers of people that may be displaced by such a project—about adequate rehabilitation schemes for people affected by the project, and so on. Big dams and other hydroelectric projects naturally bring with them the threats of submergence of hundreds of villages and the forced displacement of thousands of people. In the absence of people-friendly rehabilitation and resettlement packages, it remains questionable whether these development projects are truly worthwhile since they deprive one population of its livelihood to enhance that of another.

In this context, land acquisition by the government in the name of public purpose can be seen to raise doubt about the efficacy of such infrastructure development in the name of agrarian reform. Such issues prompted the World Bank to withdraw all funding for the still-incomplete Sardar Sarovar Project. In an attempt to steer clear of national and local controversies, IFIs have begun to finance and promote water sector restructuring projects of another kind. Highlighting the need for a "total revolution in irrigated agriculture" the government of India and the World Bank have identified the following goals for national rural development:

- Modernization of irrigation agencies to make them more autonomous and accountable.
- Improvements in irrigation systems by organizing farmers to take up operation and management responsibilities. Formation of water-user associations at the minor and distributaries levels.
- Reforms in irrigation financing in order to make state irrigation departments financially self-sufficient, rationalizing water charges, and improving collection rates.
- Institution of a system of water rights.

In the past, irrigation schemes had led to more severe environmental problems such as a rise in soil saturation and salinity in irrigated areas, which in turn brought more severe soil degradation. Not surprisingly, the World Bank came forward with new aid programs to resolve these problems, and it is now well into a second phase of water project loan disbursements. In 2001, the Bank announced two water and irrigation projects in the states of Rajasthan and Uttar Pradesh (UP). The US$140 million credit for Rajasthan and the US$149.2 million credit for Uttar Pradesh are both on standard IDA terms, with a forty-year maturity and including a ten-year grace period.

Premised on the assumption that irrigated agriculture could be the engine of agricultural growth but has been constrained by a failing public irrigation and drainage system, these two projects aim to initiate fundamental reform in water resources management and irrigation as a means to improve the living standards of the poor. The projects claim that improving agricultural productivity will generate additional jobs in the rural sector. In Rajasthan, projected aims are to benefit an estimated 250,000 farm families and stimulate demand for labour estimated at approximately 29,000 jobs per year, while in UP, the project is expected to generate additional employment for 22,000 rural farm families per year, representing a 24 percent increase in rural farm employment.

In addition, it is claimed that the formation of community groups under some of the project components will empower the rural population, particularly women and other disadvantaged people. The project also supports environmental management capacity, which will benefit affected communities by reducing pollution, preventing water-related diseases and improving public health.

These projects, with their laudable objectives, have just been initiated, and it would be instructive to monitor their implementation and progress vis-à-vis the actual impact on people in the regions affected. It must be kept in mind that the present IFI-led ventures in the sector of water are basically premised on the following two assumptions: First, in view of the impending water scarcity there is a need for water resources management in the form of large projects, for the storage and transfer of river waters. This requires huge investments that are beyond the capabilities of the government, and hence require liberal participation of the private sector. Second, in order to ensure water conservation and its proper distribution, there is a need to establish stable water markets and fair pricing. The emphasis, therefore, is on the creation of water markets, which will impinge on important issues of equity, social justice, and sustainability.

At the same time, the language being used in the water sector restructuring projects is reminiscent of the Joint Forest Management

(JFM) and its emphasis on participatory management. Under the new World Bank projects, the irrigation sector, too, is being couched in the same rhetoric of community management, though now in a less pervasive and publicized manner. In the management of tanks and lift irrigation (so-called minor irrigation) and even in the management of canal irrigation, phrases such as "participatory irrigation management" (PIM), or the more explicit "irrigation management turnover" (IMT), are the new catch phrases. Consequently, all sectoral reform programs or development projects speak of "joint management," "co-management," or "shared management."

Forestry Projects: The Relationship Between Land Reform and Environmental Sustainability

The land within a forest area relates in a unique fashion to issues of land reform. It is important to have an ecological balance among the proportions of land designated for forestry, agriculture, and nonagricultural purposes, and, ironically, land reform can help to maintain and sustain this balance. Several studies have linked the problems of reduction in area under forest cover with the historical patterns of development that result in skewed land distribution.

Hence, land reform that can ensure more equitable landownership can go a long way in relieving pressure on forests, even more than dedicated forest development programs that look on forests as a narrow environmental issue, devoid of a human dimension. The human element in forests, however, is very important, especially in several states of India where groups of populations have depended on forests for their livelihood for generations.

The concept of social forestry was originally conceived by the government of India as a response to the accelerating deforestation in India. Its objectives included assisting rural communities and landless people in meeting their needs for fodder, fuel wood, small timber, and minor produce through community planned and managed tree plantations and nurseries.

However, the social forestry projects came under criticism for failing to adequately involve local communities and rural poor, supposedly the main beneficiaries of the projects. Instead, the projects catered to urban and commercial interests through the widespread promotion of fast-growing tree species for pulp and paper manufacture, rayon production, urban fuel-wood supply, and other commercial uses. Such plantations were even encouraged on private farmlands, community lands, and wastelands.

The net result of this activity was to further reduce the access of the poor to fodder, fuel wood, and other forest products. Meanwhile, monoculture plantation of tree species, and in some cases the widespread plantation of water-consuming trees like eucalyptus, a pulpwood species and the Bank's favourite monoculture—for use in the very profitable paper and pulp sector—resulted in the degradation of soils and a falling water table. Further, these trees were not able to meet the fodder and fuel-wood need of the local forest dwellers/dependents.

Given the failure of this first round of social forestry projects, and in the face of the ongoing deterioration of the country's forest resources, the Indian government introduced a new forest policy (NFP) in 1988, which called for substantive change in the management of that sector. The NFP altered the aims of forest management, shifting them from a more commercial and industrial focus toward those that stressed the functions of environmental preservation and the preservation of basic needs for people living in or near forests.

The NFP required that forests be managed first as an ecological necessity, second as a source of goods for local populations, and, finally, as a source of wood for industries and other nonlocal consumers. This policy was pioneering to the extent that it recognized the people living in and around the forest as an essential factor in the governance of forests, considering them to be in partnership with the forestry department and giving primacy to their needs with regard to use of forest produce.

In 1990 the government directed all states to develop a participatory approach, similar to that of the NFP, in their efforts to restore the nation's degraded forests. Within seven years of this directive, seventeen states had issued orders enabling what is now known as JFM. Several states had used bilateral/multilateral funding to initiate forest sector projects, each with JFM as the guiding principle and value. By 1998, the vast majority of the states had introduced JFM programs and policies, most often with financial and technical support from the World Bank. One such project was initiated in the state of Madhya Pradesh in 1995. Its goals included increasing the productivity and quality of forests, protecting the environment, alleviating poverty, and strengthening and streamlining the policies of the forestry sector that the project hoped to achieve through the adoption of better practices and new technologies to increase forest productivity, the promotion of private sector participation in forestry sector development, the maintenance and improvement of biodiversity, and the strengthening of institutions involved in forest sector management.

This project was deemed to be successfully completed in December 1999, and the World Bank subsequently proposed a second phase, to be implemented beginning in 2002. It would be worthwhile to assess whether the earlier project did, in fact, meet the needs of the rural poor and indigenous peoples. By its own admission, the Bank now holds that the JFM project in Madhya Pradesh fell short of delivering the full measure of control and access required to alleviate the poverty of forest-dependent communities; what it now suggests is a new strategy of community forest management that envisages additional rights and responsibilities for local groups.

Returning Land Reform to the National Agenda

The present economic trends in India are negatively affecting land use and distribution in a variety of ways, some of which have been described above. Attempts to either reverse these trends or propose alternative approaches to development present a significant challenge to the landless in India. As the neoliberalization of the Indian state decreases the opportunity to resist the topdown World Bank models, there is an increased awareness of the problem with land use and distribution both within the Bank itself and among international nongovernmental organizations more generally. However, the need to sensitize people to these realities cannot be underestimated. Increasing the prominence of land reform challenges through public discourse and Indian politics is particularly important since more comprehensive agrarian reform has virtually disappeared from the popular, political, and elite radar screen throughout the country.

The growing size of the urban-based population in India presents another challenge to establishing a national, comprehensive land reform policy. Most urban dwellers perceive land in a compartmentalized and detached way, and are unable to identify with the problems of the small or marginal farmers or fathom the larger linkages of land use to the functioning of the macroeconomy.

For instance, the urban middle-class market demand for cheaper products pushes farmers toward agricultural systems that have a low-unit cost of production. This is only possible if the yield per acre is increased through the use of artificial fertilizers, pesticides that reduce crop losses, and, more recently, through genetically modified crops that claim to be more resistant to pests. All of these require access to and maintenance of capital for cashpoor farmers. Higher capital costs on the part of farmers drive the demand for borrowing from individual or credit institutions.

As farmers' debts rise, along with the frequency of bankruptcy, they are forced to sell land to richer farmers or corporate houses and move into cities in search of other jobs. Equipped with few skills, these now landless people live in the slums. The environmental and social costs of cheap agricultural produce are huge; but this scenario is largely invisible to urbanites. Few acknowledge or appreciate the link between huge entertainment complexes or wildlife sanctuaries and the fate of the displaced, or between rising urban crime and increasing rural dislocation as a result of commercialized agriculture, bankrupted farmers, and environmental degradation.

Importance of Land Reform to India's Future

From an economic perspective, the question of land is linked to critical issues of agricultural productivity, agrarian relations, industrial uses, infrastructure development, employment opportunities, housing, and other related issues. Each one of these aspects is crucial for enhancing national security by ensuring consistent economic growth, food security, goods for export, and so on, which reinforce the country's economic strength, and therefore, its bargaining power in the international community.

A National Food Security Requirement

For a country the size and population of India, food security is an especially crucial component of national security, and, until recently, it was on an upswing due to technological breakthroughs in rice and wheat production, a price policy ensuring minimum support prices, agricultural subsidies providing cheaper modern inputs, and a closed market. However, with economic liberalization has come the entry of cheaper foreign agricultural goods into the country and the removal of agricultural subsidies for Indian farmers, which will threaten food security in the future.

With a reduction in the role of the state to ensure food security and the eventual takeover by market forces, there is sure to be a decrease in the access to food for the poorest Indian citizens. Apart from its economic function, land ownership has a more profound social function, in that the distribution of land impacts the quality of the social fabric in a community and the dynamic of gender relations within that community. If the patterns of land ownership are perceived as fair and just, this, in turn, enhances an ethic of justice and equity within a community.

By contrast, skewed land distribution patterns, alienation, or poverty eventually lead to social discontentment, widespread unrest, and violent venting of frustration and anger, which could further increase volatility within a multiethnic, multireligious country such as India. Such unhappiness could also provide a fertile base for extranational powers to foment disharmony and encourage separatist tendencies in a bid to fragment the country; movements for greater autonomy or even independence from the Indian Union already place strain on Indian national security apparatus in the Northeast, Jharkhand, Punjab, and elsewhere.

It becomes imperative, therefore, to strike a balance between the economic and social functions of land. A model of development that excludes one in 86 land and agrarian reform: historical perspectives favour of the other loses out on the very basic meaning and purpose of development.

In order to envisage viable land-use patterns that ensure high agricultural production along with social justice and environmental sustainability, land must be conceived within an equity-based development strategy that is economically viable, ecologically sound, socially acceptable, and politically feasible through the creation of an institutional framework. This, of course, is easier said than done. This chapter will now turn to addressing a few of the complex issues involved in developing such a strategy for land and agrarian reform in India.

Challenge 1: Shifting Economic Imperatives

National economic development should ideally bring about an enhancement in the quality of life for all citizens within a given nation. But the question remains, are these parameters met by the present model of development? It seems, instead, that "development has become a big business, preoccupied more with its own growth and imperatives than with the people it was originally created to serve". The present economic model is premised on the centrality of markets.

But the market forces themselves are a function of economic power and control. In cases in which economic resources and opportunities are widely distributed, economic activity may best be left to individual, private initiative, and market forces, but in societies with a skewed distribution of natural resources and opportunities, a free play of market forces could marginalize an increasing proportion of people, without state intervention through reforms. In these circumstances, land reform holds a key to the removal of current socioeconomic abuses and serves as a means to break the age-old bondages of exploitation and poverty, to foster greater equity and justice.

Increasing people's access to land and creating a more equitable redistribution of land assets are important for India, particularly in view of its high and ever-increasing person-to-land ratio. Increased emphasis on industrialization should not result in an abandonment of the rural sector. For an economy that has little capital but a surplus of labour, optimal land utilization is an important component of land sustainability, and should be based on a consideration of land's labour-absorption capacity—to avoiding crowding and soil degradation— in a bid to achieve higher output per unit of land. Policies aimed at liberalizing markets and privatizing natural resources fail to address the problem of land and labour in the rural sector of India.

Challenge 2: Maintaining Ecological Balance

Forests. The case has been made above for an ecological balance between the proportion of land designated for forestry, agriculture, and nonagricultural purposes. There is a need to explore the linkages among rural poverty, landlessness, and skewed land tenure systems with particular attention to the problems of deforestation. The reduction of forests inevitably disturbs the ecological balance.

Cyclical patterns of droughts followed by floods have been clearly linked to this. At the same time, there is no guarantee that the already existing skewed distribution of land outside the forests will not be replicated. Unless the government engages in the exercise with a blueprint for land reforms in mind, fertile lands cleared by the government are most likely to be taken over by rich farmers, private companies, and state enterprises, or held by speculators as a hedge against inflation.

Traditionally, impoverished farmers moving into forests have been identified as the principal, direct agents of forest loss. Hence, land reform that can ensure more equitable landownership may well do more to relieve pressure on forests rather than any other policy of forest resource development. In this context, and as suggested above it would be helpful to explore the efficacy of social forestry programs already undertaken in states such as Andhra Pradesh.

Land Degradation. Patterns of land use also have an impact on soil erosion and land degradation. For instance, agricultural practices designed to suit market conditions presuppose a permissive use of agrochemicals to maximize productivity. When land is perceived as a commodity or investment that must be made good upon, it is rigorously exploited to generate immediate, short-term profit, often at the expense of a long-term impact in the form of severe land degradation.

In arid and semiarid regions, the introduction of perennial irrigation in order to increase yield causes salinization of the land. Irrigation on poorly drained land has waterlogged the soil, causing salts in the groundwater to rise and accumulate on the surface, turning farmland into a salt-encrusted desert. Artificial fertilizers and chemical sprays undermine the natural fertility of soils and increase its vulnerability to erosion. Of a total land expanse in India of 329 million hectares, nearly 141 million hectares (43 percent) of the land is subject to water and soil erosion.

Other types of land degradation such as waterlogging, alkaline and arid soils, salinity, ravines, and gullies affect another 34 million hectares (Vyas 1999, 18). Given the fragile nature of the ecosystem and land quality that has resulted from such a dependency on chemical inputs, care must be exercised in determining land-use patterns in the future. Agriculture is expanding to wastelands that are not suited for cultivation, hence pushing India's small farmers into a less fertile land base.

Additionally, the rising demand for irrigated agriculture has led to massive overexploitation of groundwater. And, with the demand for more water, local wells often dry up, leaving small and marginal farmers to either pay for expensive state-provided water or abandon the unproductive farm. In response to the same crisis in water access, wealthier farmers, corporations, and the state resort to expensive technology-dependent extraction of groundwater, which exacerbates the overall problem of groundwater depletion. The ecological consequences of the current dominant model of development are serious and need to be addressed.

Challenge 3: Preserving Human Diversity

Tribal Displacement and Deprivation. The concept of land as a commodity comes into conflict with traditional concepts of common property and with societies, such as those of many tribal peoples throughout India, who generally do not have a documented system of land rights. The issue of land use arises in this context because many tribal groups, 7 percent of the total Indian population, live in resource-rich regions. Consequently, both the government and the private sector have a keen interest in gaining access and control over the land or its mineral wealth. In the process, depriving tribal groups of land has become the norm, as they are routinely displaced, and, in most cases, not even able to claim compensation since they have no legal proof of ownership.

It is estimated that over 20 million people have been displaced by large projects (e.g., dams, railroads) since independence, and a majority of these people have been tribal groups. This has happened despite the fact that special legal provisions exist to protect the land and other assets of tribal people. Driven away from their homes and with little or no resettlement assistance, they join the ranks of the landless. One attempt at correcting this ongoing marginalization was the official endorsement of five principles that valued the preservation of tribal land use patterns and land distribution practices.

The Panchsheela, or five principles of tribal development, state the following:

1. Tribal people have the right to develop according to their

own culture and join the mainstream as equals, while maintaining their identity.

2. Tribal rights on tribal lands and forest will be safeguarded.
3. A team built from among tribals will develop their land.
4. State administration in tribal areas will work through traditional tribal structures.
5. Achievements in tribal areas will be judged according to human growth rather than productivity.

The Panchsheela principles have been most difficult to achieve, and in many ways they lack sufficient definition for use in policy making. The resource-rich regions of the tribal peoples in India have been drawn into the plans for national development, with its emphasis on industrialization and ever-higher productivity. Already, industries and irrigation schemes built on large dams have displaced many tribal people and transformed them into landless migrant labour. The Indian government has presented tribal development schemes as a principal tool for poverty alleviation.

However, these schemes have not taken into account the total dependence of the tribal population on land and their lack of other productive assets. It is critical that the unique existence and subsistence patterns of tribal people be empathetically understood so that economic development can be harmonized with social change. Without such understanding, India may well have to face more indigenous struggles for national identity, as it has already in Nagaland, Jharkhand, and many other regions.

Women and Land. With farms linked to the wider market economy, the condition of women's participation in farming has also undergone a change, and not for the better. Traditionally, rural women have been responsible for half of the world's food production. They remain the main producers of the world's staple crops—rice, wheat, and maize— which provide up to 90 percent of the rural poor's food intake. Their contribution to secondary-crop production, such as that of legumes and vegetables, is even greater.

Grown mainly in home gardens, these crops provide essential nutrients and are often the only food available during lean seasons or when the main harvest fails. Women's specialized knowledge of genetic resources for food and agriculture makes them essential custodians of agrobiodiversity. In the livestock sector, women feed and milk the larger animals, while raising poultry and small animals such as sheep, goats, rabbits, and guinea pigs.

Additionally, once the harvest is in, rural women provide most of the labour for postharvest activities, taking responsibility for storage, handling, stocking, processing, and marketing. However, in the market-driven agriculture, a conceptual division of labour between what are considered the productive tasks of farming and the unproductive tasks of household and reproduction recasts the women's role as "mere 'supporters' of the 'producers'" (Clunies-Ross and Hildyard 1992).

This view, however, tends to overlook the effects of the realities of the rural-urban migration of men in search of paid employment and rising mortalities attributed to health problems such as alcoholism and HIV/AIDS, which have led to a rise in the numbers of female-headed households in the developing world. This "feminization of agriculture" places a considerable burden on a woman's capacity to participate in agriculture, in view of the difficulty in their ability to gain access, control, and recognition with regard to ownership of valuable resources such as land, credit and agricultural inputs, technology, extension, training, and services.

Certain communities in India (especially in the northeast and the south) have practiced the tradition of customarily recognizing women's property rights. In these areas inheritance laws and marriage practices have been so tailored as to provide and protect these rights; many studies have been devoted to examining these practices. Several matrilineal and bilateral systems of land inheritance have also given women advantages in many respects, especially in granting them economic and social security, and considerable autonomy and equality in marital relations.

These systems, however, have eroded over time. Interventions by both colonial and postcolonial government policies, particularly in the legal and economic spheres, as well as the complex processes of social and cultural change (which the former set in motion), have degraded customary practices. Large joint family estates have fallen into disuse; formerly egalitarian tribal societies have grown economically differentiated; there has been an increasing penetration into the culture of market forces and notable shifts in the techniques of production, the social division of labour, and land relations; sexual mores have altered; and patriarchal ideologies have spread their influence.

Women, in particular, have been profoundly affected by these changes, and their customary exclusion from major authority in public bodies has meant that they are not the ones directing the change or are even in a position to effectively protect their interests. The task is a complicated one, and government intervention in the form of honest land reform could go a long way in ensuring social justice and equity for women.

Challenge 4: Complexities of Common Property Regimes

Resources, both natural and manmade, controlled and managed as common property present another challenge in the context of land-related issues. Besides private property or property owned and controlled by the state, common property such as forests, grazing lands, water, and fisheries can also be held and managed through a community resource management system. These are different from open-access land and natural resources, e.g., forest areas and lakes, where there are no rules regulating individual use rights. The system of common property operates through a "complex system of norms and conventions for regulating individual rights to use a variety of natural resources" (Runge 1992, 17). Specifying rights of joint use, common-property regimes envisage tacit cooperation among individuals.

Traditionally, common-property regimes have contributed substantially to village economies by providing a source for fodder, fuel wood, small timber, and employment in local products derived from raw material. At the same time, they have also proved to be a stable form of resource management. However, the combination of population growth, technological change, and political forces has in many cases destabilized existing common-property regimes, while the institution of common property itself has often been blamed for these problems and accused of resource mismanagement.

The imposition of private property rights has been instituted as a remedial measure. But enforcement of private property rights from outside the group or village is not a sufficient condition for optimal resource utilization and may lead to the adoption of land use patterns that are incompatible with local needs or place land use in the hands of those, such as absentee owners, with fewer incentives for efficient, equitable local management.

The scenario described above may become especially worrisome if lands are subjected to a new zoning system, in which grazing land may be redesignated as commercial land and local forests turned to conservation forests with concessions for tourism companies. In either of these cases, the access of those who have traditionally depended upon the communal land is curtailed. The worst affected are the women whose daily lives have been severely strained by the additional load of daily livelihood activities of food, fodder, fuel wood, and water collection. Alienation and involuntary migration are, again, the inevitable outcomes, as is erosion in the long-term capacity of such land development.

On the counts of efficiency and equity, common-property regimes have traditionally existed as a viable proposition for more equitable national development. This has been especially true for a developing economy in which poverty and natural resource dependency have arisen out of a skewed distribution of resources. Common-property regimes have provided a hedge against uncertainties, in times of poor crop harvests and harsh growing conditions. When facing such challenges, the pooling of resources— land in this case— ensures that at minimum larger numbers of farm families will maintain a level of subsistence.

In fact, the implications of such systems of resource management are immense since the poorest members of society, e.g., the indigent and the elderly, can obtain a share of their sustenance from the public domain while remaining connected to members of their rural communities. In these ways, common-property regimes enhance the general welfare of rural dwellers and increase the sustainability of equitable resource distribution practices.

6

The Green Revolution Changed the Face of Agriculture

Green Revolution refers to the transformation of agriculture that began in 1945, largely due to the life work of Norman Borlaug. One significant factor in this revolution was the Mexican government's request to establish an agricultural research station to develop more varieties of wheat that could be used to feed the rapidly growing population of the country.

In 1943, Mexico imported half its wheat, but by 1956, the Green Revolution had made Mexico self-sufficient; by 1964, Mexico exported half a million tons of wheat.

The associated transformation has continued as the result of programs of agricultural research, extension, and infrastructural development. These programs were instigated and largely funded by the Rockefeller Foundation along with the Ford Foundation, and other major agencies.

The Green Revolution allowed food production to enable, or keep pace with worldwide population growth. The Green Revolution has had major social and ecological impacts, making it a popular topic of study among sociologists.

The term "Green Revolution" was first used in 1968 by former USAID director William Gaud, who noted the spread of the new technologies and said,

"These and other developments in the field of agriculture contain the makings of a new revolution. It is not a violent Red Revolution like that of the Soviets, nor is it a White Revolution like that of the Shah of Iran. I call it the Green Revolution."

History

Indian Success: With the experience of agricultural development begun in Mexico by Norman Borlaug in 1943 judged as a success, the Rockefeller Foundation sought to spread it to other nations. The Office of Special Studies in Mexico became an informal international research institution in 1959, and in 1963 it formally became CIMMYT, The International Maize and Wheat Improvement Centre.

In 1961 India was on the brink of mass famine. Borlaug was invited to India by the adviser to the Indian minister of agriculture M. S. Swaminathan. Despite bureaucratic hurdles imposed by India's grain monopolies, the Ford Foundation and Indian government collaborated to import wheat seed from CIMMYT. Punjab was selected by the Indian government to be the first site to try the new crops because of its reliable water supply and a history of agricultural success. India began its own Green Revolution program of plant breeding, irrigation development, and financing of agrochemicals.

India soon adopted IR8-a semi-dwarf rice variety developed by the International Rice Research Institute (IRRI) that could produce more grains of rice per plant when grown with certain fertilizers and irrigation. In 1968, Indian agronomist S.K. De Datta published his findings that IR8 rice yielded about 5 tons per hectare with no fertilizer, and almost 10 tons per hectare under optimal conditions. This was 10 times the yield of traditional rice. IR8 was a success throughout Asia, and dubbed the "Miracle Rice". IR8 was also developed into Semi-dwarf IR36.

In the 1960s, rice yields in India were about two tons per hectare; by the mid-1990s, they had risen to six tons per hectare. In the 1970s, rice cost about $550 a ton; in 2001, it cost under $200 a ton. India became one of the world's most successful rice producers, and is now a major rice exporter, shipping nearly 4.5 million tons in 2006.

IR8 and the Philippines

In 1960, the Government of the Republic of the Philippines with Ford and Rockefeller Foundations established IRRI (International Rice Research Institute). A rice crossing between Dee-geo-woo-gen and Peta was done at IRRI in 1962. In 1966, one of the breeding lines became a new cultivar, IR8. IR8 required the use of fertilizers and pesticides, but produced substantially higher yields than the traditional cultivars. Annual rice production in the Philippines increased from 3.7 to 7.7 million tonnes in two decades. The switch to IR8 rice made the Philippines a rice exporter for the first time in the 20th century. But the heavy pesticide use reduced the number of fish and frog species found in rice paddies.

CGIAR

In 1970, foundation officials proposed a worldwide network of agricultural research centres under a permanent secretariat. This was further supported and developed by the World Bank; on May 19, 1971, the Consultative Group on International Agricultural Research was established, co-sponsored by the FAO, IFAD and UNDP. CGIAR, has added many research centres throughout the world.

CGIAR has responded, at least in part, to criticisms of Green Revolution methodologies. This began in the 1980s, and mainly was a result of pressure from donor organizations. Methods like Agroecosystem Analysis and Farming System Research have been adopted to gain a more holistic view of agriculture. Methods like Rapid Rural Appraisal and Participatory Rural Appraisal have been adopted to help scientists understand the problems faced by farmers and even give farmers a role in the development process.

Problems in Africa

There have been numerous attempts to introduce the successful concepts from the Mexican and Indian projects into Africa. These programs have generally been less successful, for a number of reasons. Reasons cited include widespread corruption, insecurity, a lack of infrastructure, and a general lack of will on the part of the governments. Yet environmental factors, such as the availability of water for irrigation, the high diversity in slope and soil types in one given area are also reasons why the Green Revolution is not so successful in Africa.

A recent program in western Africa is attempting to introduce a new high-yield variety of rice known as "New Rice for Africa"(NERICA). NERICAs yield about 30% more rice under normal conditions, and can double yields with small amounts of fertilizer and very basic irrigation. However the program has been beset by problems getting the rice into the hands of farmers, and to date the only success has been in Guinea where it currently accounts for 16% of rice cultivation.

Agricultural Production and Food Security

Technologies

The projects within the Green Revolution spread technologies that had already existed, but had not been widely used outside industrialized nations. These technologies included pesticides, irrigation projects, synthetic nitrogen fertilizer and improved crop varieties developed through the conventional, science-based methods available at the time.

The novel technological development of the Green Revolution was the production of novel wheat cultivars. Agronomists bred cultivars of maize, wheat, and rice that are generally referred to as HYVs or "high-yielding varieties". HYVs have higher nitrogen-absorbing potential than other varieties. Since cereals that absorbed extra nitrogen would typically lodge, or fall over before harvest, semi-dwarfing genes were bred into their genomes. A Japanese dwarf wheat cultivar (Norin 10 wheat), which was sent to Washington, D.C. by Cecil Salmon, was instrumental in developing Green Revolution wheat cultivars. IR8, the first widely implemented HYV rice to be developed by IRRI, was created through a cross between an Indonesian variety named "Peta" and a Chinese variety named "Dee-geo-woo-gen."

With advances in molecular genetics, the mutant genes responsible for Arabidopsis genes (GA 20-oxidase, *ga1*, *ga1-3*), wheat reduced-height genes (*Rht*) and a rice semidwarf gene (*sd1*) were cloned. These were identified as gibberellin biosynthesis genes or cellular signalling component genes. Stem growth in the mutant background is significantly reduced leading to the dwarf phenotype. Photosynthetic investment in the stem is reduced dramatically as the shorter plants are inherently more stable mechanically. Assimilates become redirected to grain production, amplifying in particular the effect of chemical fertilizers on commercial yield.

HYVs significantly outperform traditional varieties in the presence of adequate irrigation, pesticides, and fertilizers. In the absence of these inputs, traditional varieties may outperform HYVs. Therefore, several authors have challenged the apparent superiority of HYVs not only compared to the traditional varieties alone, but by contrasting the monocultural system asssociated with HYVs with the polycultural system associated with traditional ones

Production Increases

Cereal production more than doubled in developing nations between the years 1961 – 1985. Yields of rice, maize, and wheat increased steadily during that period. The production increases can be attributed roughly equally to irrigation, fertilizer, and seed development, at least in the case of Asian rice.

While agricultural output increased as a result of the Green Revolution, the energy input to produce a crop has increased faster, so that the ratio of crops produced to energy input has decreased over time. Green Revolution techniques also heavily rely on chemical fertilizers, pesticides and herbicides, some of which must be developed from fossil fuels, making agriculture increasingly reliant on petroleum products. Proponents of the Peak Oil theory fear that a future decline in oil and gas production would lead to a decline in food production or even a Malthusian catastrophe.

Effects on Food Security

The effects of the Green Revolution on global food security are difficult to understand because of the complexities involved in food systems.

The world population has grown by about four billion since the beginning of the Green Revolution and many believe that, without the Revolution, there would have been greater famine and malnutrition. India saw annual wheat production rise from 10 million tons in the 1960s to 73 million in 2006. The average person in the developing world consumes roughly 25% more calories per day now than before the Green Revolution. Between 1950 and 1984, as the Green Revolution transformed agriculture around the globe, world grain production increased by over 250%

The production increases fostered by the Green Revolution are often credited with having helped to avoid widespread famine, and for feeding billions of people.

There are many claims that the Green Revolution has decreased food security for a large number of people. One claim involves the shift of subsistence-oriented cropland to cropland oriented towards production of grain for export or animal feed. For example, the Green Revolution replaced much of the land used for pulses that fed Indian peasants for wheat, which did not make up a large portion of the peasant diet.

Criticisms

Malthusian Criticism

Some criticisms generally involve some variation of the Malthusian principle of population. Such concerns often revolve around the idea that the Green Revolution is unsustainable, and argue that humanity is now in a state of overpopulation with regards to the sustainable carrying capacity and ecological demands on the Earth.

Although 36 million people die each year as a direct or indirect result of hunger and poor nutrition, Malthus' more extreme predictions have frequently failed to materialize. In 1798 Thomas Malthus made his prediction of impending famine. The world's population had doubled by 1923 and doubled again by 1973 without fulfilling Malthus' prediction. Malthusian Paul R. Ehrlich, in his 1968 book *The Population Bomb*, said that "India couldn't possibly feed two hundred million more people by 1980" and "Hundreds of millions of people will starve to death in spite of any crash programs." Ehrlich's warnings failed to materialize when India became self-sustaining in cereal production in 1974 (six years later) as a result of the introduction of Norman Borlaug's dwarf wheat varieties.

Is Food Production Related to Famine?

To some modern Western sociologists and writers, increasing food production is not synonymous with increasing food security, and is only part of a larger equation. For example, Harvard professor Amartya Sen claimed large historic famines were not caused by decreases in food supply, but by socioeconomic dynamics and a failure of public action. However, economist Peter Bowbrick refutes that Sen's theory is incorrect as Sen relies on inconsistent arguments, and contradicting available information, including sources that Sen himself cited. Bowbrick further argues that Sen's views coincide with that of the Bengal government at the time of the Bengal famine of 1943 and the policies Sen advocates failed to relieve the famine.

Quality of Diet

Some have challenged the value of the increased food production of Green Revolution agriculture. Miguel A. Altieri, (a pioneer of agroecology and peasant-advocate), writes that the comparison between traditional systems of agriculture and Green Revolution agriculture has been unfair, because Green Revolution agriculture produces monocultures of cereal grains, while traditional agriculture usually incorporates polycultures.

These monoculture crops are often used for export, feed for animals, or conversion into biofuel. According to Emile Frison of Biodiversity International, the Green Revolution has also led to a change in dietary habits, as less people are affected by hunger and die from starvation, but many are affected by malnutrition such as iron or vitamin-A deficiencies. Frison further asserts that almost 60% of yearly deaths of children under age five in developing countries are related to malnutrition.

High-yield rice (HYR), introduced since 1964 to poverty-ridden Asian countries, (such as the Philippines), was found to have inferior flavor and be more glutinous and less savory than their native varieties. This caused its price to be lower than the average market value.

In the Philippines the introduction of heavy pesticides to rice production, in the early part of the green revolution, poisoned and killed off fish and weedy green vegetables that traditionally coexisted in rice paddies. These were nutritious food sources for many poor Filipino farmers prior to the introduction of pesticides, further impacting the diets of locals.

Political Impacts

The Green Revolution is unpopular among many leftists because of its context within the Cold War. A major critic of the Green Revolution, U.S. investigative journalist Mark Dowie, writes:

> The primary objective of the program was geopolitical: to provide food for the populace in underdeveloped countries and so bring social stability and weaken the fomenting of communist insurgency.

Citing internal Foundation documents, Dowie states that the Ford Foundation had a greater concern than Rockefeller in this area.

There is significant evidence that the Green Revolution weakened socialist movements in many nations. In countries such as India, Mexico, and the Philippines, *technological solutions* were sought as an alternative to expanding *agrarian reform* initiatives, the latter of which were often linked to socialist politics.

Socioeconomic Impacts

The transition from traditional agriculture, in which inputs were generated on-farm, to Green Revolution agriculture, which required the purchase of inputs, led to the widespread establishment of rural credit institutions. Smaller farmers often went into debt, which in many cases results in a loss of their farmland. The increased level of mechanization on larger farms made possible by the Green Revolution removed a large source of employment from the rural economy. Because wealthier farmers had better access to credit and land, the Green Revolution increased class disparities. The rich-poor gap widened due to that. Because some regions were able to adopt Green Revolution agriculture more readily than others (for political or geographical reasons), interregional economic disparities increased as well. Many small farmers are hurt by the dropping prices resulting from increased production overall.

The new economic difficulties of small holder farmers and landless farm workers led to increased rural-urban migration. The increase in food production led to a cheaper food for urban dwellers, and the increase in urban population increased the potential for industrialization.

Globalization

In the most basic sense, the Green Revolution was a product of globalization as evidenced in the creation of international agricultural research centres that shared information, and with transnational funding from groups like the Rockefeller Foundation, Ford Foundation, and United States Agency for International Development (USAID). Additionally, the inputs required in Green Revolution agriculture created new markets for seed and chemical corporations, many of which were based in the United States. For example, Standard Oil of New Jersey established hundreds of distributors in the Philippines to sell agricultural packages composed of HYV seed, fertilizer, and pesticides.

Environmental Impact

Pesticides

Green Revolution agriculture relies on extensive use of pesticides, which are necessary to limit the high levels of pest damage that inevitably occur in monocropping-the practice of producing or growing one single crop over a wide area.

Water

Industrialized agriculture with its high yield varieties are extremely water intensive. In the US, agriculture consumes 85% of all fresh water resources. For example, the Southwest uses 36% of the nations water while at the same time only receiving 6% of the country's rainfall. Only 60% of the water used for irrigation comes from surface water supplies. The other 40% comes from underground aquifers that are being used up in a way similar to topsoil that makes the aquifers, as Pfeiffer says, "for all intents and purposes non renewable resources." The Ogallala Aquifer is essential to a huge portion of central and southwest plain states, but has been at annual overdrafts of 130-160% in excess of replacement. This irrigation source for America's bread basket will become entirely unproductive in another 30 years or so.

Likewise, rivers are drying up at an alarming rate. In 1997, the lower parts of China's Yellow River were dry for a record 226 days. Over the past ten years, it has gone dry an average of 70 days a year. Famous lifelines such as the Nile and Ganges along with countless other rivers are sharing in the same fate. The Aral Sea has lost half its area and two-thirds its volume due to river diversion for cotton production. Also the water quality is being compromised. In the Aral Sea, water salinization has wiped out all native fish, leaving an economy even more dependent on the agricultural model that originated the problem.

Fish are disappearing through another form of agricultural run off as well. When nitrogen-intensive fertilizers wash into waterways it results in an explosion of algae and other microorganisms that lead to oxygen depletion resulting in "dead zones", killing off fish and other creatures.

Biodiversity

The spread of Green Revolution agriculture affected both

agricultural biodiversity and wild biodiversity. There is little disagreement that the Green Revolution acted to reduce agricultural biodiversity, as it relied on just a few high-yield varieties of each crop.

This has led to concerns about the susceptibility of a food supply to pathogens that cannot be controlled by agrochemicals, as well as the permanent loss of many valuable genetic traits bred into traditional varieties over thousands of years. To address these concerns, massive seed banks such as Consultative Group on International Agricultural Research's (CGIAR) International Plant Genetic Resources Institute (now Bioversity International) have been established.

There are varying opinions about the effect of the Green Revolution on wild biodiversity. One hypothesis speculates that by increasing production per unit of land area, agriculture will not need to expand into new, uncultivated areas to feed a growing human population. However, land degradation and soil nutrients depletion have forced farmers to clear up formerly forested areas in order to keep up with production. A counter-hypothesis speculates that biodiversity was sacrificed because traditional systems of agriculture that were displaced sometimes incorporated practices to preserve wild biodiversity, and because the Green Revolution expanded agricultural development into new areas where it was once unprofitable or too arid. For example, the development of wheat varieties tolerant to acid soil conditions with high aluminium content, permitted the introduction of agriculture in the Amazonian Cerrado ecosystem in Brazil.

Nevertheless, the world community has clearly acknowledged the negative aspects of agricultural expansion as the 1992 Rio Treaty, signed by 189 nations, has generated numerous national Biodiversity Action Plans which assign significant biodiversity loss to agriculture's expansion into new domains.

Health Impact

The consumption of the chemicals and pesticides used to kill pests by humans in some cases may be increasing the likelihood of cancer in some of the rural villages using them. Poor farming practices including non-compliance to usage of masks and over-usage of the chemicals by un-educated farmers in poor countries compound this situation.

Pesticides and Cancer

Long term exposure to pesticides such as organochlorines, creosote, and sulfallate have been correlated with higher cancer rates and organochlorines DDT, chlordane, and lindane as tumor promoters in animals. Contradictory epidemiologic studies in humans have linked phenoxy acid herbicides or contaminants in them with soft tissue sarcoma (STS) and malignant lymphoma, organochlorine insecticides with STS, non-Hodgkin's lymphoma (NHL), leukemia, and, less consistently, with cancers of the lung and breast, organophosphorous compounds with NHL and leukemia, and triazine herbicides with ovarian cancer.

Punjab Case

The Indian state of Punjab pioneered green revolution among the other states transforming India into a food-surplus country. The state is witnessing serious consequences of intensive farming using chemicals and pesticide. A comprehensive study conducted by Post Graduate Institute of Medical Education and Research (PGIMER) has underlined the direct relationship between indiscriminate use of these chemicals and increased incidence of cancer in this region. Increase in the number of cancer cases has been reported in several villages including Jhariwala, Koharwala, Puckka, Bhimawali, Khara.

Ecologist Vandana Shiva has written extensively about the social, political and economic impacts of the Green Revolution in Punjab. She has shown how the Green Revolution's reliance on heavy use of chemical inputs and monocultures has resulted in a precarious situation of water scarcity, vulnerability to pests, and incidence of violent conflict and social marginalization.

Organic Farming

About four decades after the Green Revolution widely helped the world to be able to produce food in sufficient levels, a small percentage of farmers in India have chosen to employ organic farming methods in response to side effects from their adoption of modern agriculture techniques.

However, the techniques which these farmers perceive as harmful enough to sacrifice as much as a half of their food production are often not properly applied in the way they were developed, many conventional Indian farmers misuse concentrated chemicals in ways such as not wearing protective clothing or equipment, re-using pesticide containers as kitchen containers, and using more pesticide and fertilizer than necessary to maximize yield.

Norman Borlaug's Response to Criticism

He dismissed certain claims of critics, but did take other concerns seriously and stated that his work has been: "a change in the right direction, but it has not transformed the world into a Utopia".

Of environmental lobbyists he said: "some of the environmental lobbyists of the Western nations are the salt of the earth, but many of them are elitists. They've never experienced the physical sensation of hunger. They do their lobbying from comfortable office suites in Washington or Brussels...If they lived just one month amid the misery of the developing world, as I have for fifty years, they'd be crying out for tractors and fertilizer and irrigation canals and be outraged that fashionable elitists back home were trying to deny them these things".

Why Green Revolution

The world's worst recorded food disaster happened in 1943 in British-ruled India. Known as the Bengal Famine, an estimated four million people died of hunger that year alone in eastern India (that included today's Bangladesh). The initial theory put forward to 'explain' that catastrophe was that there as an acute shortfall in food production in the area. However, Indian economist Amartya Sen (recipient of the Nobel Prize for Economics, 1998) has established that while food shortage was a contributor to the problem, a more potent factor was the result of hysteria related to World War II which made food supply a low priority for the British rulers. The hysteria was further exploited by Indian traders who hoarded food in order to sell at higher prices.

Nevertheless, when the British left India four years later in 1947, India continued to be haunted by memories of the Bengal Famine. It was therefore natural that food security was a paramount item on free India's agenda. This awareness led, on one hand, to the Green Revolution in India and, on the other, legislative measures to ensure that businessmen would never again be able to hoard food for reasons of profit.

However, the term "Green Revolution" is applied to the period from 1967 to 1978. Between 1947 and 1967, efforts at achieving food self-sufficiency were not entirely successful. Efforts until 1967 largely concentrated on expanding the farming areas. But starvation deaths were still being reported in the newspapers. In a perfect case of Malthusian economics, population was growing at a much faster rate than food production. This called for drastic action to increase yield. The action came in the form of the Green Revolution.

The term "Green Revolution" is a general one that is applied to successful agricultural experiments in many Third World countries. It is NOT specific to India. But it was most successful in India.

What was the Green Revolution in India?

There were three basic elements in the method of the Green Revolution:

(1) Continued expansion of farming areas;
(2) Double-cropping existing farmland;
(3) Using seeds with improved genetics.

Continued Expansion of Farming Areas

As mentioned above, the area of land under cultivation was being increased right from 1947. But this was not enough in meeting with rising demand. Other methods were required. Yet, the expansion of cultivable land also had to continue. So, the Green Revolution continued with this quantitative expansion of farmlands. However, this is NOT the most striking feature of the Revolution.

Double-Cropping Existing Farmland

Double-cropping was a primary feature of the Green Revolution. Instead of one crop season per year, the decision was made to have two crop seasons per year. The one-season-per-year practice was based on the fact that there is only natural monsoon per year. This was correct. So, there had to be two "monsoons" per year. One would be the natural monsoon and the other an artificial 'monsoon.'

The artificial monsoon came in the form of huge irrigation facilities. Dams were built to arrest large volumes of natural monsoon water which were earlier being wasted. Simple irrigation techniques were also adopted.

Using Seeds with Superior Genetics

This was the scientific aspect of the Green Revolution. The Indian Council for Agricultural Research (which was established by the British in 1929 but was not known to have done any significant research) was re-organized in 1965 and then again in 1973. It developed new strains of high yield value (HYV) seeds, mainly wheat and rice but also millet and corn. The most noteworthy HYV seed was the K68 variety for wheat. The credit for developing this strain goes to Dr. M.P. Singh who is also regarded as the hero of India's Green revolution.

Statistical Results of the Green Revolution:

(1) The Green Revolution resulted in a record grain output of 131 million tons in 1978-79. This established India as one of the world's biggest agricultural producers. No other country in the world which attempted the Green Revolution recorded such level of success. India also became an exporter of food grains around that time.

(2) Yield per unit of farmland improved by more than 30 per cent between 1947 (when India gained political independence) and 1979 when the Green Revolution was considered to have delivered its goods.

(3) The crop area under HYV varieties grew from seven per cent to 22 per cent of the total cultivated area during the 10 years of the Green Revolution. More than 70 per cent of the wheat crop area, 35 per cent of the rice crop area and 20 per cent of the millet and corn crop area, used the HYV seeds.

Economic Results of the Green Revolution:

(1) Crop areas under high-yield varieties needed more water, more fertilizer, more pesticides, fungicides and certain other chemicals. This spurred the growth of the local manufacturing sector. Such industrial growth created new jobs and contributed to the country's GDP.

(2) The increase in irrigation created need for new dams to harness monsoon water. The water stored was used to create hydro-electric power. This in turn boosted industrial

growth, created jobs and improved the quality of life of the people in villages.

(3) India paid back all loans it had taken from the World Bank and its affiliates for the purpose of the Green Revolution. This improved India's creditworthiness in the eyes of the lending agencies.

4) Some developed countries, especially Canada, which were facing a shortage in agricultural labour, were so impressed by the results of India's Green Revolution that they asked the Indian government to supply them with farmers experienced in the methods of the Green Revolution. Many farmers from Punjab and Haryana states in northern India were thus sent to Canada where they settled (That's why Canada today has many Punjabi-speaking citizens of Indian origin). These people remitted part of their incomes to their relatives in India. This not only helped the relatives but also added, albeit modestly, to India's foreign exchange earnings.

Sociological Results of the Green Revolution

The Green Revolution created plenty of jobs not only for agricultural workers but also industrial workers by the creation of lateral facilities such as factories and hydro-electric power stations as explained above.

Political Results of the Green Revolution:

(1) India transformed itself from a starving nation to an exporter of food. This earned admiration for India in the comity of nations, especially in the Third World.

(2) The Green Revolution was one factor that made Mrs. Indira Gandhi (1917-84) and her party, the Indian National Congress, a very powerful political force in India (*it would however be wrong to say that it was the only reason*).

Limitations of the Green Revolution:

(1) Even today, India's agricultural output sometimes falls short of demand. The Green Revolution, howsoever impressive, has thus NOT succeeded in making India totally and permanently self-sufficient in food. In 1979 and 1987, India faced severe drought conditions due to poor monsoon; this raised questions about the whether

the Green Revolution was really a long-term achievement. In 1998, India had to import onions. Last year, India imported sugar.

However, in today's globalized economic scenario, 100 per cent self-sufficiency is not considered as vital a target as it was when the world political climate was more dangerous due to the Cold War.

(2) India has failed to extend the concept of high-yield value seeds to all crops or all regions. In terms of crops, it remain largely confined to foodgrains only, not to all kinds of agricultural produce. In regional terms, only Punjab and Haryana states showed the best results of the Green Revolution. The eastern plains of the River Ganges in West Bengal state also showed reasonably good results. But results were less impressive in other parts of India.

(3) Nothing like the Bengal Famine can happen in India again. But it is disturbing to note that even today, there are places like Kalahandi (in India's eastern state of Orissa) where famine-like conditions have been existing for many years and where some starvation deaths have also been reported. Of course, this is due to reasons other than availability of food in India, but the very fact that some people are still starving in India (whatever the reason may be), brings into question whether the Green Revolution has failed in its overall social objectives though it has been a resounding success in terms of agricultural production.

(4) The Green Revolution cannot therefore be considered to be a 100 percent success

The Green Revolution

The world's worst recorded food disaster occurred in 1943 in British-ruled India. Known as the Bengal Famine, an estimated 4 million people died of hunger that year in eastern India (which included today's Bangladesh). Initially, this catastrophe was attributed to an acute shortfall in food production in the area. However, Indian economist Amartya Sen (recipient of the Nobel Prize for Economics, 1998) has established that while food shortage was a contributor to the problem, a more potent factor was the result of hysteria related to World War II, which made food supply a low priority for the British rulers.

When the British left India in 1947, India continued to be haunted by memories of the Bengal Famine. It was therefore natural that food security was one of the main items on free India's agenda. This awareness led, on one hand, to the Green Revolution in India and, on the other, legislative measures to ensure that businessmen would never again be able to hoard food for reasons of profit.

The Green Revolution, spreading over the period from1967/68 to 1977/78, changed India's status from a food-deficient country to one of the world's leading agricultural nations. Until 1967 the government largely concentrated on expanding the farming areas. But the population was growing at a much faster rate than food production. This called for an immediate and drastic action to increase yield. The action came in the form of the Green Revolution. The term 'Green Revolution' is a general one that is applied to successful agricultural experiments in many developing countries. India is one of the countries where it was most successful.

There were three basic elements in the method of the Green Revolution:

- Continuing expansion of farming areas
- Double-cropping in the existing farmland
- Using seeds with improved genetics.

The area of land under cultivation was being increased from 1947 itself. But this was not enough to meet the rising demand. Though other methods were required, the expansion of cultivable land also had to continue. So, the Green Revolution continued with this quantitative expansion of farmlands.

Double cropping was a primary feature of the Green Revolution. Instead of one crop season per year, the decision was made to have two crop seasons per year. The one-season-per-year practice was based on the fact that there is only one rainy season annually. Water for the second phase now came from huge irrigation projects. Dams were built and other simple irrigation techniques were also adopted.

Using seeds with superior genetics was the scientific aspect of the Green Revolution. The Indian Council for Agricultural Research (which was established by the British in 1929) was reorganized in 1965 and then again in 1973. It developed new strains of high yield variety seeds, mainly wheat and rice and also millet and corn. The Green Revolution was a technology package comprising material components of improved high yielding varieties of two staple cereals (rice and wheat), irrigation or controlled water supply and improved moisture utilization, fertilizers, and pesticides, and associated management skills.

Benefits

Thanks to the new seeds, tens of millions of extra tonnes of grain a year are being harvested.

The Green Revolution resulted in a record grain output of 131 million tonnes in 1978/79. This established India as one of the world's biggest agricultural producers. Yield per unit of farmland improved by more than 30% between 1947 (when India gained political independence) and 1979. The crop area under high yielding varieties of wheat and rice grew considerably during the Green Revolution.

The Green Revolution also created plenty of jobs not only for agricultural workers but also industrial workers by the creation of related facilities such as factories and hydroelectric power stations.

Shortcomings

In spite of this, India's agricultural output sometimes falls short of demand even today. India has failed to extend the concept of high yield value seeds to all crops or all regions. In terms of crops, it remains largely confined to foodgrains only, not to all kinds of agricultural produce.

In regional terms, only the states of Punjab and Haryana showed the best results of the Green Revolution. The eastern plains of the River Ganges in West Bengal also showed reasonably good results. But results were less impressive in other parts of India.

The Green Revolution has created some problems mainly to adverse impacts on the environment. The increasing use of agrochemical-based pest and weed control in some crops has affected the surrounding environment as well as human health. Increase in the area under irrigation has led to rise in the salinity of the land. Although high yielding varieties had their plus points, it has led to significant genetic erosion.

Since the beginning of agriculture, people have been working to improving seed quality and variety. But the term 'Green Revolution' was coined in the 1960s after improved varieties of wheat dramatically increased yields in test plots in northwest Mexico. The reason why these 'modern varieties' produced more than traditional varieties was that they were more responsive to controlled irrigation and to petrochemical fertilizers. With a big boost from the international agricultural research centres created by the Rockefeller and Ford Foundations, the 'miracle' seeds quickly spread to Asia, and soon new strains of rice and corn were developed as well.

By the 1970s the new seeds, accompanied by chemical fertilizers, pesticides, and, for the most part, irrigation, had replaced the traditional farming practices of millions of farmers in developing countries. By the 1990s, almost 75% of the area under rice cultivation in Aisa was growing these new varieties. The same was true for almost half of the wheat planted in Africa and more than half of that in Latin America and Asia, and more than 50% of the world's corn as well.

The mission of India's Green Revolution may have been to give it time to plan its long term strategy.

India's food-grains production has hovered around a fifth of a billion tonnes mark in recent years. More than self-sufficient, India frequently exports its surpluses. India in 55 years has emerged from famine ridden colonial times, as a famine free Republic. Its population has nearly tripled in that period. More significantly, India in 1947, lost some of its most fertile lands. But she has managed to stand up and falsify many prophesies of doom. India was the greatest success story of the Green Revolution. Although today her agriculture is at a crossroads again, the Green Revolution of the sixties gained some crucial decades for India in which to rethink her way forward. The Revolution is also worth remembering for India's capacity for collective action. Pause a while therefore, before you decry India's administration for every ill in the land.

Famine Kingdom

If the shame of the German Reich was the Holocaust, the British Empire —the Reich's great adversary— matched it with the Bengal Famine. Both occurred around the same time and the scores were about even: 3 million dead in each. As a consequence of heartlessness and inept governance, the Great Famine of 1943-44 has no equal. Heavily taxed and left to themselves and the monsoons, India's farmers began the forties with falling, failing crops. The 'war effort' meant seizure of farm produce, banning of grain trade and turning the gaze away from the countryside. Result was, destitute folk began to arrive in Kolkata looking for food. Fearing that declaring an official famine would mandate supplying food diverted from its armed forces, the Empire simply let people die in the streets. And then within three years, with the war won, the British upped and left a traumatised, dismembered India.

The young nation was the object of much mockery worldwide. "Starving millions" was the phrase flung at it for an identity. Though the Indian farmer was back plying his heartache trade, shortages recurred. India was a massive importer, the tonnage peaking at 10 million in 1966. Humiliation was heaped upon it in a book: "Famine 1975" [Paddock and Paddock, 1965]. The authors predicted that by 1975 Indians would die in their millions. They suggested that the world turn its attention away from this hopeless land. Thomas Malthus probably concurred from his grave. Many nations of course helped, notably the USA with its massive PL-480 programme. The Indian government gamely coped with the times. It was a decade of much hardship and morale sapping pessimism.

The Tide Turns

The story of how what came to be called the Green Revolution began is an exciting one. The story's moral is that hope is always buried within tragedy. Shortly after the Bengal Famine, MacArthur's victorious US army marched into Japan. In the huge occupation force was S. Cecil Salmon of the US Agricultural Research Service [ARS]. Many initiatives were being considered for rebuilding Japan. Salmon was focused on agriculture and that was how he chanced upon the legendary Norin strain of wheat that was to trigger the Revolution.

Norin was a dwarf variety with little foliage and a heavy head of grain. Salmon sent this to the US for further study. In Washington State University at Pullman, a team under Orville Vogel researched the dwarf wheat. They bred many prototypes and finally created in 1959 the Gaines dwarf. It had been 13 long years of experimentation. Norman Borlaug —that icon of the Green Revolution— picked up Gaines and crossed it with Mexico's best varieties at the International Maize and Wheat Research Centre there. He had the magic bullet — he waited to unleash the Revolution.

By the 1960's India was desperate for a breakthrough. The nation's self-confidence was at an ebb. The Chinese had delivered a military lesson. Nehru was aging. Political uncertainty loomed. Food crises were endemic. Total food production hung around about 50 million tonnes. Marginal increases were only through bringing more land area under cultivation and not through increases in productivity. Food reserves were nil. India was just about meeting its deficit with imports. Clearly a quantum leap was needed.

It was then that India discovered Borlaug and the Norin dwarf. A small field at Pusa was seeded and the results were dramatic. It was what India had been waiting for. What then followed was a display of commitment and implementation that has stood to inspire India in many other fields. It is a milestone to cherish. Though the Green Revolution was a worldwide phenomenon its most successful revolutionaries were India's political leadership, bureaucrats, scientists and of course the farmers.

Once Borlaug and India were convinced that they had a solution, the realisation of what needed to be done dawned. It was a formidable task. But India had its men in place. Of the ones that are easily named are C. Subramaniam, B. P. Pal and M.S.Swaminathan. In the end however, literally millions of Indians were active parts of the Revolution.

C. Subramaniam was in 1965, the Union Minister for Agriculture. He had trudged a long road, as a Gandhi devotee, freedom fighter and as a member of India's Constituent Assembly. Most of all he was a modern mind and a man of action. Swaminathan was an entirely home-grown plant genetist of repute. He emerged as Subramaniam's able lieutenant. In 1996, Subramaniam took the politically bold decision of importing 18,000 tonnes of the dwarf wheat seeds of the Lerma Rojo 64A and Sonora 64 variety.

The induction of an agricultural technology is not a mere question of buying seeds. Conducive policies and delivery systems have to exist. Subramaniam piloted the necessary reforms. To disseminate information Krishi Vigyan Kendras, model farms and district block development offices were put in place. Seed farms were developed. To augment research the Indian Council for Agricultural Research [ICAR] was reorganised. As the dwarf variety was chemicals and fertiliser intensive new industrial units were licenced. To encourage two crops a year and monsoon-independence, irrigation canals and deep water wells were created. Policy was changed to assure guaranteed prices and markets. Food stock storages were created.

The results were not long to come. Land under active cultivation began to grow from 1.9 million hectares [mHa] in 1960 to 15.5mHa [1970], 43mHa [1980] and 64mHa [1990]. As for the Paddocks' prophesied demise of India in 1975 well, it didn't happen: India weighed in that year with over 110 million tonnes of food grains.

	1950	1960	1970	1980	1990	2000
Food grain production [mT]	50.8	82.0	108.4	129.6	176.4	201.8
Food grain import [mT]	4.8	10.4	7.5	0.8	0.3	-
Buffer stock [mT]	-	2.0	-	15.5	20.8	40.0
Population [m]	361	439	548	683	846	1000

It is also well to remember that India continued its own adaptive research on high yielding varieties [HYV]. The Revolution was not about just importing seeds. At the Indian Agricultural Research Institute [IARI], Benjamin Peary Pal developed the New Pusa 809, a hardy Indian wheat variety. A genial man who did his doctorate at Cambridge in 1933, B.P.Pal is easily the father of post-modern research in India's agriculture. He was a painter, a rose fancier and a patron of arts. He built a large team, groomed many scientists and extended the HYV research in crops other than wheat. Indian Council for Agricultural Research [ICAR] of which he was the first Director General, proceeded to synthesise and broadcast many HYV seeds like Pusa Sonara, Malavika, Kalyan Sona. Many of these are popular today in Pakistan, other SAARC countries, Afghanistan, Sudan and Syria.

The success was not agriculture's alone. There were many spin-offs. Infrastructure improved. With increasing production India paid back all her loans on time; this increased its standing in the world. Vast employment opportunities opened up. Demand for consumer and industrial goods were triggered. Science-mindedness —and mechanics!— sprouted everywhere. Amazed by the doughty farmers of Punjab and Haryana —the real real heroes of the Revolution— Canada came wooing them to settle and farm its lands. Indians came to esteem themselves better. India had shaken off her colonial hang-over and defied the mould assigned for her.

The Next Road

So let us say, "Long live the Revolution!" Why? Is it dying? No, but no Revolution is permanent. We began by observing that 'hope is always buried in tragedy'. Maybe strife in return arrives with success. The Green Revolution has thrown up its own set of problems. There has been a toll on soil fertility. The HYVs call for heavy dosages of chemicals — fertilisers and pesticides. Prolonged use of these has depleted our soils and poisoned our environment. The once thrifty farmer has become a profligate user of power and water.

Also because this form of agriculture is capital intensive, it is the farmer of means who most benefits from it. Therefore, while India's food problem may have been solved, not so the hunger problem of its poor. The profits of the Revolution have not spread evenly in society and the poor have little means to buy the huge stocks with the government. Worst of all yields are beginning to fall. We may have basked for too long in the glow of the Revolution.

So, India is at a crossroads again. Which road is it to take. A tempting sign points to transgenic crops, also known as genetically modified [GM] crops. These are promoted as being the spear-heads of the next Green Revolution. They are said to need fewer inputs, display greater immunity to pests and yield high. But there are many sober voices that dispute these claims. Their views too are justified because in the past, multinational companies have hastily jumped in to reap their profits with dubious products leaving the farmer to harvest sorrow. Objective scientific assessment of the claims made for GM crops is not yet complete. So the time may not be ripe yet to induct these promising technologies.

The more sensible road to take is the one to eco-sensitive farming. India needs to re-evaluate proven, ancient ways of harmoniously maintaining soil fertility. Dependance on chemicals has to be minmised. Esteem for carefully selected native strains has to be encouraged if the small farmer is to be freed from malevolent seed companies. Conservation and optimal use of water is an important issue. Most of all, agricultural pricing and market policies need to be reviewed to favour the small farmer. There are signs of an emerging awareness all around. Many farmers in Kerala and Karnataka are turning to organic farming on a large scale. Most significantly Swaminathan, that star of the Green Revolution is today an advocate of 'sustainable agriculture'.

So let's put the Green Revolution in context again. It is undoubtedly a great Indian success story. But its unspoken mission may have been to give us a fresh breath with which to codify Indian farmers' traditional wisdom. Today technologies and Indian technologists are available — as was not the case in the sixties— to compile 'best practices' and disseminate them widely. It is in the nature of revolutions that they are never 'final solutions' but place-holders till the next one comes along.

Norman Borlaug

Norman Ernest Borlaug (March 25, 1914 – September 12, 2009) was an American agronomist, humanitarian, and Nobel laureate who has been deemed the father of the Green Revolution. Borlaug was one of only six people to have won the Nobel Peace Prize, the Presidential Medal of Freedom and the Congressional Gold Medal. He was also a recipient of the Padma Vibhushan, India's second highest civilian honour.

Borlaug received his Ph.D. in plant pathology and genetics from the University of Minnesota in 1942. He took up an agricultural research position in Mexico, where he developed semi-dwarf, high-yield, disease-resistant wheat varieties.

During the mid-20th century, Borlaug led the introduction of these high-yielding varieties combined with modern agricultural production techniques to Mexico, Pakistan, and India. As a result, Mexico became a net exporter of wheat by 1963. Between 1965 and 1970, wheat yields nearly doubled in Pakistan and India, greatly improving the food security in those nations. These collective increases in yield have been labelled the Green Revolution, and Borlaug is often credited with saving over a billion people worldwide from starvation. He was awarded the Nobel Peace Prize in 1970 in recognition of his contributions to world peace through increasing food supply.

Later in his life, he helped apply these methods of increasing food production to Asia and Africa.

Early Life, Education, and Family

Borlaug was the great-grandchild of Norwegian immigrants to the United States. Ole Olson Dybevig and Solveig Thomasdotter Rinde, from Leikanger, Norway, emigrated to Dane, Wisconsin, in 1854. The family eventually moved to the small Norwegian-American community of Saude, near Cresco, Iowa. The family became a member of the Saude Lutheran Church where Norman was both baptized and confirmed.

The eldest of four children — his three younger sisters were Palma Lillian (Behrens; 1916–2004), Charlotte (Culbert; b. 1919) and Helen (1921–1921) — Borlaug was born to Henry Oliver (1889–1971) and Clara (Vaala) Borlaug (1888–1972) on his grandparents' farm in Saude in 1914. From age seven to nineteen, he worked on the 106 acre (43 hectare) family farm west of Protivin, Iowa, fishing, hunting, and raising maize, oats, timothy-grass, cattle, pigs and chickens. He attended the one-teacher, one-room New Oregon #8 rural school in Howard County up through eighth grade. Today, the school building, built in 1865, is owned by the Norman Borlaug Heritage Foundation as part of "Project Borlaug Legacy". At Cresco High School, Borlaug played on the football, baseball and wrestling teams, on the latter of which his coach, Dave Barthelma, continually encouraged him to "give 105%".

He attributed his decision to leave the farm and pursue further education to his grandfather, Nels Olson Borlaug (1859 to 1935), who strongly encouraged Borlaug's learning, once saying, "You're wiser to fill your head now if you want to fill your belly later on." Through a Depression-era program known as the National Youth Administration, he was able to enroll at the University of Minnesota in 1933. Initially, Borlaug failed the entrance exam, but was accepted to the school's newly created two-year General College. After two quarters, he transferred to the College of Agriculture's forestry program.

While at the University of Minnesota, he was a member of the varsity wrestling team, reaching the Big Ten semifinals, and helped introduce the sport to Minnesota high schools by putting on exhibition matches around the state. "Wrestling taught me some valuable lessons ... I always figured I could hold my own against the best in the world. It made me tough. Many times, I drew on that strength. It's an inappropriate crutch perhaps, but that's the way I'm made". Borlaug was inducted into the National Wrestling Hall of Fame in Stillwater, Oklahoma, in 1992.

To finance his studies, Borlaug periodically had to put his education on hold and take a job. One of these jobs, in 1935, was as a leader in the Civilian Conservation Corps, working with the unemployed on U.S. federal projects. Many of the people who worked for him were starving. He later recalled, "I saw how food changed them ... All of this left scars on me". From 1935 to 1938, before and after receiving his Bachelor of Science forestry degree in 1937, Borlaug worked for the United States Forestry Service at stations in Massachusetts and Idaho. He spent one summer in the middle fork of Idaho's Salmon River, the most isolated piece of wilderness in the lower 48 states at the time.

In the last months of his undergraduate education, Borlaug attended a Sigma Xi lecture by Elvin Charles Stakman, a professor and soon-to-be head of the plant pathology group at the University of Minnesota. The event was pivotal for Borlaug's future life. Stakman, in his speech titled "These Shifty Little Enemies that Destroy our Food Crops", discussed the manifestation of the plant disease rust, a parasitic fungus that feeds on phytonutrients, in wheat, oat, and barley crops across the U.S. He had discovered that special plant breeding methods created plants resistant to rust.

His research greatly interested Borlaug, and when Borlaug's job at the Forest Service was eliminated due to budget cuts, he asked Stakman if he should go into forest pathology. Stakman advised him to focus on plant pathology instead, and Borlaug subsequently re-enrolled to the University to study plant pathology under Stakman. Borlaug received his Master of Science degree in 1940 and Ph.D. in plant pathology and genetics in 1942.

Borlaug was a member of the Alpha Gamma Rho fraternity. He met his wife, Margaret Gibson, while in college, as he waited tables at a university Dinkytown coffee shop where they both worked. They had three children, Norma Jean "Jeanie" Laube, Scotty (who died soon after birth due to spina bifida), and William Borlaug, five grandchildren, and six great-grandchildren. On March 8, 2007, Margaret Borlaug died at the age of 95, following a fall.

They had been married for 69 years. Borlaug spent the last years of his life in northern Dallas although, as a result of his global humanitarian efforts, he actually resided there only a few weeks of the year.

Career

From 1942 to 1944, Borlaug was employed as a microbiologist at DuPont in Wilmington, Delaware. It was planned that he would lead research on industrial and agricultural bacteriocides, fungicides, and preservatives. However, following the December 7, 1941 attack on Pearl Harbor, Borlaug tried to enlist in the military, but was rejected under wartime labour regulations; his lab was converted to conduct research for the United States armed forces. One of his first projects was to develop glue that could withstand the warm saltwater of the South Pacific. The Imperial Japanese Navy had gained control of the island of Guadalcanal, and patrolled the sky and sea by day.

The only way that U.S. forces could supply the troops stranded on the island was by approaching at night by speedboat, and jettisoning boxes of canned food and other supplies into the surf to wash ashore. The problem was that the glue holding these containers together disintegrated in saltwater. Within weeks, Borlaug and his colleagues had developed an adhesive that resisted corrosion, allowing food and supplies to reach the stranded Marines. Other tasks included work with camouflage, canteen disinfectants, DDT to control malaria, and insulation for small electronics.

In 1940, the Avila Camacho administration took office in Mexico. The administration's primary goal for Mexican agriculture was augmenting the nation's industrialization and economic growth. U.S. Vice President-Elect Henry Wallace, who was instrumental in persuading the Rockefeller Foundation to work with the Mexican government in agricultural development, saw Avila Camacho's ambitions as beneficial to U.S. economic and military interests.

The Rockefeller Foundation contacted E.C. Stakman and two other leading agronomists. They developed a proposal for a new organization, the Office of Special Studies, as part of the Mexican Government, but directed by the Rockefeller Foundation. It was to be staffed with both U.S. and Mexican scientists, focusing on soil development, maize and wheat production, and plant pathology.

Stakman chose Dr. J. George "Dutch" Harrar as project leader. Harrar immediately set out to hire Borlaug as head of the newly established Cooperative Wheat Research and Production Program in Mexico; Borlaug declined, choosing to finish his war service at DuPont. In July 1944, after rejecting DuPont's offer to double his salary, and temporarily leaving behind his pregnant wife and 14-month old daughter, he flew to Mexico City to head the new program as a geneticist and plant pathologist.

In 1964, he was made the director of the International Wheat Improvement Program at El Batán, Texcoco, on the eastern fringes of Mexico City, as part of the newly established Consultative Group on International Agricultural Research's International Maize and Wheat Improvement Centre (*Centro Internacional de Mejoramiento de Maíz y Trigo,* or CIMMYT), an autonomous international research training institute developed from the Cooperative Wheat Research Production Program, with funding jointly undertaken by the Ford and Rockefeller Foundations and the Mexican government.

Borlaug officially retired from the position in 1979. But he remained a senior consultant at the CIMMYT and continued to be involved in plant research at CIMMYT with wheat, triticale, barley, maize, and high-altitude sorghum, in addition to taking up charitable and educational roles.

Borlaug taught and researched at Texas A&M University from 1984 till his death. He was the Distinguished Professor of International Agriculture at the university and the holder of the Eugene Butler Endowed Chair in Agricultural Biotechnology.

Wheat Research in Mexico

The Cooperative Wheat Research Production Program, a joint venture by the Rockefeller Foundation and the Mexican Ministry of Agriculture, involved research in genetics, plant breeding, plant pathology, entomology, agronomy, soil science, and cereal technology. The goal of the project was to boost wheat production in Mexico, which at the time was importing a large portion of its grain. George Harrar, a plant pathologist, recruited and assembled the wheat research team in late 1944. The four other members were Edward Wellhausen, maize breeder, John Niederhauser, potato breeder, William Colwell, and Norman Borlaug, all from the United States. Borlaug would remain with the project for sixteen years. During this time, he bred a series of remarkably successful high-yield, disease-resistant, semi-dwarf wheat.

Borlaug said that his first couple of years in Mexico were difficult. He lacked trained scientists and equipment. Native farmers were hostile toward the wheat program because of serious crop losses from 1939 to 1941 due to stem rust. "It often appeared to me that I had made a dreadful mistake in accepting the position in Mexico," he wrote in the epilogue to his book, *Norman Borlaug on World Hunger*. He spent the first 10 years breeding wheat cultivars resistant to disease, including rust. In that time, his group made 6,000 individual crossings of wheat.

Double Wheat Season

Initially, his work had been concentrated in the central highlands, in the village of Chapingo near Texcoco, where the problems with rust and poor soil were most prevalent. But he realized that he could speed up breeding by taking advantage of the country's two growing seasons. In the summer he would breed wheat in the central highlands as usual, then immediately take the seeds north to the Yaqui Valley research station near Ciudad Obregón, Sonora. The difference in altitudes and temperatures would allow more crops to be grown each year.

His boss, George Harrar, was against this expansion. Besides the extra costs of doubling the work, Borlaug's plan went against a then-held principle of agronomy that has since been disproved. It was believed that seeds needed a rest period after harvesting, in order to store energy for germination before being planted. Harrar vetoed his plan, causing Borlaug to resign. Elvin Stakman, who was visiting the project, calmed the situation, talking Borlaug into withdrawing his resignation and Harrar into allowing the double wheat season. As of 1945, wheat would then be bred at locations 700 miles (1000 km) apart, 10 degrees apart in latitude, and 8500 feet (2600 m) apart in altitude. This was called "shuttle breeding".

Locations of Borlaug's Research Stations, at Yaqui Valley and Chapingo

As an unexpected benefit of the double wheat season, the new breeds did not have problems with photoperiodism. Normally, wheat varieties cannot adapt to new environments, due to the changing periods of sunlight. Borlaug later recalled, "As it worked out, in the north, we were planting when the days were getting shorter, at low elevation and high temperature. Then we'd take the seed from the best plants south and plant it at high elevation, when days were getting longer and there was lots of rain. Soon we had varieties that fit the whole range of conditions. That wasn't supposed to happen by the books". This meant that the project wouldn't need to start separate breeding programs for each geographic region of the planet.

Increasing Disease Resistance Through Multiline Varieties

Because pureline (genotypically identical) plant varieties often only have one or a few major genes for disease resistance, and plant diseases such as rust are continuously producing new races that can overcome a pureline's resistance, multiline varieties were developed. Multiline varieties are mixtures of several phenotypically similar purelines which each have different genes for disease resistance. By having similar heights, flowering and maturity dates, seed colours, and agronomic characteristics, they remain compatible with each other, and do not reduce yields when grown together on the field.

In 1953, Borlaug extended this technique by suggesting that several purelines with different resistance genes should be developed through backcross methods using one recurrent parent. Backcrossing involves crossing a hybrid and subsequent generations with a recurrent parent. As a result, the genotype of the backcrossed progeny becomes increasingly similar to that of the recurrent parent.

Borlaug's method would allow the various different disease-resistant genes from several donor parents to be transferred into a single recurrent parent. To make sure each line has different resistant genes, each donor parent is used in a separate backcross program. Between five and ten of these lines may then be mixed depending upon the races of pathogen present in the region. As this process is repeated, some lines will become susceptible to the pathogen. These lines can easily be replaced with new resistant lines. As new sources of resistance become available, new lines are developed. In this way, the loss of crops is kept to a minimum, because only one or a few lines become susceptible to a pathogen within a given season, and all other crops are unaffected by the disease. Because the disease would spread more slowly than if the entire population were susceptible, this also reduces the damage to susceptible lines. There is still the possibility that a new race of pathogen will develop to which all lines are susceptible, however.

Dwarfing

Dwarfing is an important agronomic quality for wheat; dwarf plants produce thick stems. The cultivars Borlaug worked with had tall, thin stalks. Taller wheat grasses better compete for sunlight, but tend to collapse under the weight of the extra grain—a trait called lodging— from the rapid growth spurts induced by nitrogen fertilizer Borlaug used in the poor soil.

To prevent this, he bred wheat to favour shorter, stronger stalks that could better support larger seed heads. In 1953, he acquired a Japanese dwarf variety of wheat called Norin 10 developed by Orville Vogel, that had been crossed with a high-yielding American cultivar called Brevor 14. Norin 10/Brevor is semi-dwarf (one-half to two-thirds the height of standard varieties) and produces more stalks and thus more heads of grain per plant. Also, larger amounts of assimilate were partitioned into the actual grains, further increasing the yield. Borlaug crossbred the semi-dwarf Norin 10/Brevor cultivar with his disease-resistant cultivars to produce wheat varieties that were adapted to tropical and sub-tropical climates.

Borlaug's new semi-dwarf, disease-resistant varieties, called Pitic 62 and Penjamo 62, changed the potential yield of spring wheat dramatically. By 1963, 95% of Mexico's wheat crops used the semi-dwarf varieties developed by Borlaug. That year, the harvest was six times larger than in 1944, the year Borlaug arrived in Mexico. Mexico had become fully self-sufficient in wheat production, and a net exporter of wheat. Four other high yield varieties were also released, in 1964: Lerma Rojo 64, Siete Cerros, Sonora 64, and Super X.

Expansion to South Asia: The Green Revolution

In 1961 to 1962, Borlaug's dwarf spring wheat strains were sent for multilocation testing in the International Wheat Rust Nursery, organized by the U.S. Department of Agriculture. In

March 1962, a few of these strains were grown in the fields of the Indian Agricultural Research Institute in Pusa, New Delhi, India. In May 1962, M. S. Swaminathan, a member of IARI's wheat program, requested of Dr. B. P. Pal, Director of IARI, to arrange for the visit of Borlaug to India and to obtain a wide range of dwarf wheat seed possessing the Norin 10 dwarfing genes.

The letter was forwarded to the Indian Ministry of Agriculture, which arranged with the Rockefeller Foundation for Borlaug's visit. In March 1963, the Rockefeller Foundation and the Mexican government sent Borlaug and Dr. Robert Glenn Anderson to India to continue his work. He supplied 100 kg (220 lb) of seed from each of the four most promising strains and 630 promising selections in advanced generations to the IARI in October 1963, and test plots were subsequently planted at Delhi, Ludhiana, Pant Nagar, Kanpur, Pune and Indore. Anderson stayed as head of the Rockefeller Foundation Wheat Program in New Delhi until 1975.

During the mid-1960s, the Indian subcontinent was at war, and experiencing widespread famine and starvation, even though the U.S. was making emergency shipments of millions of tons of grain, including over one fifth of its total wheat, to the region. The Indian and Pakistani bureaucracies and the region's cultural opposition to new agricultural techniques initially prevented Borlaug from fulfilling his desire to immediately plant the new wheat strains there. By the summer of 1965, the famine became so acute that the governments stepped in and allowed his projects to go forward.

Biologist Paul R. Ehrlich wrote in his 1968 bestseller *The Population Bomb*, "The battle to feed all of humanity is over ... In the 1970s and 1980s hundreds of millions of people will starve to death in spite of any crash programs embarked upon now." Ehrlich said, "I have yet to meet anyone familiar with the situation who thinks India will be self-sufficient in food by 1971," and "India couldn't possibly feed two hundred million more people by 1980."

In 1965, after extensive testing, Borlaug's team, under Anderson, began its effort by importing about 450 tons of Lerma Rojo and Sonora 64 semi-dwarf seed varieties: 250 tons went to Pakistan and 200 to India. They encountered many obstacles. Their first shipment of wheat was held up in Mexican customs and so could not be shipped from the port at Guaymas in time for proper planting. Instead, it was sent via a 30-truck convoy from Mexico to the U.S. port in Los Angeles, encountering delays at the Mexico-United States border. Once the convoy entered the U.S., it had to take a detour, as the U.S. National Guard had closed the freeway due to Watts riots in Los Angeles.

When the seeds reached Los Angeles, a Mexican bank refused to honour Pakistan treasury's payment of US$100,000, because the check contained three misspelled words. Still, the seed was loaded onto a freighter destined for Bombay, India, and Karachi, Pakistan. Twelve hours into the freighter's voyage, war broke out between India and Pakistan over the Kashmir region. Borlaug received a telegraph from the Pakistani minister of agriculture, Malik Khuda Bakhsh Bucha: "I'm sorry to hear you are having trouble with my check, but I've got troubles, too. Bombs are falling on my front lawn. Be patient, the money is in the bank ..."

These delays prevented Borlaug's group from conducting the germination tests needed to determine seed quality and proper seeding levels. They started planting immediately, and often worked in sight of artillery flashes. A week later, Borlaug discovered that his seeds were germinating at less than half the normal rate. It later turned out that the seeds had been damaged in a Mexican warehouse by over-fumigation with a pesticide. He immediately ordered all locations to double their seeding rates.

The initial yields of Borlaug's crops were higher than any ever harvested in South Asia. The countries subsequently committed to importing large quantities of both the Lerma Rojo 64 and Sonora 64 varieties.

In 1966, India imported 18,000 tons —the largest purchase and import of any seed in the world at that time. In 1967, Pakistan imported 42,000 tons, and Turkey 21,000 tons. Pakistan's import, planted on 1.5 million acres (6,100 km^2), produced enough wheat to seed the entire nation's wheatland the following year.

By 1968, when Ehrlich's book was released, William Gaud of the United States Agency for International Development was calling Borlaug's work a "Green Revolution". High yields led to a shortage of various utilities — labour to harvest the crops, bullock carts to haul it to the threshing floor, jute bags, trucks, rail cars, and grain storage facilities. Some local governments were forced to close school buildings temporarily to use them for grain storage.

Wheat Yields in Developing Countries, 1950 to 2004, kg/HA Baseline 500

In Pakistan, wheat yields nearly doubled, from 4.6 million tons in 1965 to 7.3 million tons in 1970; Pakistan was self-sufficient in wheat production by 1968. Yields were over 21 million tons by 2000. In India, yields increased from 12.3 million tons in 1965 to 20.1 million tons in 1970. By 1974, India was self-sufficient in the production of all cereals. By 2000, India was harvesting a record 76.4 million tons (2.81 billion bushels) of wheat. Since the 1960s, food production in both nations has increased faster than the rate of population growth.

Paul Waggoner, of the Connecticut Agricultural Experiment Station, calculates that India's use of high-yield farming has prevented 100 million acres (400,000 km^2) of virgin land from being converted into farmland—an area about the size of California, or 13.6% of the total area of India. The use of these wheat varieties has also had a substantial effect on production in six Latin American countries, six countries in the Near and Middle East, and several others in Africa.

Borlaug's work with wheat led to the development of high-yield semi-dwarf *indica* and *japonica* rice cultivars at the International Rice Research Institute, started by the Ford and Rockefeller Foundations, and at China's Hunan Rice Research Institute. Borlaug's colleagues at the Consultative Group on International Agricultural Research also developed and introduced a high-yield variety of rice throughout most of Asia. Land devoted to the semi-dwarf wheat and rice varieties in Asia expanded from 200 acres (0.8 km^2) in 1965 to over 40 million acres (160,000 km^2) in 1970. In 1970, this land accounted for over 10% of the more productive cereal land in Asia.

Nobel Peace Prize

For his contributions to the world food supply, Borlaug was awarded the Nobel Peace Prize in 1970. Norwegian officials notified his wife in Mexico City at 4:00 am, but Borlaug had already left for the test fields in the Toluca valley, about 40 miles (65 km) west of Mexico City. A chauffeur took her to the fields to inform her husband. According to his daughter, Jeanie Laube, "My mom said, 'You won the Nobel Peace Prize,' and he said, 'No, I haven't', ...

It took some convincing ... He thought the whole thing was a hoax".

He was awarded the prize on December 10. In his Nobel Lecture the following day, he speculated on his award: "When the Nobel Peace Prize Committee designated me the recipient of the 1970 award for my contribution to the 'green revolution', they were in effect, I believe, selecting an individual to symbolize the vital role of agriculture and food production in a world that is hungry, both for bread and for peace".

Borlaug Hypothesis

Borlaug continually advocated increasing crop yields as a means to curb deforestation. The large role he played in both increasing crop yields and promoting this view has led to this methodology being called by agricultural economists the "Borlaug hypothesis", namely that *increasing the productivity of agriculture on the best farmland can help control deforestation by reducing the demand for new farmland.*

According to this view, assuming that global food demand is on the rise, restricting crop usage to traditional low-yield methods would also require at least one of the following: the world population to decrease, either voluntarily or as a result of mass starvations; or the conversion of forest land into crop land. It is thus argued that high-yield techniques are ultimately saving ecosystems from destruction.

On a global scale, this view holds strictly true ceteris paribus, if all land either consists of forests or is used for agriculture. But other land uses exist, such as urban areas, pasture, or fallow, so further research is necessary to ascertain what land has been converted for what purposes, in order to determine how true this view remains. Increased profits from high-yield production may also induce cropland expansion in any case, although as world food needs decrease, this expansion may decrease as well.

Criticisms and his View of Critics

Borlaug's name is nearly synonymous with the Green Revolution, against which many criticisms have been mounted over the decades by environmentalists, nutritionists, progressives, and economists. Throughout his years of research, Borlaug's programs often faced opposition by people who consider genetic crossbreeding to be unnatural or to have negative effects. Borlaug's work has been criticized for bringing large-scale monoculture, input-intensive farming techniques to countries that had previously relied on subsistence farming.

These farming techniques reap large profits for U.S. agribusiness and agrochemical corporations such as Monsanto Company and have been criticized for widening social inequality in the countries owing to uneven food distribution while forcing a capitalist agenda of U.S. corporations onto countries that had undergone land reform. Other concerns of his critics and critics of biotechnology in general include: that the construction of roads in populated third-world areas could lead to the destruction of wilderness; the crossing of genetic barriers; the inability of crops to fulfil all nutritional requirements; the decreased biodiversity from planting a small number of varieties; the environmental and economic effects of inorganic fertilizer and pesticides; the amount of herbicide sprayed on fields of herbicide-resistant crops.

Borlaug dismissed most claims of critics, but did take certain concerns seriously. He stated that his work has been "a change in the right direction, but it has not transformed the world into a Utopia". Of environmental lobbyists he stated, "some of the environmental lobbyists of the Western nations are the salt of the earth, but many of them are elitists. They've never experienced the physical sensation of hunger. They do their lobbying from comfortable office suites in Washington or Brussels. If they lived just one month amid the misery of the developing world, as I have for fifty years, they'd be crying out for tractors and fertilizer and irrigation canals and be outraged that fashionable elitists back home were trying to deny them these things".

Later Roles

Following his retirement, Borlaug had continued to participate actively in teaching, research and activism. He spent much of the year based at CIMMYT in Mexico, conducting research, and four months of the year serving at Texas A&M University, where he had been a distinguished professor of international agriculture since 1984. In 1999, the university's Board of Regents named its US$16 million Centre for Southern Crop Improvement in honour of Borlaug. He worked in the building's Heep Centre, and taught one semester each year.

Production in Africa

In the early 1980s, environmental groups that were opposed to Borlaug's methods campaigned against his planned expansion of efforts into Africa. They prompted the Rockefeller and Ford Foundations and the World Bank to stop funding most of his African agriculture projects. Western European governments were persuaded to stop supplying fertilizer to Africa. According to David Seckler, former Director General of the International Water Management Institute, "the environmental community in the 1980s went crazy pressuring the donor countries and the big foundations not to support ideas like inorganic fertilizers for Africa."

In 1984, during the Ethiopian famine, Ryoichi Sasakawa, the chairman of the Japan Shipbuilding Industry Foundation (now the Nippon Foundation), contacted the semi-retired Borlaug, wondering why the methods used in Asia were not extended to Africa, and hoping Borlaug could help. He managed to convince Borlaug to help with this new effort, and subsequently founded the Sasakawa Africa Association (SAA) to coordinate the project.

The SAA is a research and extension organization that aims to increase food production in African countries that are struggling with food shortages. "I assumed we'd do a few years of research first," Borlaug later recalled, "but after I saw the terrible circumstances there, I said, 'Let's just start growing'." Soon, Borlaug and the SAA had projects in seven countries. Yields of maize and sorghum in developed African countries doubled between 1983 and 1985. Yields of wheat, cassava, and cowpeas also increased in these countries. At present, program activities are under way in Benin, Burkina Faso, Ethiopia, Ghana, Guinea, Mali, Malawi, Mozambique, Nigeria, Tanzania, and Uganda.

From 1986 to 2009, Borlaug was the President of the SAA. That year, a joint venture between The Carter Centre and SAA was launched called Sasakawa-Global 2000 (SG 2000). The program focuses on food, population and agricultural policy. Since then, more than 8 million African, small-scale farmers in 15 countries have been trained in SAA farming techniques, which have helped them to double or triple grain production. Those elements that allowed Borlaug's projects to succeed in India and Pakistan, such as well-organized economies and transportation and irrigation systems, are severely lacking throughout Africa, posing additional obstacles to increasing yields. Because of this, Borlaug's initial projects were restricted to developed regions of the continent.

Despite these setbacks, Borlaug found encouragement. Visiting Ethiopia in 1994, Jimmy Carter won Prime Minister Meles Zenawi's support for a campaign seeking to aid farmers, using the fertilizer diammonium phosphate and Borlaug's methods. The following season, Ethiopia recorded the largest harvests of major crops in history, with a 32% increase in production, and a 15% increase in average yield over the previous season. For Borlaug, the rapid increase in yields suggests that there is still hope for higher food production throughout sub-Saharan Africa.

World Food Prize

The World Food Prize is an international award recognizing the achievements of individuals who have advanced human development by improving the quality, quantity or availability of food in the world. The prize was created in 1986 by Norman Borlaug, as a way to recognize personal accomplishments, and as a means of education by using the Prize to establish role models for others. The first prize was given to Borlaug's former colleague, M. S. Swaminathan, in 1987, for his work in India. The next year, Swaminathan used the US$250,000 prize to start the MS Swaminathan Research Foundation for research on sustainable development topics.

Online Education

At the DuPont Agriculture & Nutrition Media Day held in Des Moines, Iowa, on September 25, 2000, Borlaug announced the launch of Norman Borlaug University, an Internet-based learning company for the agriculture and food industry personnel. The University was unable to expand the necessary content or customer base, and since late 2001 has been defunct.

The Future of Global Farming and Food Supply

The limited potential for land expansion for cultivation worried Borlaug, who, in March 2005, stated that, "we will have to double the world food supply by 2050." With 85% of future growth in food production having to come from lands already in use, he recommends a multidisciplinary research focus to further increase yields, mainly through increased crop immunity to large-scale diseases, such as the rust fungus, which affects all cereals but rice.

His dream is to "transfer rice immunity to cereals such as wheat, maize, sorghum and barley, and transfer bread-wheat proteins (gliadin and glutenin) to other cereals, especially rice and maize".

Borlaug believed that genetic manipulation of organisms (GMO) was the only way to increase food production as the world runs out of unused arable land. GMOs were not inherently dangerous "because we've been genetically modifying plants and animals for a long time. Long before we called it science, people were selecting the best breeds."

According to Borlaug, "Africa, the former Soviet republics, and the cerrado are the last frontiers. After they are in use, the world will have no additional sizable blocks of arable land left to put into production, unless you are willing to level whole forests, which you should not do. So, future food-production increases will have to come from higher yields. And though I have no doubt yields will keep going up, whether they can go up enough to feed the population monster is another matter. Unless progress with agricultural yields remains very strong, the next century will experience sheer human misery that, on a numerical scale, will exceed the worst of everything that has come before".

Besides increasing the worldwide food supply, early in his career Borlaug stated that taking steps to decrease the rate of population growth will also be necessary to prevent food shortages. In his Nobel Lecture of 1970, Borlaug stated, "Most people still fail to comprehend the magnitude and menace of the 'Population Monster' ... If it continues to increase at the estimated present rate of two percent a year, the world population will reach 6.5 billion by the year 2000. Currently, with each second, or tick of the clock, about 2.2 additional people are added to the world population.

The rhythm of increase will accelerate to 2.7, 3.3, and 4.0 for each tick of the clock by 1980, 1990, and 2000, respectively, unless man becomes more realistic and preoccupied about this impending doom. The tick-tock of the clock will continually grow louder and more menacing each decade. Where will it all end?" However, by the 1990s Borlaug had changed his position on population control, believing it was not necessary. In 2000 he stated: "I now say that the world has the technology — either available or well advanced in the research pipeline — to feed on a sustainable basis a population of 10 billion people.

The more pertinent question today is whether farmers and ranchers will be permitted to use this new technology? While the affluent nations can certainly afford to adopt ultra low-risk positions, and pay more for food produced by the so-called 'organic' methods, the one billion chronically undernourished people of the low income, food-deficit nations cannot."

Death

Borlaug died at the age of 95, on September 12, 2009, in his Dallas home. He died of lymphoma. Borlaug's children released a statement saying,

We would like his life to be a model for making a difference in the lives of others and to bring about efforts to end human misery for all mankind.

Prime Minister of India Manmohan Singh and President of India Pratibha Patil paid tribute to Borlaug saying,

Borlaug's life and achievement are testimony to the far-reaching contribution that one man's towering intellect, persistence and scientific vision can make to human peace and progress.

United Nations' Food and Agriculture Organization (FAO) described Borlaug as

... a towering scientist whose work rivals that of the 20th century's other great scientific benefactors of humankind.

Kofi Annan, former Secretary-General of the United Nations said,

As we celebrate Dr. Borlaug's long and remarkable life, we also celebrate the long and productive lives that his achievements have made possible for so many millions of people around the world... we will continue to be inspired by his enduring devotion to the poor, needy and vulnerable of our world.

Honours and Recognition

In 1968, Borlaug received what he considered an especially satisfying tribute when the people of Ciudad Obregón, where some of his earliest experiments were undertaken, named a street after him. Also in that year, he became a member of the U.S. National Academy of Sciences.

In 1970, he was given an honorary doctorate by the Agricultural University of Norway.

In 1970, he was awarded the Nobel Peace Prize by the Norwegian Nobel Committee "for his contributions to the "green revolution" that was having such an impact on food production particularly in Asia and in Latin America."

In 1975, he was named a Distinguished Fellow of the Iowa Academy of Science.

In 1980, he was elected honorary member of the Hungarian Academy of Sciences.

In 1984, his name was placed in the National Agricultural Hall of Fame at the national centre in Bonner Springs, Kansas. Also that year, he was recognized for sustained service to humanity through outstanding contributions in plant breeding from the Governors Conference on Agriculture Innovations in Little Rock, Arkansas. Also in 1984, he received the Henry G. Bennet Distinguished Service Award at commencement ceremonies at Oklahoma State University. He recently received the Charles A. Black Award for his contributions to public policy and the public understanding of science.

In 1985, the University of Minnesota named a wing of the new science building in Borlaug's honour, calling it "Borlaug Hall."

In addition to the Nobel Prize, Borlaug received the 1977 U.S. Presidential Medal of Freedom, the 2002 Public Welfare Medal from the U.S. National Academy of Sciences, the 2002 Rotary International Award for World Understanding and Peace, and the 2004 National Medal of Science. As of January 2004, Borlaug had received 49 honorary degrees from as many universities, in 18 countries, the most recent from Dartmouth College on June 12, 2005, and was a foreign or honorary member of 22 international Academies of Sciences. In Iowa and Minnesota, "World Food Day", October 16, is referred to as "Norman Borlaug World Food Prize Day". Throughout the United States, it is referred to as "World Food Prize Day".

The Government of India, where he is known as the Father of India's Green Revolution, conferred the Padma Vibhushan, its second highest civilian award on him in 2006. Dr. Borlaug also received the National Medal of Science, the United States' highest scientific honour, from U.S. President George W. Bush on February 13, 2006. He was awarded the Danforth Award for Plant Science by the Donald Danforth Plant Science Centre, St. Louis, Missouri in recognition of his life-long commitment to increasing global agricultural production through plant science.

Several research institutions and buildings have been named in his honour, including: the Norman E. Borlaug Centre for Farmer Training and Education, Santa Cruz de la Sierra, Bolivia, in 1983; Borlaug Hall, on the St. Paul Campus of the University of Minnesota in 1985; Borlaug Building at the International Maize and Wheat Improvement Centre (CIMMYT) headquarters in 1986; the Norman Borlaug Institute for Plant Science Research at De Montfort University, Leicester, United Kingdom in 1997; and the Norman E. Borlaug Centre for Southern Crop Improvement, at Texas A&M University in 1999. In 2006, the Texas A&M University System created the Norman Borlaug Institute for International Agriculture to be a premier institution for agricultural development and to continue the legacy of Dr. Borlaug.

The stained-glass "World Peace Window" at St. Mark's Episcopal Cathedral in Minneapolis, Minnesota, depicts "peace makers" of the 20th century, including Norman Borlaug. Borlaug was also prominently mentioned in an episode ("In this White House") of the *The West Wing* television show. The president of a fictional African country describes the kind of "miracle" needed to save his country from the ravages or AIDS by referencing an American scientist who was able to save the world from hunger through the development of a new type of wheat. The U.S. president replies by providing Borlaug's name.

Borlaug was also featured in an episode of *Penn & Teller: Bullshit!*, where he was referred to as the "Greatest Human Being That Ever Lived". In that episode, Penn & Teller play a card game where each card depicts a great person in history. Each player picks a few cards at random, and bets on whether one thinks one's card shows a greater person than the other players' cards based on a characterization such as humanitarianism or scientific achievement. Penn gets Norman Borlaug, and proceeds to bet all his chips, his house, his rings, his watch, and essentially everything he's ever owned. He wins because, as he says, "Norman is the greatest human being, and you've probably never heard of him." In the episode — the topic of which was genetically altered food — he is credited with saving the lives of over a billion people.

In August 2006, Dr. Leon Hesser published *The Man Who Fed*

the World: Nobel Peace Prize Laureate Norman Borlaug and His Battle to End World Hunger, an account of Borlaug's life and work. On August 4, the book received the 2006 Print of Peace award, as part of International Read For Peace Week.

On September 27, 2006, the United States Senate by unanimous consent passed the Congressional Tribute to Dr. Norman E. Borlaug Act of 2006. The act authorizes that Borlaug be awarded America's highest civilian award, the Congressional Gold Medal. On December 6, 2006, the House of Representatives passed the measure by voice vote. President George Bush signed the bill into law on December 14, 2006, and it became Public Law Number 109–395. According to the act, "the number of lives Dr. Borlaug has saved [is] more than a billion people" The act authorizes the Secretary of the Treasury to strike and sell duplicates of the medal in bronze. He was presented with the medal on July 17, 2007.

Borlaug was a foreign fellow of the Bangladesh Academy of Sciences.

Norman Borlaug: The Nobel Peace Prize 1970

Biography

A central figure in the "green revolution", Norman Ernest Borlaug (March 25, 1914-) was born on a farm near Cresco, Iowa, to Henry and Clara Borlaug. For the past twenty-seven years he has collaborated with Mexican scientists on problems of wheat improvement; for the last ten or so of those years he has also collaborated with scientists from other parts of the world, especially from India and Pakistan, in adapting the new wheats to new lands and in gaining acceptance for their production.

An eclectic, pragmatic, goal-oriented scientist, he accepts and discards methods or results in a constant search for more fruitful and effective ones, while at the same time avoiding the pursuit of what he calls "academic butterflies". A vigorous man who can perform prodigies of manual labour in the fields, he brings to his work the body and competitive spirit of the trained athlete, which indeed he was in his high school and college days.

After completing his primary and secondary education in Cresco, Borlaug enrolled in the University of Minnesota where he studied forestry. Immediately before and immediately after receiving his Bachelor of Science degree in 1937, he worked for the U.S. Forestry Service at stations in Massachusetts and Idaho. Returning to the University of Minnesota to study plant pathology, he received the master's degree in 1939 and the doctorate in 1942.

From 1942 to 1944, he was a microbiologist on the staff of the du Pont de Nemours Foundation where he was in charge of research on industrial and agricultural bactericides, fungicides, and preservatives.

In 1944 he accepted an appointment as geneticist and plant pathologist assigned the task of organizing and directing the Cooperative Wheat Research and Production Program in Mexico. This program, a joint undertaking by the Mexican government and the Rockefeller Foundation, involved scientific research in genetics, plant breeding, plant pathology, entomology, agronomy, soil science, and cereal technology. Within twenty years he was spectacularly successful in finding a high-yielding short-strawed, disease-resistant wheat.

To his scientific goal he soon added that of the practical humanitarian: arranging to put the new cereal strains into extensive production in order to feed the hungry people of the world-and thus providing, as he says, "a temporary success in man's war against hunger and deprivation," a breathing space in which to deal with the "Population Monster" and the subsequent environmental and social ills that too often lead to conflict between men and between nations.

Statistics on the vast acreage planted with the new wheat and on the revolutionary yields harvested in Mexico, India, and Pakistan are given in the presentation speech by Mrs. Lionaes and in the Nobel lecture by Dr. Borlaug. Well advanced, also, is the use of the new wheat in six Latin American countries, six in the Near and Middle East, several in Africa.

When the Rockefeller and Ford Foundations in cooperation with the Mexican government established the International Maize and Wheat Improvement Centre (CIMMYT), an autonomous international research training institute having an international board of trustees and staff, Dr. Borlaug was made director of its International Wheat Improvement Program.

In this capacity he has been able to realize more fully a third objective, that of training young scientists in research and production methods. From his earliest days in Mexico he has, to be sure, carried on an intern program, but with the establishment of the Centre, he has been able to reach out internationally. In the last seven years some 1940 young scientists from sixteen or so countries (the figures constantly move upward) have studied and worked at the Centre.

Dr. Borlaug is presently participating in extensive experimentation with triticale, a man-made species of grain derived from a cross between wheat rye that shows promise of being superior to either wheat or rye in productivity and nutritional quality.

In addition to the Nobel Peace Prize, Dr. Borlaug has received extensive recognition from universities and organizations in six countries: Canada, India, Mexico, Norway, Pakistan, the United States. In 1968 he received an especially satisfying tribute when the people of Ciudad Obregon, Sonora, Mexico, in whose area he did some of his first experimenting, named a street in his honour.

Norman Borlaug

Norman Ernest Borlaug (25 March 1914 – 12 September 2009) was an American agricultural scientist, and humanitarian. He is considered by some to be the "father of modern agriculture" and the father of the green revolution. He won the 1970 Nobel Peace Prize for his life's work.

Sourced

- "You can't build a peaceful world on empty stomachs and human misery."
    - From "Eat This!", an episode of Penn and Teller's *Bullshit!*.
- "There can be no permanent progress in the battle against hunger until the agencies that fight for increased food production and those that fight for population control unite in a common effort."
    - 1970 Nobel Peace Prize acceptance speech.
- "It is a sad fact that on this earth at this late date there are still two worlds, "the privileged world" and "the forgotten world". The privileged world consists of the affluent, developed nations, comprising twenty-five to thirty percent of the world population, in which most of

the people live in a luxury never before experienced by man outside the Garden of Eden. The forgotten world is made up primarily of the developing nations, where most of the people, comprising more than fifty percent of the total world population, live in poverty, with hunger as a constant companion and fear of famine a continual menace."

- o From his 1970 Nobel Lecture.

- "I now say that the world has the technology – either available or well advanced in the research pipeline – to feed on a sustainable basis a population of 10 billion people. The more pertinent question today is whether farmers and ranchers will be permitted to use this new technology? While the affluent nations can certainly afford to adopt ultra low-risk positions, and pay more for food produced by the so-called "organic" methods, the one billion chronically undernourished people of the low income, food-deficit nations cannot."
  - o 30th Anniversary Lecture, The Norwegian Nobel Institute, Oslo, September 8, 2000.
  - "Producing food for 6.2 billion people, adding a population of 80 million more a year, is not simple. We better develop an ever improved science and technology, including the new biotechnology, to produce the food that's needed for the world today." In response to the fraction of the world population that could be fed if current farmland was convered to organic-only crops: "We are 6.6 billion people now. We can only feed 4 billion. I don't see 2 billion volunteers to disappear." In response to extreme critics: "These are utopian people that live on Cloud 9 and come into the third world and cause all kinds of confusion and negative impacts on the developing countries."
  - o Transcript of all comments from "Eat This!", an episode of Penn and Teller's *Bullshit!*.
- "Reach for the stars. Although you will never touch them, if you reach hard enough, you will find that you get a little star dust on you in the process."

- o Reported by Ed Runge, retired head of Texas A&M's department of soil and crop sciences, who persuaded Borlaug to teach at the school.

Quotes about Norman Borlaug:

- "Some credit him with saving more human lives than any other person in history."
  - o Bruce Alberts, President, National Academy of Sciences, U.S.
- "At a time when doom-sayers were hopping around saying everyone was going to starve, Norman was working. He moved to Mexico and lived among the people there until he figured out how to improve the output of the farmers. So that saved a million lives. Then he packed up his family and moved to India, where in spite of a war with Pakistan, he managed to introduce new wheat strains that quadrupled their food output. So that saved another million. You get it? But he wasn't done. He did the same thing with a new rice in China. He's doing the same thing in Africa-as much of Africa as he's allowed to visit. When he won the Nobel Prize in 1970, they said he had saved a *billion* people. That's *BILLION*! BUH! That's Carl Sagan *BILLION* with a "B"! And most of them were a different race from him. Norman is the greatest human being-and you've probably never heard of him."
  - o Penn Jillette, on the show *Penn & Teller: Bullshit.*
- "Though barely known in the country of his birth, elsewhere in the world Norman Borlaug is widely considered to be among the leading Americans of our age... Norman Borlaug has already saved more lives than any other person who ever lived... Borlaug is responsible for the fact that throughout the postwar era, except in sub-Saharan Africa, global food production has expanded faster than the human population, averting the mass starvations that were widely predicted — for example, in the 1967 best seller Famine — 1975! The form of agriculture that Borlaug preaches may have prevented a billion deaths."
  - o Gregg Easterbrook in *The Atlantic Monthly.*
- "Norman Borlaug is the living embodiment of the human quest for a hunger free world. His life is his message."

- Professor M. S. Swaminathan, M.S. Swaminathan Research Foundation (India).

- "Borlaug's work saved the Indian sub-continent from mass starvation. In his 90 years on this planet its human population has grown from about one billion to more than six billion. Without the hybrid wheats it was Borlaug's life's mission to develop and promote among the world's poorest farmers, few believe that this population could have been sustained."
  - Matthew Parris, The Times (UK).
- "It is very likely that Dr. Borlaug is directly responsible for saving more lives than anyone else in the twentieth century... Dr. Borlaug has never stopped fighting, teaching, inventing, or caring... The world owes Dr. Borlaug endless amounts of gratitude"
  - Senator 'Kit' Bond I, Missouri, in a congressional record in honour of Borlaug's 90th birthday.
- "Dr. Norman Borlaug was the father of the Green Revolution that transformed much of the hungry Third World. As U.S. Food for Peace Administrator in the 1960s, I shipped 4 million tons of food aid per year to India; now it can export food. Dr. Borlaug's scientific leadership not only saved people from starvation, but the high-yield seeds he bred saved millions of square miles of wildlife from being plowed down. He is one of the great men of our age."
  - George McGovern, Former US Senator, UN "Ambassador to the Hungry".
- "For fifty-two years, Dr. Norman Borlaug has been helping to provide more food to the most needy areas of the world. But perhaps of greater importance, this distinguished scientist-philosopher has been demonstrating practical ways to give people of the entire world a higher quality of life... The passion that drives Dr. Borlaug's life is an inspiration for all of us to follow. Since 1986, we've worked together through Global 2000 of The Carter Centre and the Sasakawa Africa Association to help small-scale farmers to improve agricultural productivity and crop quality, sometimes two or even

threefold. It has been an honour to collaborate with Dr. Borlaug. He is a true humanitarian and a dear friend."

- o Jimmy Carter, 39th president of the United States and 2002 Nobel Peace Prize Laureate.

- "It gives me great pleasure to add my voice to all those paying tribute to Dr. Norman E. Borlaug on his 90th birthday. As we celebrate Dr. Borlaug's long and remarkable life, we also celebrate the long and productive lives that his achievements have made possible for so many millions of people around the world. And as the United Nations continues its efforts to reach the ambitious but achievable Millennium Development Goal of reducing, by half, by the year 2015, the proportion of people who suffer from hunger, we will continue to be inspired by his enduring devotion to the poor, needy and vulnerable of our world. Dr. Borlaug, for your many contributions to the work of the United Nations, please accept my best wishes on this happy occasion."
  - o Kofi Annan, Secretary General of the United Nations.
- "Dr. Norman Borlaug holds the record for longevity as a "persistent pioneer" in the development of a new cooperative approach among the countries of the world in the alleviation of hunger."
  - o Dr. Edwin J. Wellhausen, First Director General of CIMMYT, Mexico, 1996.
- "Dr. Norman Borlaug is the first person in history to save a billion human lives. But he must also get credit for saving the wild creatures and diverse plant species on 12 million square miles of global forest that would long since have been plowed down without the high-yield farming he pioneered. The two accomplishments combined make him dramatically unique. I am proud to work with the Centre for Global Food Issues, of which he is Chairman Emeritus."
  - o Senator Rudy Boschwitz, R-MN, former member of the US Senate Agriculture Committee.
- "'The battle to feed all of humanity is over," biologist Paul Ehrlich famously wrote in his 1968 bestseller The Population Bomb... But Borlaug and his team were already

engaged in the kind of crash program that Ehrlich declared wouldn't work. Their dwarf wheat varieties resisted a wide spectrum of plant pests and diseases and produced two to three times more grain than the traditional varieties... Borlaug, who unfortunately is far less well-known than doomsayer Ehrlich, is responsible for much of the progress humanity has made against hunger."

- o Ronald Bailey, Reason Magazine.

- "Thanks to the Green Revolution, the real price of food is half or less than it was in 1960 which means those who spend the highest portion of their income on food-the urban and non-farm rural poor — garner the most benefit from it."

- o Thomas R. DeGregori, University of Houston.

- "As a result of [Borlaug's] work, a billion people now exist who otherwise would have starved to death, died of starvation-related diseases, or never have been born."

  - o Gregory Pence and Joyce Hsu, Birmingham News.

- "Borlaug is one of the great humanitarians of the 20th Century-and winner of the Nobel Peace Prize in 1970 for a lifetime of work feeding a hungry world. The breeds of wheat he developed-with strong disease resistance, high yield potential and the ability to withstand poor growing conditions-led the "Green Revolution" that saved literally hundreds of millions of lives in developing nations that were prone to terrible famines."

  - o James Glassman, Tech Central Station.

- "He is credited with starting the Green Revolution in the mid-1960s and saving millions of lives from starvation. Since 1984, he has been a professor of international agriculture at Texas A&M, where he teaches one semester every year. But he is by no means semi-retired. At 86, he remains as active as ever-carrying his brand of prairie pragmatism to fight hunger around the world and in the classroom. Think big. Fight complacency. That is the essence of his message, whether he's talking to heads of state or college freshmen."

  - o David Tarrant, Dallas Morning News.

- "Scientist. Teacher. Humanitarian. Nobel Laureate. Father of the Green Revolution. Those terms describe Dr. Norman Borlaug, who is distinguished professor of international agriculture at Texas A&M University, but they can't possibly capture the magnitude of his accomplishments."
    - o Ellen Ritter, Texas A&M University.
- "If there's one thread running through Borlaug's life it's doing — acting with fierce determination. Working on a problem as fundamental as world hunger is a complicated business, and Borlaug is a complicated man, somehow balancing contradictions... He is the scientist and the dirt farmer; the advocate of common sense and the master of political subtleties; the humanitarian and the pugnacious fighter; the idealist and the consultant to governments of every political ideology. He has been called a peaceful revolutionary, and the tension in that term-between benevolence and aggressiveness-seems particularly apt."
    - o From the University of Minnesota College of Agriculture, Food and Environmental Science.

Norman Borlaug Biography

In 1970 Norman E. Borlaug was awarded the Nobel Peace Prize for a lifetime of work to feed a hungry world. Although a scientist with outstanding contributions, perhaps Dr. Borlaug's greatest achievement has been his unending struggle to integrate the various streams of agricultural research into viable technologies and to convince political leaders to bring these advances to fruition.

Born of Norwegian descent, Dr. Borlaug was raised in Cresco, a small farming community in northeast Iowa. He learned his work ethic on a small mixed crop and livestock family farm and obtained initial education in a one-room rural school house.

Dr. Borlaug's skills as an athlete (mainly in wrestling) opened the door for him to attend the University of Minnesota, where he studied to be a forester, wrestled, and worked various odd jobs. After graduating in 1937 with a BS in Forestry, he went to work for the United States Forest Service, initially in Idaho and later in Massachusetts and Connecticut. He returned to graduate school at the University of Minnesota, and took up the study of plant pathology, receiving his Ph.D. in 1942. Years later, the University of Minnesota would house its plant pathology and agronomy programs in Borlaug Hall.

After graduation, Dr. Borlaug worked as a Microbiologist for E.I. Dupont de Nemours, until being released from his wartime service.

In 1944, Dr. Borlaug participated in the Rockefeller Foundation's pioneering technical assistance program in Mexico, where he was a research scientist in charge of wheat improvement. For the next sixteen years, he worked to solve a series of wheat production problems that were limiting wheat cultivation in Mexico and to help train a whole generation of young Mexican scientists.

The work in Mexico not only had a profound impact on Dr. Borlaug's life and philosophy of agriculture research and development, but also on agricultural production, first in Mexico and later in many parts of the world.

It was on the research stations and farmers' fields of Mexico that Dr. Borlaug developed successive generations of wheat varieties with broad and stable disease resistance, broad adaptation to growing conditions across many degrees of latitude, and with exceedingly high yield potential.

These new wheat varieties and improved crop management practices transformed agricultural production in Mexico during the 1940's and 1950's and later in Asia and Latin America, sparking what today is known as the "Green Revolution." Because of his achievements to prevent hunger, famine and misery around the world, it is said that Dr. Borlaug has "saved more lives than any other person who has ever lived

M. S. Swaminathan

Monkombu Sambasivan Swaminathan is an Indian agriculture scientist, born August 7, 1925, in Kumbakonam, Tamilnadu. He was the second of four sons of a doctor. His ancestral home is the island village of Monkompu, Alleppey District, Kerala. He is known as the "Father of the Green Revolution in India", for his leadership and success in introducing and further developing high-yielding varieties of wheat in India. He is the founder and Chairman of the MS Swaminathan Research Foundation.

His stated vision is to rid the world of hunger and poverty. Dr. Swaminathan is an advocate of moving India to sustainable development, especially using environmentally sustainable agriculture, sustainable food security and the preservation of biodiversity, which he calls an "evergreen revolution"

Education and Personal Life

M. S. Swaminathan was born on August 7, 1925. His father died when Swaminathan was 11. His early schooling was at the Native High School and later at the Little Flower Catholic High School in Kumbakonam. He went to college at Maharajas College in Ernakulam and earned a Bachelor of Science degree (B.Sc.) in zoology.

Swaminathan was strongly influenced by Mahatma Gandhi's belief in ahinsa or non-violence to achieve Purna swaraj (total freedom) and swadeshi, (self-reliance) on both a personal and national level. During this time of wartime food shortages he chose a career in agriculture and enrolled in Coimbatore Agricultural College where he graduated as valedictorian with another B.Sc, this time in Agricultural Science. In 1947, the year of Indian independence he moved to the Indian Agricultural Research Institute (IARI) in New Delhi as a post-graduate student in genetics and plant breeding and obtained a post-graduate degree with high distinction in Cytogenetics in 1949.

He received a UNESCO Fellowship to continue his IARI research on potato genetics at the Wageningen Agricultural University, Institute of Genetics in the Netherlands. Here he succeeded in standardizing procedures for transferring genes from a wide range of wild species of *Solanum* to the cultivated potato, *Solanum tuberosum*. In 1950, he moved to study at the Plant Breeding Institute of the University of Cambridge School of Agriculture. He earned a Doctor of Philosophy (Ph.D) degree in 1952, for his thesis, "*Species Differentiation, and the Nature of Polyploidy in certain species of the genus* Solanum – *section Tuberarium*". His work presented a new concept of the species relationships within the tuber-bearing *Solanum*. He reside in Chennai, Tamil Nadu.

Swaminathan then accepted a post-doctoral research associateship at the University of Wisconsin, Department of Genetics to help set up a USDA Potato Research Station. Despite his strong personal and professional satisfaction with the research work in Wisconsin, he declined the offer of a full time faculty position, returning to India in early 1954.

M. S. Swaminathan is married to Mina Swaminathan who he met in 1951 while they were both studying at Cambridge. They have three daughters: Soumya Swaminathan, Madhura Swaminathan and Nitya Rao. Dr. Swaminathan lives in Chennai, Tamil Nadu with his wife, and has five grandchildren-Anandi, Shreya, Kalyani, Akshay and Madhav.

Professional Achievements

Dr. Swaminathan has worked worldwide in collaboration with colleagues and students on a wide range of problems in basic and applied plant breeding, agricultural research and development and the conservation of natural resources.

His professional career began in 1949: mmmm:

- 1949-55-Research on potato (Solanum tuberosum), wheat (Triticum aestivum), rice (Oryza sativa), and jute genetics.
- 1955–72-Field research on Mexican dwarf wheat varieties. Teach Cytogenetics, Radiation Genetics, and Mutation Breeding and build up the wheat and rice germplasm collections at Indian Agricultural Research Institute IARI.
- 1970–80-Director-General, Indian Council of Agricultural Research (ICAR),
  - Established the National Bureau of Plant, Animal, and Fish Genetic Resources of India.,
  - Established the International Plant Genetic Resources Institute (changed in 2006 to Bioversity International)).

Principal Secretary in the Ministry of Agriculture, Government of India, Transformed the Pre-investment Forest Survey Programme into the Forest Survey of India.

- 1981–85-Independent Chairman, Food and Agriculture Organization (FAO) Council, Rome, played a significant role in establishing the Commission on Plant Genetic Resources.

Developed the concept of Farmers' Rights and the text of the International Undertaking on Plant Genetic Resources (IUPGR).

President of the International Congress of Genetics. (1983):

- 1982–88-Director General, International Rice Research Institute (IRRI), organized the International Rice Germplasm Centre, now named International Rice Genebank.

- 1984-90-President of the International Union for Conservation of Nature and Natural Resources IUCN, develop the Convention on Biological Diversity CBD.
- 1986-99-Chairman of the editorial advisory board, World Resources Institute, Washington, D. C., conceived and produced the first "World Resources Report".
- 1988-91-Chairman of the International Steering Committee of the Keystone International Dialogue on Plant Genetic Resources, regarding the availability, use, exchange and protection of plant germplasm.
- 1988-96-President, World Wide Fund for Nature–India WWF, Organized the Indira Gandhi Conservation Monitoring Centre.. Organize the Community Biodiversity Conservation Programme..
- 1988-99-Chairman/Trustee, Commonwealth Secretariat Expert Group, organized the Iwokrama International Centre for Rainforest Conservation and Development, for the sustainable and equitable management of tropical rainforests in Guyana. The President of Guyana wrote in 1994 *"there would have been no Iwokrama without Swaminathan."*
- 1990-93-Founder/President, International Society for Mangrove Ecosystems (ISME)
- 1988-98-Chaired various committees of the Government of India to prepare draft legislations relating to biodiversity (Biodiversity Act) and breeders' and farmers' rights (Protection of Plant Varieties and Farmers' Rights Act).
- 1994-Chairman of the Commission on Genetic Diversity of the World Humanity Action Trust.. Established a Technical Resource Centre at MSSRF for the implementation of equity provisions of CBD and FAO's Farmers' Rights.
- 1994 onwards-Chairman of the Genetic Resources Policy Committee (GRPC) of the Consultative Group on International Agricultural Research (CGIAR), development of policies for the management of the ex situ collections of International Agricultural Research Centres.
- 1999-Introduced the concept of trusteeship management of Biosphere reserves. Implemented the Gulf of Mannar

Biosphere Reserve Trust, with financial support from the Global Environment Facility (GEF).

- 2001-Chairman of the Regional Steering Committee for the India – Bangladesh joint Project on Biodiversity Management in the Sundarbans World Heritage Site, funded by the UN Foundation and UNDP.
- 2002-President of the Nobel Peace Prize-winning Pugwash Conferences on Science and World Affairs which work towards reducing the danger of armed conflict and to seek solutions to global security threats.
- 2002-2005-Co-chairman with Dr. Pedro Sanchezof the UN Millennium Task Force on Hunger,, a comprehensive global action plan for fighting poverty, disease and environmental degradation in developing countries.
- Over 68 students have done their Ph.D thesis work under his guidance:

On the occasion of Dr. Norman Borlaug's receipt of the Nobel Peace Prize in 1970, he said of Dr. Swaminathan: "*The green revolution has been a team effort and much of the credit for its spectacular development must go to Indian officials, Organizations, Scientists and farmers. However, to you, Dr. Swaminathan, a great deal of the credit must go for first recognizing the potential value of the Mexican dwarfs. Had this not occurred, it is quite possible that there would not have been a green revolution in Asia*".

On the occasion of the presentation of the First World Food Prize to Dr. Swaminathan in October 1987, Mr. Javier Perez de Cuellar-Secretary General of the United Nations, wrote: "*Dr. Swaminathan is a living legend. His contributions to Agricultural Science have made an indelible mark on food production in India and elsewhere in the developing world. By any standards, he will go into the annals of history as a world scientist of rare distinction*".

Swaminathan has been described by the United Nations Environment Programme as "*the Father of Economic Ecology*".

He was one of three from India included in TIME Magazine's 1999 list of the "*20 most influential Asian people of the 20th century*", the other two being Mahatma Gandhi and Rabindranath Tagore..

Following the 2004 Indian Ocean earthquake, he advised India to plant new mangrove groves along the shoreline to minimize damage from future tsunamis.

Dr. Swaminathan was the featured speaker at The 2006 Norman E. Borlaug International Symposium: in Des Moines, Iowa on, October 19, 2006. He was sponsored by Humanities Iowa, an affiliate of the National Endowment for the Humanities. Dr. Swaminathan presented The *"Third Annual Governor's Lecture"* and spoke on *"THE GREEN REVOLUTION REDUX: Can we replicate the single greatest period of food production in all human history?"* Powerpoint Presentation, Hear: about the cultural and social foundations of the Green Revolution in India and the role of historic leaders in India, such as Mahatma Gandhi, in inspiring the Green Revolution there by calling for the alleviation of widespread hunger. He also talked about the links between Gandhi and the great Iowa scientist George Washington Carver.,

Swaminathan is a Fellow of the Royal Society of London the U. S. National Academy of Sciences, the Russian Academy of Sciences, the Chinese Academy of Sciences, and the Italian Academy of Sciences.

Controversy

A scientific paper in which Swaminathan and his team claimed to have produced a mutant breed of wheat by gamma irradiation of a Mexican variety (Sonora 64) resulting in *Sharbati Sonora,* claimed to have a very high lysine content led to a major controversy. The case was discussed as a classic example of scientific misdemeanor and was claimed to be an error made by the laboratory assistant. The episode was also compounded by the suicide of an agricultural scientist. Recent workers have also studied it as part of a systemic problem in Indian agriculture research.

Publications

Dr Swaminathan is a prolific scientific researcher and writer. He published 46 single author papers between 1950 and 1980. Out of 118 two author papers, he was first author of 80. Out of 63 three author papers he was first author of 15. Out of 21 four author papers he was first author of 9. In total he had 254 papers to his credit, 155 of which he was the single author or first author. His scientific papers are in the fields of crop improvement (95), cytogenetics and genetics (87) and phylogenetics (72). His most frequent publishers were: Indian Journal of Genetics (46), Current Science (36), Nature (12) and Radiation Botany (12). Some of the papers are listed below.

In addition he has written a few books around the general theme of his life's work, biodiversity and sustainable agriculture for alleviation of hunger.

Dr. Swaminathan's books include:

- *"An Evergreen Revolution"*, 2006.
- *"I Predict: A Century of Hope Towards an Era of Harmony with Nature and Freedom from Hunger"*, (1999)
- *"Gender Dimensions in Biodiversity Management"*, (ed.) (1998)
- *"Implementing the Benefit Sharing Provisions of the Convention on Biological Diversity: Challenges and opportunities"* (1997)
- *"Agrobiodiversity and Farmers' Rights"*, 1996
- *"Sustainable Agriculture: Towards Food Security"*
- *"Farmers' Rights and Plant Genetic Resources: A dialogue."* (ed.) (1995)
- *"Wheat Revolution: a Dialogue"* (ed) (1993).

Awards and Recognition

Dr. Swaminathan has received several outstanding awards and prizes. These prizes include large sums of money, which has helped sustain and expand his work.

- H.K. Firodia award for excellence in Science & Technology
- Four Freedoms Award for demonstrating achievement of the principles of Freedom of speech, Freedom of Religion, Freedom from want and Freedom from fear, 2000
- Planet and Humanity Medal of the International Geographical Union awarded *"in recognition of his* unique success in outstanding scientific research and its application, leading to Asia's Green Revolution. His endeavours to combat hunger and food shortages by promoting new seed varieties and applying these with ecologically sound principles and sustainable agriculture are all part of his profound humanitarian ethos, which reminds scientists and politicians worldwide of their responsibilities for stewardship of nature and humanity on our common Planet Earth." *2000*
- UNEP Sasakawa Environment Prize Laureate for outstanding contributions to the protection and management of the environment. Co-winner with Paul and Anne Ehrlich 1994, $200,000 prize.

- The Tyler Prize for Environmental Achievement "in recognition of life-long contributions to increasing biological productivity on an ecologically sustainable basis, and to promoting the conservation of biological diversity" 1991.
- Honda Prize, for achieving outstanding results in the field of ecotechnology, 1991
- Padma Vibhushan 1989
- World Food Prize for advancing human development through increased quantity, guality or accessibility of food, 1987
- Golden Heart Presidential Award of the Philippines, conferred by President Corazon Aquino "*in* recognition of his contribution in resolving a wide range of problems in basic and applied genetics and agricultural research and development in the Philippines, for his accomplishments in the area of agricultural science and research highly beneficial to Filipino farmers, and for having expanded considerably the International Rice Research Institute's capacity for upstream research to bring the fruits of recent advances in science and technology to Asian rice farmers."*1987*
- Albert Einstein World Science Award by the World Cultural Council for research which has brought true benefit and well being to mankind.. 1986.

Ramon Magsaysay Award:

- Borlaug Award, given by Coromandel Fertilizers in profound appreciation of his catalytic role in providing deep insights and inspiring fellow scientists to set goals... for evolving a strategy for agriculture rooted in science, but tempered by a concern for ecology and human values 1979
- Padma Bhushan 1972
- Ramon Magsaysay Award for Community Leadership 1971
- Padma Shri 1967
- Foreign Fellow of Bangladesh Academy of Sciences.

He holds 58 honorary Doctorate degrees from universities around the world.

National Awards

He has been honoured with several awards in India for his work to benefit the country:

- Karmaveer Puraskaar Noble Laureates, March, 2007 by iCONGO-Confederation of NGOs.
- Dupont-Solae Award for his contribution to the field of food and nutrition security 2004
- Life Time Achievement Award from BioSpectrum 2003
- Indira Gandhi Gold Plaque by the Asiatic Society for his significant contribution towards human progress. 2002
- Indira Gandhi Prize for Peace, Disarmament and Development *"for his outstanding contribution in the domain of plant genetics and ensuring food security to hundreds of millions of citizens in the developing world."* This prestigious award honours those outstanding global citizens who have made a significant contribution to humanity's material and cultural progress. 2000
- The Indian National Science Academy awarded him Millennium Scientist Award 2001, Asutosh Mookerjee Memorial Award for 1999-2000, Shatabdi Puraskar award in the field of Agricultural Sciences 1999, Jawaharlal Nehru Birth Centenary Award 1992, B.P. Pal Memorial Award of the 1998, Meghnad Saha Medal 1981, Silver Jubilee Commemoration Medal for contributions to genetics and agricultural research 1971.
- Lokmanya Tilak Award by the Tilak Smarak Trust, in recognition of his contribution to the green revolution in India and for his outstanding scientific and environmental works. 2001
- Indira Gandhi Prize for Peace, Disarmament and Development in recognition of creative efforts toward promoting international peace, development and a new international economic order; ensuring that scientific discoveries are used for the larger good of humanity, and enlarging the scope of freedom. 2000
- Millennium Alumnus Award by the Tamil Nadu Agricultural University 2000
- Prof P N Mehra Memorial Award 1999

- Legend in his Lifetime Award by the World Wilderness Trust-India 1999
- Dr. B.P. Pal Medal for unique contributions to agricultural research and development of the National Academy of Agricultural Sciences, India 1997
- V. Gangadharan Award for outstanding contributions to National Development 1997
- Dr. B.P. Pal Medal for unique contributions to agricultural research and development of the National Academy of Agricultural Sciences, India 1997
- V. Gangadharan Award for outstanding contributions to National Development 1997
- Lal Bahadur Shastri Deshgaurav Samman 1992
- Dr. J.C. Bose Medal, Bose Institute 1989
- Krishi Ratna Award for "devotion to the cause of agroscience, and for being the benefactor of the farming community," instituted by the Bharat Krishak Samaj (Indian Farmer's Society)/World Agriculture Fair Memorial Trust Society, and presented by President Giani Zail Singh of India 1986
- Rathindranath Tagore Prize of Visva Bharati University 1981
- R.D. Misra Medal of the Indian Environmental Society 1981
- Barclay Medal of the Asiatic Society for contributions to genetics 1978
- Moudgil Prize of the Bureau of Indian Standards for contributions to standardisation 1978
- Birbal Sahni Medal of the Indian Botanical Society for contributions to Applied Botany 1965.
- Shanti Swarup Bhatnagar Award for contributions to Biological Sciences 1961.

International Awards

He has been honoured with recognition from several international organizations for spreading the benefits of his work to other countries.

- UNESCO Mahatma Gandhi Gold Medal for his

outstanding work in extending the benefits of biotechnology to marginalized and poverty-stricken populations in developing countries and in securing a sound basis for sustainable agricultural, environmental and rural development 1999

- Henry Shaw Medal awarded by the Board of Trustees of the Missouri Botanical Garden in consideration of important service to humanity through emphasis on sustainability in agriculture-USA 1998
- Ordre du Merite Agricole, Govt of France to honour services of the highest quality rendered to the cause of agriculture 1997
- Highest award for International Cooperation on Environment and Development, Govt of China for outstanding contributions to the lofty cause of environmental protection and development, and for his signal accomplishments in the field of international cooperation 1997
- Global Environmental Leadership Award "for encouraging village-level responses to environmental issues" by the Climate Institute 1995
- World Academy of Art and Science 1994
- Asian Regional Award by the Asian Productivity Organization APO 1994
- Charles Darwin International Science and Environment Medal 1993
- Commandeur of the Order of the Golden Ark of the Netherlands 1990
- The VOLVO Environment Prize for his outstanding research and devoted work in turning Indian food production from a deficit to a much increased supply. 1990.
- Association for Women's Rights in Development (AWID) international award for significant contributions to promoting the knowledge, skill, and technological empowerment of women in agriculture and for his pioneering role in mainstreaming gender considerations in agriculture and rural development 1985.

- Bicentenary Medal of the University of Georgia, U.S.A. 1985
- Bennett Commonwealth Prize of the Royal Society of Arts for significant contributions to Household Nutrition Security 1984
- Mendel Memorial Medal of the Czechoslovak Academy of Sciences for contributions to Plant Genetics 1965.

Critics

Despite these awards and honours, the credibility of Swaminathan and his promotion of biotechnology remains open to question by some. His record retains some controversy. There are cases of scientific fraud and scandals involving the suicide of a fellow scientist at the (ICAR).

The first among those who came to expose many of the claims made by MS Swaminathan was Claude Alvares. In his article *The Great Gene Robbery* 23 March 1986 The Illustrated Weekly. [26] Alvares provided enough evidences to show that most of the research that were initiated by him and International Rice Research Institute were not original.

In the recent years Shiv Vishwanathan in an EPW [27]article writes *he is a sociological phenomenon.*

He is paradigm, exemplar, dissenter, critic and alternative......Swaminathan always assimilates the new. Earlier Claude Alvares had given a better picture as follows

Strangely, he has become more and more akin to HYV of the seeds he sells. Like them, he is capable of high-yielding varieties of phrase and word.

At a Gandhi seminar, he will speak of the relevance of Gandhi. At a meeting in Madras on the necessity of combine harvesters. At another meeting on appropriate technology, he will plump for organic manures. At a talk in London, he will speak on the necessity of chemical fertilizers.

He will label slum dwellers 'ecological refugees', and advertise his career as a quest for 'imparting an ecological basis to productivity improvement.' This, after presiding over, and indiscriminately furthering, one of the ecologically most devastating technologies of modern times– the HYV package of the Green revolution

The Father of the Green Revolution used his Skills in Genetic Engineering and his Powers

If you travel by land from any Asian metropolis, it doesn't take long to hit a timeless landscape carpeted with fields of rice, wheat, millet or maize. Whether you're at the rice paddies of Kuttanad, Kerala in southern India or the wheat bowl of central China, farmers tend fields as their ancestors did, harvesting grain for their families and countrymen.

But beneath the soil of those seemingly unaltered tableaux is a high-tech invention that changed not only Asia but the world. The seeds planted today by farmers from Punjab to Pusan are nothing like those used by their ancestors. If they were, the entire continent would either be starving or enslaved to the outside world for food or financing.

That turn of history, one of the truly astonishing transformations of the century, is now known as the Green Revolution. It relied heavily on the work of a diminutive Indian geneticist named Monkombu Sambasivan Swaminathan. As godfather of the Green Revolution, Swaminathan, 74, is modest about his own achievements but forthright about his work's impact on his native land and the planet Earth. "Our history," he says, "changed from that time."

Swaminathan, together with colleagues in India and around the world, managed in a few short years to demolish the dire Malthusian worldview that was so prevalent, and pertinent, four decades ago. Asia's populations were growing uncontrollably. None of the largest countries was self-sufficient in food. China lost as many as 30 million people to famine from 1958 to '62 during and after the Great Leap Forward, and postwar India lived a "ship-to-mouth" existence, subsisting on foodgrains imported from the U.S. Too many mouths, ever more pregnancies, the same farmers growing the same crops—something had to give.

Instead of tragedy, though, a miracle was born in the mid-'60s at Swaminathan's laboratory in New Delhi—and, a few years later, at the International Rice Research Institute in the Philippines which he later headed. Swaminathan brought into India seeds developed in Mexico by U.S. agricultural guru Norman Borlaug and, after cross-breeding them with local species, created a wheat plant that yielded much more grain than traditional types. Scientists at IRRI accomplished the same miracle for rice. Imminent tragedy turned to a new era of hope for Asia, paving the way for the Asian economic miracle of the 1980s and '90s.

As with all great revolutions, though, the seed was but the starting point. Swaminathan combined all the great components of a revolutionary: vision, dedication, energy and follow-through. He was born in what is now the southern Indian state of Tamil Nadu. His physician father was an ardent follower of Mohandas Gandhi, and the young Swaminathan was brought to a rally in which British cloth was burned. (Gandhi exhorted Indians to end their dependence on imported goods.) It was a lesson the boy would never forget. In college, he eschewed more lucrative professions and studied agriculture. "I believed I had to serve the nation," he says from his Madras-based M.S.

Swaminathan Research Foundation, which is involved in a range of activities, including ways to hook farmers up to the Internet. He almost became a police officer, but a 1949 fellowship to study genetics in the Netherlands changed his career path. In 1952 he earned his Ph.D from Cambridge University, then crossed the Atlantic on the liner Queen Elizabeth to do further studies in Wisconsin. There he turned down a professorship. "I asked myself, why did I study genetics? It was to produce enough food in India. So I came back."

Swaminathan's poor, overpopulated homeland was importing vast amounts of grain. "Importing food was like importing unemployment," he recalls. "Seventy percent of our people were employed in agriculture. We were supporting farmers in other countries." By 1966, Swaminathan was director of the Indian Agricultural Research Institute in New Delhi, spending his time in fields with farmers trying to help improve their productivity. Fertilizers were a dead end: when the wheat plant's pod grew more seeds, its stalk collapsed under the weight. With help from the Rockefeller Foundation, Swaminathan found a cross-bred wheat seed, part-Japanese and part-Mexican, that was both fruitful and staunch. (He would later marry this plant to an Indian variety to produce the golden-colored grain favoured by Indians.)

That was the breakthrough in the Green Revolution, but there was a lot more work to be done. Indian farmers, immersed in traditional ways, had to be convinced to grow the new wheat. In

1966, Swaminathan set up 2,000 model farms in villages outside New Delhi to show farmers what his seed could do. Then came the hardest part. He needed the government to help—specifically, to import 18,000 tons of the Mexican seed at a time of fiscal hardship. Swaminathan lobbied then-Prime Minister Lal Bahadur Shastri. "He probably thought nothing could be worse," Swaminathan recalls. "Famine was imminent. There was a willingness to take risks." The first harvest with the new seeds was three times greater than the previous year's.

But the revolution was still incomplete. Only Punjab state had the right irrigation for the new technologies, the state-run food collection and distribution networks were notoriously inefficient, and new fertilizers and pesticides were needed, along with credit lines for small farmers. Political leadership was vital to solve that tangle of problems, and Swaminathan found it in Shastri's successor. "Indira Gandhi was a strong nationalist," he recalls. "She wanted an independent foreign policy, and food was a political weapon." Gandhi bluntly asked him how India could be free of imports and gave Swaminathan a free hand to organize a new agricultural program. Today, India grows some 70 million tons of wheat a year, compared to 12 million tons in the early '60s.

Swaminathan now believes farmers must adopt more eco-friendly methods, and he's using his influence to spread the message. And although populations continue to mushroom, he maintains that still greater harvests are possible. All that's needed, he says, is "inspiration, perspiration and luck." The greatest stroke of luck for hundreds of millions of Asians has been Swaminathan's revolution

Operation Flood

Operation Flood was a rural development programme started by India's National Dairy Development Board (NDDB) in 1970. One of the largest of its kind, the programme objective was to create a nationwide milk grid.

It resulted in making India the largest producer of milk and milk products, and hence is also called the White Revolution of India. It also helped reduce malpractices by milk traders and merchants. This revolution followed the Indian green revolution and helped in alleviating poverty and famine levels from their dangerous proportions in India during the era. Gujarat-based Amul (Anand Milk Union Limited) was the engine behind the success of Operation Flood and in turn became a mega company based on the cooperative approach. Verghese Kurien (chairman of NDDB at that time), then 33, gave the professional management skills and necessary thrust to the cooperative, and is considered the architect of India's 'White Revolution' (Operation Flood). His work has been recognised by the award of a Padma Bhushan, the Ramon Magsaysay Award for Community Leadership, the Carnegie-Wateler World Peace Prize, and the World Food Prize.

Operation Flood has helped dairy farmers, direct their own development, placing control of the resources they create in their own hands. A 'National Milk Grid', links milk producers throughout India with consumers in over 700 towns and cities, reducing seasonal and regional price variations while ensuring that the producer gets a major share of the price consumers pay.

The bedrock of Operation Flood has been village milk producers' cooperatives, which procure milk and provide inputs and services, making modern management and technology available to members. Operation Flood's objectives included :

- Increase milk production ("a flood of milk")
- Augment rural incomes
- Fair prices for consumers.

Programme Implementation

Operation Flood was implemented in three phases.

Phase I

Phase I (1970–1980) was financed by the sale of skimmed milk powder and butter oil donated by the European Union (then the European Economic Community) through the World Food Programme. NDDB planned the programme and negotiated the details of EEC assistance. During its first phase, Operation Flood linked 18 of India's premier milksheds with consumers in India's major metropolitan cities: Delhi, Mumbai, Kolkata and Chennai. Thus establishing mother dairies in four metros.

Operation flood, also referred to as "White Revolution" is a gigantic project propounded by Government of India for developing dairy industry in the country. The Operation Flood – 1 originally meant to be completed in 1975, actually the period of about nine years from 1970-79, at a total cost of Rs.116 corers. As start of operation Flood-1 in 1970 certain set of aims were kept in view for the implementation of the programmers. Improvement by milk marketing the organized dairy sector in the metropolitan cities Bombay, Calcutta, Madras, Delhi. The objectives of commanding share of milk market and speed up development of dairy animals respectively hinter lands of rural areas with a view to increase both production and procurement.

Phase II

Operation Flood Phase II (1981–1985) increased the milksheds from 18 to 136; 290 urban markets expanded the outlets for milk. By the end of 1985, a self-sustaining system of 43,000 village cooperatives with 42.5 lakh milk producers were covered. Domestic milk powder production increased from 22,000 tons in the pre-project year to 140,000 tons by 1989, all of the increase coming from dairies set up under Operation Flood. In this way EEC gifts and World Bank loan helped promote self-reliance. Direct marketing of milk by producers' cooperatives increased by several million litres a day.

Phase III

Phase III (1985–1996) enabled dairy cooperatives to expand and strengthen the infrastructure required to procure and market increasing volumes of milk. Veterinary first-aid health care services, feed and artificial insemination services for cooperative members were extended, along with intensified member education.

Operation Flood's Phase III consolidated India's dairy cooperative movement, adding 30,000 new dairy cooperatives to the 42,000 existing societies organized during Phase II. Milksheds peaked to 173 in 1988-89 with the numbers of women members and Women's Dairy Cooperative Societies increasing significantly. Phase III gave increased emphasis to research and development in animal health and animal nutrition. Innovations like vaccine for Theileriosis, bypassing protein feed and urea-molasses mineral blocks, all contributed to the enhanced productivity of milch animals.

Criticisms

Some critics of the project (cf. Ramdas and Ghotge, 2006) argue that the emphasis on foreign cow breeds has been instrumental in the decimation of Indian breeds. Foreign breeds give higher yields, but require more feed and are not suited to Indian conditions. Critics also argue that the focus on the dairy sector during this period came at the expense of development, research, and extension work in other areas of Indian agriculture. There is also the criticism that the product from the White Revolution, namely milk and dairy products (like foodgrains from the harvests using Green Revolution methods and practices) is qualitatively, not exactly 'technically', inferior to the product obtained employing traditional methods and practices geared to smaller population levels which had only to be 'scaled up' for larger populations

States Reorganisation Act

The States Reorganisation Act of 1956 was a major reform of the boundaries and governance of India's states and territories. The act reorganised the boundaries of India's states along linguistic lines, and amended the Indian Constitution to replace the three types of states, known as Parts A, B, and C states, with a single type of state. Although additional changes to India's state boundaries have been made since 1956, the States Reorganisation Act of 1956 remains the single most extensive change in state boundaries since the independence of India in 1947.

Political Integration after Independence and the Constitution of 1950

South Indian states prior to the *States Reorganisation Act.*

British India, which included most of present day India as well as Pakistan and Bangladesh, was divided into two types of territories: provinces, which were governed directly by British officials, responsible to the Governor-General of India; and princely states, under the rule of local hereditary rulers who recognised British sovereignty in return for local autonomy, as established by treaty.

As a result of the reforms of the early 20th century, most of the provinces had elected legislatures and governors, although some of the smaller provinces were governed by a chief commissioner appointed by the Governor-General. The 20th century reforms of British India also established the principle of federalism, also known in British India as "dyarchy", which was carried forward into the governance of independent India. On August 15, 1947, British India was granted independence as the separate dominions of India and Pakistan. The British dissolved their treaty relations with the over 600 princely states, who were encouraged to accede to either India or Pakistan. Most of the states acceded to India, and a few to Pakistan. Bhutan and Hyderabad opted for independence, although the armed intervention of India brought Hyderabad into the Indian Union.

During the 1947-1950 period, the territories of the princely states were politically integrated into the Indian Union. Most were merged into the existing provinces; others were organised into new provinces, like Rajputana, Himachal Pradesh, Madhya Bharat, and Vindhya Pradesh made up of multiple princely states; a few, including Mysore, Hyderabad, Bhopal, and Bilaspur, became separate provinces. The Government of India Act 1935 remained the constitutional law of India pending adoption of a new Constitution.

The Constitution of India, which went into effect on January 26, 1950, made India a sovereign, democratic republic, and a union of states (replacing provinces) and territories. The states would have extensive autonomy and complete democracy in the Union, while the Union territories would be administered by the Government of India. The constitution of 1950 distinguished between three types of states.

Part A states, which were the former governors' provinces of British India, were ruled by an elected governor and state legislature. The nine Part A states were Assam, West Bengal, Bihar, Bombay, Madhya Pradesh (formerly Central Provinces and Berar), Madras, Orissa, Punjab, and Uttar Pradesh (formerly United Provinces).

The eight Part B states were former princely states or groups of princely states, governed by a rajpramukh, who was often a former prince, along with an elected legislature. The rajpramukh was appointed by the President of India. The Part B states were Hyderabad, Saurashtra, Mysore, Travancore-Cochin, Madhya Bharat, Vindhya Pradesh, Patiala and East Punjab States Union (PEPSU), and Rajasthan.

The ten Part C states included both the former chief commissioners' provinces and princely states, and were governed by a chief commissioner. The chief commissioner was appointed by the President of India. The Part C states included Delhi, Kutch, Himachal Pradesh, Bilaspur, Coorg, Bhopal, Manipur, Ajmer-Merwara, and Tripura.

Jammu and Kashmir had special status until 1957. The Andaman and Nicobar Islands was established as a union territory, ruled by a lieutenant governor appointed by the central government.

The States Reorganisation Commission

In December 1953, Prime Minister Jawaharlal Nehru appointed the States Reorganisation Commission to prepare for the creation of states on linguistic lines. This was headed by Justice Fazal Ali and the commission itself was also known as the *Fazal Ali Commission.* The efforts of this commission were overseen by Govind Ballabh Pant, who served as Home Minister from December 1954. The commission created a report in 1955 recommending the reorganisation of India's states.

The States Reorganisation Act

The States Reorganisation Act of 1956, which went into effect on November 1, eliminated the distinction between part A, B, and C states. It also reorganised the state boundaries and created or dissolved states and union territories.

Changes to States and Union Territories

On November 1, 1956, India was divided into the following states and union territories:

States

1. Andhra Pradesh: Andhra was renamed Andhra Pradesh, and enlarged by the addition of the Telangana region of erstwhile Hyderabad State.
2. Assam
3. Bihar
4. Bombay State: the state was enlarged by the addition of Saurashtra and Kutch, the Marathi-speaking districts of Nagpur Division of Madhya Pradesh, and the Marathwada region of Hyderabad. The southernmost districts of Bombay were transferred to Mysore State. (In 1960, the

state was split into the modern states of Maharashtra and Gujarat.)

5. Jammu and Kashmir
6. Kerala: formed by the merger of Travancore-Cochin state with the Malabar District of Madras State and adding southern part of travancore (kanyakumari) to Madras state.
7. Madhya Pradesh: Madhya Bharat, Vindhya Pradesh, and Bhopal were merged into Madhya Pradesh, and the Marathi-speaking districts of Nagpur Division were transferred to Bombay State.
8. Madras State: the state was reduced to its present boundaries by the transfer of Malabar District to the new state of Kerala. The southern part of Travancore (kanyakumari district) was added to the state.(The state was renamed Tamil Nadu in 1969.)
9. Mysore State: enlarged by the addition of Coorg state and the Kannada speaking districts from southern Bombay state and western Hyderabad state. (The state was renamed Karnataka in 1973.)
10. Orissa: enlarged by the addition of 28 princely states including two princely states of Saraikela and Kharsawan, but later these two states merged with Bihar.
11. Punjab: the Patiala and East Punjab States Union (PEPSU) was merged into Punjab.
12. Rajasthan: Rajputana was renamed Rajasthan, and enlarged by the addition of Ajmer-Merwara state.
13. Uttar Pradesh
14. West Bengal.

Union Territories

1. Andaman and Nicobar Islands
2. Delhi
3. Himachal Pradesh
4. Lakshadweep
5. Pondicherry
6. Tripura
7. Manipur.

7

States and Territories of India

India is a federal union of states comprising twenty-eight states and seven union territories. The states and territories are further subdivided into districts and so on.

List of States and Territories

Administrative divisions of India, including 28 states and 7 union territories.

States:

1. Andhra Pradesh
2. Arunachal Pradesh
3. Assam
4. Bihar
5. Chhattisgarh
6. Goa
8. Gujarat
   Haryana
9. Himachal Pradesh
10. Jammu and Kashmir
11. Jharkhand
12. Karnataka
13. Kerala
15. Madhya Pradesh
    Maharashtra
16. Manipur
17. Meghalaya

18. Mizoram
19. Nagaland
20. Orissa
22. Punjab
    Rajasthan
23. Sikkim
24. Tamil Nadu
25. Tripura
26. Uttar Pradesh
27. Uttarakhand
28. West Bengal.

Union Territories:

A. Andaman and Nicobar Islands
B. Chandigarh
C. Dadra and Nagar Haveli
D. Daman and Diu
A. Lakshadweep
B. National Capital Territory of Delhi
C. Puducherry

Responsibilities and Authorities of the States Compared to the National Government

The Constitution of India distributes the sovereign powers exercisable with respect to the territory of any State between the Union and that State. "Article 73 broadly stated, provides that the executive power of the Union shall extend to the matters with respect to which Parliament has power to make laws. Article 162 similarly provides that the executive power of a State shall extend to the matters with respect to which the Legislature of a State has power to make laws. The Supreme Court has reiterated this position when it ruled in *Ramanaiah case* that the executive power of the Union or of the State broadly speaking, is coextensive and coterminus with its respective legislative power." (italics in original)

History

Pre-1956

The subcontinent of India has been ruled by many different

ethnic groups throughout its history, each imposing their own administrative divisions on the region. Modern India's current administrative divisions are fairly recent developments, which began to develop during British occupation of India. British India included almost all of present-day India, Pakistan, and Bangladesh.

During this period, regions of India were either directly ruled by the British or as Princely States ruled by local rajas. Independence in 1947 largely preserved these divisions, with the provinces of Punjab and Bengal being divided between India and Pakistan. One of the first challenges for the new nation was the integration of the multitude of princely states into the union.

Following independence, however, instability soon arose in India. Many of the provinces had been created by the British to serve their colonial purposes and as such did not reflect either the will of India's citizens or the ethnic divisions found throughout the subcontinent. Ethnic tensions spurred the Indian Parliament to reorganize the country along ethnic and linguistic lines in 1956 by means of the States Reorganisation Act.

After 1956

The former French and Portuguese colonies in India were incorporated into the Republic as the union territories of Pondicherry, Dadra, Nagar Haveli, Goa, Daman, and Diu in 1962.

Several new states and union territories have been created out of existing states since 1956. Bombay State was split into the linguistic states of Gujarat and Maharashtra on 1 May 1960 by the Bombay Reorganization Act. Nagaland was made a state on 1 December 1963.. The Punjab Reorganization Act of 1966 divided the Punjab along linguistic and religious lines, creating a new Hindu and Hindi-speaking state of Haryana on 1 November, transferring the northern districts of Punjab to Himachal Pradesh, and designating Chandigarh, the shared capital of Punjab and Haryana, a union territory.

Statehood was conferred upon Himachal Pradesh on 25 January 1971, Manipur, Meghalaya and Tripura on 21 January 1972. The Kingdom of Sikkim joined the Indian Union as a state on 26 April 1975. In 1987, Arunachal Pradesh and Mizoram became states on 20 February, followed by Goa on 30 May, while Goa's northern exclaves of Daman and Diu became a separate union territory.

In 2000 three new states were created; Chhattisgarh (November 1, 2000) was created out of eastern Madhya Pradesh, Uttaranchal (November 9, 2000), since renamed Uttarakhand, was created out of the Hilly regions of northwest Uttar Pradesh, and Jharkhand (15 November 2000) was created out of the southern districts of Bihar. The Union Territories of Delhi and Pondicherry (renamed to Puducherry) have since been given the right to elect their own legislatures and they are now counted as small states

Late 2009

Ahead of the 2009 General Elections in India all the major parties in Andhra Pradesh supported Telangana statehood.

On Dec 9th 2009, 11:30 PM, Mr. P. Chidambaram, Union Minister of Home Affairs, on behalf of the Government of India announced that a resolution in the Andhra Pradesh assembly for the creation of a separate Telangana state will be passed. Mr. Chidambaram also informed that process for the formation of a separate Telangana state will be initiated.

As a result of this unilateral decision made by the Government of India, Several members of Andhra Pradesh's legislature submitted their resignations to protest the creation of the new state. As of 11 December, at least 117 legislators and many Members of Parliament had resigned in protest of the Government's decision to carve out a new state of Telangana. Most of this Legislators/ MPs' resigned belong to Andhra/Rayalaseema region.

Due to unexpected turn of events, after the parties which promised support to the Telangana state formation on December 7, 2009 in a unanimous all-party meeting at the State level, presided by CM, Rosaiah, and later the party members of these parties made a U-turn on their support following the December 9th statement by the Home Minister Chidambaram, in support of Telangana state process initiation, the Centre gave another statement on December 23rd to take consultations from all groups, political and non-political before moving forward. This December 23rd statement created a new wave of agitations in the Telangana region and the movement kept on taking more momentum.

Linguistic States India

The constitution and various other government documents are purposely vague in defining such terms as national languages and official languages and in distinguishing either one from officially adopted regional languages. States are free to adopt their own language of administration and educational instruction from among the country's officially recognized languages, the Scheduled Languages. Further, all citizens have the right to primary education in their native tongue, although the constitution does not stipulate how this objective is to be accomplished.

As drafted, the constitution provided that Hindi and English were to be the languages of communication for the central government until 1965, when the switch to Hindi was mandated. The Official Languages Act of 1963, pursuing this mandate, said that Hindi would become the sole official national language in 1965. English, however, would continue as an "associate additional official language."

After ten years, a parlia-mentary committee was to consider the situation and whether the status of English should continue if the knowledge of Hindi among peoples of other native languages had not progressed sufficiently. The act, however, was ambiguous about whether Hindi could be imposed on unwilling states by 1975. In 1964 the Ministry of Home Affairs requested all central ministries to state their progress on the switch to Hindi and their plans for the period after the transition date in 1965.

The news of this directive led to massive riots and self-immolations in Tamil Nadu in late 1964 and early 1965, leading the central government, then run by the Congress, to back away from its stand. A conference of Congress leaders, cabinet ministers, and chief ministers of all the states was held in New Delhi in June 1965. Non-Hindi-speaking states were assured that Hindi would not be imposed as the sole language of communication between the central government and the states as long as even one state objected. In addition any of the Scheduled Languages could be used in taking examinations for entry into the central government services.

Before independence in 1947, the Congress was committed to redrawing state boundaries to correspond with linguistics. The States Reorganisation Commission, which was formed in 1953 to study the problems involved in redrawing state boundaries, viewed language as an important, although by no means the sole, factor. Other factors, such as economic viability and geographic realities, had to be taken into account. The commission issued its report in 1955; the government's request for comments from the populace generated a flood of petitions and letters. The final bill, passed in 1956 and amended several times in the 1960s, by no means resolved even the individual states' linguistic problems.

Even regions with a long history of agitation for a linguistic state sometimes have found the actual transition less than smooth. For example, proponents began lobbying for a Te-lugu-speaking state in the early twentieth century. In 1956 the central government formed a single state, Andhra Pradesh, composed of the predominantly Telugu-speaking parts of what in British India had been the Madras Presidency and the large polyglot princely state of Hyderabad.

Although more than 80 percent of the residents (some 53 million people as of 1991) of Andhra Pradesh speak Telugu, like most linguistic states it has a sizable linguistic minority. In this case, the minority consists of Urdu speakers centred in the state's capital, Hyderabad, where nearly 40 percent (some 1.7 million people in 1991) of the population speak that language. Linguistic affinity did not form a firm basis for unity between the two regions from which the state had been formed because they were separated by cultural and economic differences. Although there were riots in the late 1960s and early 1970s in support of the formation of two separate states, the separation did not occur.

The violence that broke out in the state of Assam in the early 1980s reflected the complexities of linguistic and ethnic politics in South Asia. The state has a significant number of Bengali-speaking Muslims—immigrants and their descendants who began settling the region in the late nineteenth and early twentieth centuries. The Muslims came in response to a British-initiated colonization plan to bring under cultivation land left fallow by the Assamese. By the 1931 census, the Assamese not only had lost a hefty portion of their land but also had become a disadvantaged minority in their traditional homeland. They represented less than 33 percent of the total population of Assam, and the Muslim immigrants (who accounted for roughly 25 percent of the population) dominated commerce and the government bureaucracy.

Assamese-Bengali rioting started in 1950, and in the 1951

census many Bengalis listed Assamese as their native tongue in an effort to placate the Assamese. Further immigration of Bengali speakers after the formation of Bangladesh in 1971 and a resurgence of pro-Bengali feeling among earlier immigrants and their descendants reawakened Assamese fears of being outnumbered. Renewed violence in the early and mid-1980s was sufficiently serious for the central government to avoid holding general elections in Assam during December 1984.

The Social Context of Language

Contemporary languages and dialects, as they figure in the lives of most Indians, are a far cry from the stylized literary forms of Indo-Aryan or Dravidian languages. North India especially can be viewed as a continuum of village dialects. As a proverb has it, "Every two miles the water changes, every four miles the speech." Spoken dialects of more distant villages will be less and less mutually understandable and finally become simply mutually unintelligible outside the immediate region. In some cases, a variety of caste dialects coexist in the same village or region. In addition, there are numerous regional dialects that villagers use when doing business in nearby towns or bazaars.

Since the late eighteenth and early nineteenth centuries, regional languages, such as Bengali, Punjabi, and Marathi, have become relatively standardized and are now used throughout their respective states for most levels of administration, business, and social intercourse. Each is associated with a body of literature. British rule was an impetus for the official codification of these regional tongues. British colonial administrators and missionaries learned regional languages and often studied their literatures, and their translations of English-language materials and the Bible encouraged the development of written, standard languages.

To provide teaching materials, prose compositions, grammars, and textbooks were often commissioned and, in some cases, were closer to everyday speech than was the standard literary language. Industrialization, modernization, and printing gave a major boost to the vocabulary and standardization of regional tongues, especially by making possible the wide dissemination of dictionaries.

Such written forms still often differ widely from spoken vernaculars and village dialects. Diglossia—the coexistence of a highly elaborate, formal language alongside a more colloquial form of the same tongue—occurs in many instances. For example, spoken Bengali is so divergent from written Bengali as to be nearly another tongue. Similarly, Telugu scholars waged a bitter battle in the early twentieth century over proper language style.

Reformers favoured a simplified prose format for written Telugu, while traditional classicists wished to continue using a classical literary poetic form. In the end, the classicists won, although a more colloquial written form eventually began to appear in the mass media. Diglossia reinforces social barriers because only a fraction of the populace is sufficiently educated to master the more literary form of the language.

The standard regional language may be the household tongue of only a small group of educated inhabitants of the region's major urban centre that has long exercised politico-economic hegemony in a region. Even literate villagers may have difficulty understanding it. The more socially isolated—women and Dalits—tend to be more parochial in their speech than people of higher caste, who are often able to use a colloquial form of the regional dialect, the caste patois, and the regional standard dialect.

An educated person may master several different speech forms that are often so different as to be considered separate languages. Western-educated scholars may well use the regional standard language mixed with English vocabulary with their colleagues at work. At home, a man may switch to a more colloquial vernacular, particularly if his wife is uneducated. Even the highly educated frequently communicate in their village dialects at home.

Only around 3 percent of the population (about 28 million people in 1995) is truly fluent in both English and an Indian language. By necessity, a substantial minority are able to speak two Indian languages; even in the so-called linguistic states, there are minorities who do not speak the official language as their native tongue and must therefore learn it as a second language. Many tribal people are bilingual. Rural-urban migrants are frequently bilingual in the regional standard language as well as in their village dialect.

In Bombay, for example, many migrants speak Hindi or Marathi in addition to their native tongue. Religious celebrations, popular festivals, and political meetings are typically carried on in the regional language, which may be unintelligible to many attendees. Bilingualism in India, however, is inextricably linked to social context. South Asia's long history of foreign rule has fostered what Clarence Maloney terms "the linguistic flight of the elite." Language—either Sanskrit, Persian, or English—has formed a barrier to advancement that only a few have been fortunate enough to overcome.

Throughout the twentieth century, radio, television, and the print media have fostered standardization of regional dialects, if only to facilitate communication. Linguistic standardization has contributed to ethnic or regional differentiation insofar as language has served as a cultural marker. Mass communication forces the adoption of a single standard regional tongue; typically, the choice is the dialect of the majority in the region or of the region's preeminent business or cultural centre.

The use of less standard forms clearly labels speakers outside their immediate home base. To fulfil its purposes, the regional language must be standardized and taught to an increasing percentage of the population, thereby encroaching both on its own dialects and the minority languages of the region. The language of instruction and administration affects the economic and career interests and the self-respect of an ever-greater proportion of the population

The First Linguistic State - Andhra Pradesh-was Born:

In 1953, the movement that led to the creation of the state of Andhra Pradesh. This act was consistent with Gandhi's wishes and with established Congress policy, yet it grated with the Prime Minister of the day. He could see that the formation of Andhra would lead to similar demands by other linguistic groups. "You will observe," wrote Jawaharlal Nehru archly to a Cabinet colleague, "that we have disturbed the hornet's nest and I believe most of us are likely to be badly stung."

The success of the Andhras did embolden other communities to come out stinging. There was now a major campaign for Samyukta or Greater Karnataka, aiming to unite Kannada speakers spread across the states of Madras, Mysore and Hyderabad. The Malayalis wanted a province of their own, bringing together the erstwhile princely states of Cochin and Travancore with Malabar. There was also a Mahagujarat movement. But, in terms of mass base and popular appeal, the most significant of the post-Andhra linguistic struggles was that which spoke for Samyukta Maharashtra.

After Andhra, the Government of India set up a States Reorganisation Committee (SRC). Its report, submitted in 1955, pretty much conceded that India would be reorganised according to linguistic provinces. But some ticklish questions remained. The most serious was the future of India's most prosperous city, Bombay. Would it go to Maharashtra, since it had more Marathi speakers than speakers of other languages, and since the areas contiguous to it would anyway form part of the state? Or would it go to Gujarat, since the Gujaratis had invested so heavily in its development? Or, since there were many other linguistic groups in Bombay, would it be constituted as some kind of autonomous, multicultural city-state?

The Battle of Bombay

The question of Bombay's future came up for discussion in the Lok Sabha on November 15, 1955. Strongly pushing the city-state alternative was the Marathi-speaking M.P. from Bombay, S.K. Patil. His city, said Patil, had a "cosmopolitan population in every respect; it had been built upon the labour of everybody". It was, he continued, cosmopolitan in theory as well as in practice: here "everybody thinks in terms of common citizenship".

This is what Patil said in Parliament, and he later expanded on the theme in a newspaper interview. The prospective city-state of Bombay, he told the paper, would "be a miniature India run on international standards... (A) melting pot which will evolve a glorious new civilisation... And it is an extraordinary coincidence that the population of the city should be exactly one per cent of the population of the whole country. This one per cent drawn from all parts of the country will set the pace for other states in the practice of secularism and mutual understanding."

Patil asked the Maharashtrians to give up their claim on Bombay in the spirit of compromise. The plea was rejected in ringing tones by the M.P. from Pune, N.V. Gadgil. Speaking immediately after Patil in the Lok Sabha, Gadgil insisted that while he was in favour of compromise, "there is a limit. That limit is, nobody can compromise one's self-respect, no woman can compromise her chastity and no country its freedom". The reports of protest meetings should make it clear "that anything short of Samyukta Maharashtra with the city of Bombay as capital will not be acceptable". If these sentiments went unheeded, warned Gadgil, then the future of Bombay would be decided on the streets of Bombay.

The Maharashtrians were being urged to accept the loss of Bombay in the name of national unity. Gadgil protested against this unsubtle attempt at blackmail. The last 150 years, he said, had seen Maharashtrians contributing selflessly to the growth of national feeling. Marathi speakers founded the first schools and universities, and helped found the Indian National Congress.

The Mahrattas were "the pioneers of violent action" against the British. Later, in the early 20th Century, when the Congress party languished, "who was it that brought in new life? Who propounded the new tenets and new philosophy? It was Lokmanya Tilak. In the Home Rule movement he led and in the 1920 movement we were behind none and ahead of many provinces... I will merely quote the certificate given to us by no less a person than Mahatma Gandhi that Maharashtra is the believe of (national) workers". Even now, in independent India, it was a Maharashtrian, Vinoba Bhave, who was "carrying the flag of Gandhian philosophy and spreading his message from place to place".

In the case of Bombay, the Maharashtrians were being lectured on the need to "work for the unity and safety and good of the country". But, said the Pune M.P. bitterly, all these years "we have done nothing else". His Lok Sabha was altogether a wonderful and moving peroration — and the last line was the best: "To ask us to serve the nation is to ask chandan (sandalwood) to be fragrant." Note that both S.K. Patil and V.N. Gadgil belonged to the same party, the Congress. The party's High Command finally decided to recommend to the Government of India that Bombay be made a city-state. Regional sentiments were disregarded, sparking widespread protests. In the 1957 elections the Congress was routed by an opposition front uniting under the banner of Samyukta Maharashtra. The anger spilled over into the streets. In 1960, the Government of India conceded the right of the Maharashtrians over Bombay.

To recall the debate between Patil and Gadgil is to remember a time when Indian parliamentarians were both independent-minded and intelligent. Patil's case, for retaining Bombay's cosmopolitan character, was made with logic and eloquence. But Gadgil's case, for the centrality of the city to Maharashtrian identity, was compelling as well. Here were politicians from Maharashtra who could argue on the basis of principle, and believe in what they said, too.

In some ways one can still hear the echoes of that old Lok Sabha debate. For, tragically, what was to N.V. Gadgil a matter or legitimate cultural pride has degenerated, under a different kind of Maharashtrian leadership, into an insular parochialism. The battle for Bombay continues. On the one side are those who see it as a truly cosmopolitan city, which can still "set the pace for other states in the practice of secularism and mutual understanding". On the other side are the visceral chauvinists of Bal Thackeray's Shiv Sena.

Other States-Assam

In the case of Andhra Pradesh, the minority consists of Urdu speakers centred in the state's capital, Hyderabad, where nearly 40 percent (some 1.7 million people in 1991) of the population speak that language. Linguistic affinity did not form a firm basis for unity between the two regions from which the state had been formed because they were separated by cultural and economic differences. Although there were riots in the late 1960s and early 1970s in support of the formation of two separate states, the separation did not occur.

The violence that broke out in the state of Assam in the early 1980s reflected the complexities of linguistic and ethnic politics in South Asia. The state has a significant number of Bengali-speaking Muslims — immigrants and their descendants who began settling the region in the late nineteenth and early twentieth centuries. The Muslims came in response to a British-initiated colonization plan to bring under cultivation land left fallow by the Assamese.

By the 1931 census, the Assamese not only had lost a hefty portion of their land but also had become a disadvantaged minority in their traditional homeland. They represented less than 33 percent of the total population of Assam, and the Muslim immigrants (who accounted for roughly 25 percent of the population) dominated commerce and the government bureaucracy.

Assamese-Bengali rioting started in 1950, and in the 1951 census many Bengalis listed Assamese as their native tongue in an effort to placate the Assamese. Further immigration of Bengali speakers after the formation of Bangladesh in 1971 and a resurgence of pro-Bengali feeling among earlier immigrants and their descendants reawakened Assamese fears of being outnumbered. Renewed violence in the early and mid-1980s was sufficiently serious for the central government to avoid holding general elections in Assam during December 1984.

Punjab

In the compound of Amritsar's Golden Temple, holy of holies to India's 6,000,000 Sikhs, long lines of tall, bearded and turbaned Sikh men and slender Sikh women passed slowly by a small wooden hut.

When they reached the hut, each Sikh dropped a coin or a bill in an offering box, then peered through a tiny glass window. Inside, on a hard mattress, lay Sant Fateh Singh, 50-year-old Sikh holy man. While doctors and disciples stood anxious watch, Sant Fateh Singh was carrying on a hunger strike. Its aim: to compel the Indian government to create a separate linguistic state in the Punjab, traditional home of the Sikhs.

In May, 1960 the Indian government arrested the Sikhs' wily political leader, Master Tara Singh, for advocating a Sikh march on New Delhi to demand statehood. Before disappearing behind prison walls, Tara Singh designated Sant Fateh Singh as his successor. For weeks stretching into months, young Sikhs, shouting "Punjabi Suba Zindabad" (Long live Punjabi state), had poured out of the Golden Temple at Amritsar and the Sikh temple at New Delhi—into the waiting arms of tough Indian police, who hustled them off to prison. At one time India's overburdened detention camps held 20,000 Sikhs.

About the last week of December, 1960 Sant Fateh Singh decided that even more effort was required to force a grant of separate statehood. A husky 260-pounder, he announced that he was embarking on a "fast unto death," would take water but no food of any kind until New Delhi gave in. By last week the holy man was down to 243 lbs., and daily health bulletins, issued with Jim Hagerty-like detail, were emphasizing the presence of ketones in the urine, indicating imminent uremic poisoning.

For India's Prime Minister Jawaharlal Nehru, keeping in anxious touch with developments while making a tour of Uttar Pradesh, the fast—and the whole Sikh effort—presented a number of galling ironies. In the first place, fasting as a political weapon was developed by Nehru's nationalist mentor, Mahatma Gandhi, but is now regarded by New Delhi as in bad taste. Secondly, to justify keeping Master Tara Singh in jail without proof of crime, Nehru a month ago had to insist on a further extension of the same Preventive-Detention Act passed originally under British rule to allow the imprisonment of Gandhi, Nehru himself and other Indian freedom fighters. After the bill was rammed through by a 165-10-33 vote, loud cries of "Shame! Shame!" reverberated in the Lower House chamber.

Finally, the Sikh demand for a separate state is an embarrassing end result of Nehru's own mistakes. After the Prime Minister backed down spring and allowed the division of Bombay State between the Marathi and Gujarati language groups, the Punjabi-speaking Sikhs became the only one of India's 14 major constitutionally recognized linguistic groups without a separate state. Nehru and the reigning Congress Party contend that the Sikhs are less a linguistic entity than a religious community.

Reorganisation of the State

The demand for the formation of a Telangana state has been voiced for more than fifty years now. Soon after the creation of Andhra Pradesh in 1956 as the first linguistic State in post-Independence India, Telangana, a major region within the State, began to witness the demand for political autonomy and cultural identity within the broader parameters of federal polity and political economy of development.

The Congress leadership's decision to initiate a process to grant statehood for Telangana brings to the fore a number of issues concerning the rationale for creating newer and smaller states in contemporary India. In order to make a better sense of the new demands for statehood, we need to revisit the States reorganisation process carried out between 1950 and 1956 and in the following decades.

The States Reorganisation Commission (SRC) appointed by Jawaharlal Nehru in 1953 was initially against the unification of Telangana with Andhra. The SRC Report, submitted in 1955, states:

"One of the principle causes of opposition to Vishalandhra also seems due to the apprehensions felt by the educationally backward people of Telangana that they may be swamped and exploited by the more advanced people of the coastal area.

The real fear of the people of Telangana is that if they join Andhra, they will be unequally placed in relation to the people of Andhra and, in this partnership, the major partner will derive all the advantages immediately while Telangana itself may be converted into a colony by the enterprising Andhras" (Para 378).

Nehru ridiculed the idea of merging Telangana with the Andhra State, fearing a "tint of expansionist imperialism" in it. Later, he compared the merger to a matrimonial alliance having "provisions for divorce" if the partners in the alliance cannot get on well. The merger was facilitated by many promises and constitutional safeguards.

However, the demand for separate statehood for Telangana has rested on factors such as the scale of inter-regional inequalities causing socioeconomic backwardness of the region, inadequate industrial infrastructure, lack of educational and employment opportunities, diversion of water and natural resources of Telangana to the coastal region of Andhra, the hegemonic control of the coastal capitalist class over the Telangana region, the hegemony of upper castes and upper classes through the Congress party leaders in the State, and the distinctive historical and cultural identity of the region.

On the basis of the SRC's recommendations, the linguistic reorganisation of 14 States and six Centrally-administered territories was partially completed in 1956, with several other States to be reorganised later on. This was a massive state rationalisation exercise, not simply to establish newer modes of power and authority but to rearrange social, cultural, regional and linguistic diversities into more manageable enclaves of state power. The deep-seated linguistic-cultural diversity and differences within different States and the regions had to be negotiated carefully during the early years of state formation.

The interface between political geography and cultural politics culminated in the consolidation of specific caste and class interests, strengthening the ideology of the nation-state building exercise, in various parts of the country on the one hand, and disintegrated the political architecture of the colonial state on the other. The story of the "integration of states" in post-colonial India is also a story of the disintegration and reintegration of various States and regions into more uniform and administratively rationalised units of state power.

Even before India achieved Independence, the nationalist leaders wanted to reorganise political and administrative boundaries of their country in consonance with its diverse geo-linguistic and cultural diversity to regenerate nationalist sentiments for unity among people belonging to different regions and communities. This attempt required an in-depth study of the regional and local bases of power and their cultural-historical pasts to understand the geographical locations of power.

The historical experiment with territorial re-demarcation began in the 1920s, when Mahatma Gandhi proposed to reorganise the Congress provincial committees on the principles of cultural-linguistic and geographical contiguity. The idea was to strengthen cultural consolidation and political participation of the regions in the national movement. This was partially in response to the colonial state's arbitrary realignment of provincial boundaries and borders by disregarding their historical cultural cohesiveness and bases of power.

Soon after Independence, the nation-building exercise of the new state had to be based on a more robust, democratic and participative pattern. The newly established federal democratic political structure needed to reconcile the balance of power between a relatively strong Centre and weaker States. The States, however, needed to be reconstructed and reconstituted in this long process of political consolidation and formation of the Indian nation. Attaining independence along with the partition of the country made some national leaders like Nehru and Vallabhbhai Patel apprehensive about the reorganisation process, which, in their view, could pose the danger of fragmentation of the new state.

The process of reorganisation was based on lessons learnt much from three decades of experimentation with the idea of the possibility of the creation of linguistic states. A number of language-centred identity movements that emerged during this period in regions comprising the Madras, Bombay and Bengal Presidencies, and parts of the United Provinces focused on reorganising the new States on the principles of linguistic-cultural distinctiveness, economic viability and geographical unity along with the federal political and administrative rationality.

Nehru's initial fears and scepticism about the disintegrative effects of this experiment disappeared with his consent for the creation of Andhra Pradesh as the first linguistic State. Though the SRC considered issues such as size, economic viability, economic planning, geo-linguistic durability and even the status of riparian states, it focused more on redrawing the map of India along linguistic lines. On the other hand, the linguistic reorganisation of States in 1956 also created newer conflicts and contests among different States.

The following decades continued to witness the process of reorganisation, with the creation of Maharashtra and Gujarat in 1960, Chandigarh, Haryana and Punjab in 1966, Himachal Pradesh in 1971, various States in the north-eastern region between 1960 and 1980, Goa in 1987 and Chhattisgarh, Jharkhand and Uttarakhand in 2000. The creation of Chhattisgarh, Jharkhand and Uttarakhand, which was made possible by disintegrating regional boundaries and political territories from within the existing States of Madhya Pradesh, Bihar and Uttar Pradesh, respectively, was not along the same criteria laid out for the earlier reorganisation of States.

The political history of independent India needs to be conceptualised by locating it within the political demands for democratic representation and legitimation of authority, on the one hand, and modes of negotiation over and redistribution of rights and resources of the State and its constituents, on the other. The idea of large States and small States had a dominant concern over the political economy of these States.

Some argued that larger States would be better governed with the mechanism of Central planning by the strong interventionist state that would ensure a proper balance between developed and underdeveloped regions through an equitable flow of capital and labour in these States. On the other hand, those favouring smaller states were worried about the excessive control over resources by larger states, resulting in the deepening of regional economic inequalities and hierarchies of power. The reorganisation process tells us a story wherein the state attempted to strike a balance between linguistic-cultural plurality and political centrality on the one hand, and strategies to refashion the scales of social, cultural and political hierarchies of regions and States on the other. The process recreated as well as remapped the given hierarchies of cultural and social geographies of castes, classes, regions, economies and cultures, which in turn, were reconstructed for specific political reasons.

Within a decade of reorganisation, it became obvious that language alone could not be a satisfactory basis for the division of States. Political scientists, public policy analysts, sociologists and even historians began to doubt the integrative effects of the process of reorganisation in this new polity.

If Selig Harrison called these years "the most dangerous decades", Joan Boundurant and others linked up the process of linguistic regionalism with "India's political problem of creating a sense of national citizenship" that needed to be guarded against the parochial tendencies of linguistic chauvinism.

Myron Weiner considered the problem of political integration as not just a territorial one but one being part of the national identity, which should also be seen in the context of territorial control, public security, public accountability and the proper balance between the rulers and the ruled. These states were considered to have ushered in the phenomenon of regional cultural renaissance.

The process also resulted in the recreation of linguistic-cultural minorities in all large States demanding recognition of their language and cultural identity, such as the Bodos in Assam, the Coorgis in Karnataka and the Nepalese in West Bengal.

The expansion of the Eighth Schedule from 12 languages in 1950 to 22 languages reflects the increasing demands and aspirations of these linguistic-cultural communities for recognition as distinctive political collectives. Is the linguistic principle a better basis to reorganise the States, and if so, to what extent has it created a federal structure satisfying the aspirations of the cultural groups? Has language provided a bond to form durable cultural identities in States such as Uttar Pradesh and Madhya Pradesh?

Such questions worried the State officials for quite some time in the initial decades after Independence.

These reorganised States had to negotiate their cultural-linguistic borders with their neighbours – issues arose between Karnataka and Maharashtra, Maharashtra and Gujarat, Haryana and Punjab, Orissa and West Bengal and between Andhra Pradesh and parts of Madras Presidency, among others. Not only this, the dominant linguistic communities in these States had their own specific regional and cultural forms of power.

The specific regional linguistic identity provided cultural and economic capital and resources that were now institutionalised through a complex network of state patronage and recognition. These newly formed States had to deal with the large proportion of the population considered part of the cultural-linguistic minorities belonging to languages other than the State/official or regionally dominant and acceptable languages of power and privilege.

The principle of linguistic-cultural homogeneity along with the criteria of economic viability, administrative efficiency and geographical contiguity did not succeed in curtailing the future demands of cultural autonomy based again on cultural and linguistic differences among various groups and communities in these States. From the very beginning, the fears of the linguistic minorities were not unwarranted as the dominant language elites in these newly created States began to exercise cultural and political hegemony in the spheres of education, economy, social mobility, administration, judiciary and employment.

In this context, the present demand for 35 more languages to be included in the Eighth Schedule needs to be kept in mind. The state rationale, therefore, began to conjoin demands of cultural autonomy with developmental polity and regional inequalities – economic and cultural – within a uniform agenda of political economy of development.

A number of ethnic, state autonomy, sub-national and sons of the soil movements emerged in different States and regions in the following decades. The institutionalisation of cultural pluralism of this kind began to reinforce the cultural hierarchies, leading to the emergence of, what Myron Weiner has called, two political cultures, that is, elite culture and mass culture with newer forms of subordination and domination.

The demand for the creation of new states clearly indicates the complex relationship between political legitimation of power, on the one hand, and the actual social and cultural diversity and its representation and recognition, on the other. The non-congruence between these two realms is one of the reasons arguing for more states in different parts of the country.

What is important for our analysis is that the principle of linguistic-cultural homogeneity favoured by the SRC had cultural, educational, political and economic manifestations.

The Indian experience of state formation through an extensive exercise of redrawing the boundaries and territories reveals the processes of identity formation of regions, sub-regions and of various communities and groups. The story of integration of states, as V.P. Menon pointed out, was also a story of the simultaneous disintegration of states. The new linguistic States were considered to have ushered in the phenomenon of regional cultural renaissance resulting from the consequences of the redrawing of boundaries culminating in the indigenisation and democratisation of provincial politics, further leading to the development of diverse regional political cultures.

The rise of regional political parties is closely tied up with the emergence of regional consciousness and region-based identity movements as an offshoot of the reorganisation process itself. These political parties and their local bases of power have posed newer challenges of governance and political stability at the Centre in the post-Congress era.

However, the experience of the last 50 years shows that the pace of economic development has not been achieved uniformly across regions and has instead increased regional disparities and inequalities.

Furthermore, these disparities have increased during the post-reform period between and within these States. Liberalisation facilitated the processes in the formation of an all-India market and increasing competition among States for private investment – both domestic and foreign – putting the backward States at a distinct disadvantage.

Therefore, greater attention needs to be paid to the specific needs of the backward regions and States to allocate adequate and more equitable investment of scarce resources.

Factors such as political instability during coalition governments, consolidation of vote-bank politics within and across States, the growing significance of regional political parties in capturing power in the States, the impact of globalisation on the national spaces of economy and labour, and the increasing assertion of lower class/caste communities in the democratic functioning of the Indian state have acquired significance and given way to administrative and political reasons behind the idea of the territorial redrawing of the existing States. The political initiatives of renaming of the States, redrawing their territorial boundaries and creating newer states and districts from within the existing ones have to be carefully planned and executed, keeping in mind the historical processes of contestations over the categories of regions and states in the identity politics of modern India.

The proposed second SRC not only needs to look carefully into the demands for carving out newer and smaller states such as Bhojpur (Uttar Pradesh and Bihar), Bodoland (Assam), Bundelkhand (Uttar Pradesh and Madhya Pradesh), Coorg (Karnataka), Gorkhaland (West Bengal), Harit Pradesh (Uttar Pradesh), Marathwada (Maharashtra), Mahakaushal (Orissa), Mithilanchal (Bihar), Muru Pradesh (Rajasthan), Poorvanchal (Uttar Pradesh), Saurashtra (Gujarat), Telangana (Andhra Pradesh) and Vidarbha (Maharashtra) but also take into account the complex relationship between regional autonomy and political viability of these regions, and their cultural and political consolidation within a more democratic, plural, secular and participative developmental politics in contemporary India.

Only then will it be possible to ensure better and equitable economic distribution of resources within and between States, better protection of the most marginalised sections of the population, more decentralised governance, political accountability to some extent, and the restraints.

Formation of Andhra Pradesh – 1947 to 1956

The years 1947 to 1956 were very crucial in the history of Andhra Pradesh.

Even as India got independence on August 15, 1947, the three distinct regions of Andhra Pradesh – Coastal Andhra and Rayalaseema belonged to Madras state and Telangana was part of Hyderabad state, which was independent. Andhra Pradesh witnessed many struggles before it emerged as the first linguistic state on November 1, 1956.

Telugu Speaking People's Dream of Separate State

The Telugu speaking people struggled for the formation of a separate Andhra province since the British period, but they could not succeed. After India attained Independence, Andhra leaders put forth the desire for a separate Andhra State on several occasions before the Prime Minister Jawaharlal Nehru and the Deputy Prime Minister Sardar Vallabhai Patel.The Government of India formed 'The Dar Commission' under the Chairmanship of S.K.Dar, which did not recommend the creation of States on the linguistic criteria.

This drew adverse reactions in the Telugu speaking regions. The Congress Party immediately constituted an unofficial Committee consisting Jawaharlal Nehru, Vallabhbhai Patel and Pattabhi Sitaramaiah, popularly known as the J.V.P. Committee. In April 1949, the Committee recommended that the creation of linguistic provinces should be postponed by few years.

Nizam's Ambitious Desire

Though India got Independence, there was nothing to cheer about for the people of Hyderabad state. During the years 1946 to 1948, Telugu speaking people were concerned about the developments in the state of Hyderabad. The Seventh and the last Nizam of Hyderabad, Nawab Mir Osman Ali Khan was very anxious to become independent, resisting Indian government's efforts to merge Hyderabad state into the Indian Union. With the help of Khasim Razvi of the Ittehadul Muslimeen and its militia called the Razakars, he spread violence to achieve his desire.

Telangana Revolt

To counter Razakars and Nizam Police, the Communists led peasant revolt by organizing village defence squads to protect the villagers. This revolt began in 1946 in the Nalgonda district and spread to Warangal and Bidar (which was then part of Hyderabad state) districts quickly. Farmers and labourers revolted against the Nizam and his loyal local feudal landlords using guerrilla tactics.

With the cooperation of a few patriotic Muslims, the Hindus who were more than 90 percent of the population of Hyderabad state launched 'Join India' movement to integrate the state with the Indian Union. Swami Ramanand Tirtha led the state congress leaders and took part in the movement actively.

Merger of Hyderabad State into Indian Union

Indian Union's negotiations with the Nizam were abortive. The Nizam Government refused to accede his territory to India Union. Government of India launched 'Police Action' code named 'Operation Polo' on September 13, 1948 against Nizam. Nizam's forces surrendered within five days on 18 September 1948 and the merger of Hyderabad state into the Indian Union announced formally.

Until the end of 1949, Major-General J.N.Chaudhuri was the Military Governor of Hyderabad. M.K.Vellodi, a Senior Civil Servant acted as the Chief Minister of the State and the Nizam was designated 'Raj Pramukh' in January 1950. Burgula Rama Krishna Rao took charge of the state after 1952 general elections.

Coastal Andhra and Rayalaseema form Andhra State

Potti Sri Ramulu one of the strong leaders of the separate Andhra movement, took indefinite fasting from October 19, 1952 demanding for a separate Andhra state from the Madras state for the Telugus. On December 15, Potti Sri Ramulu breathed his last breath in the fasting camp. As the news of his death broke, violence spread all over the southern parts of the country. As a result of Potti Sri Ramulu's sacrifice, the Prime Minister Jawaharlal Nehru inaugurated the Andhra state consisting eleven districts of Coastal Andhra and Rayalaseema on October 1, 1953 with Kurnool as its capital city.

The Formation of Andhra Pradesh

However, Telugu speaking people demanded for their long cherished Visalandhra formation, but people of Hyderabad state were unanimous in their demand for splitting the state into three parts. The States Reorganization Commission headed by Syed Fazal Ali heard the views of different people and organizations. Based on the Commission's conclusions, the Congress Party High Command preferred Visalandhra and enlarged the state by including nine Telugu speaking districts of Hyderabad state to eleven districts of Andhra state to form Andhra Pradesh with 20 districts.In the process, the Hyderabad state was split among Maharashtra, Karnataka and Andhra State.

Aurangabad division merged with Maharashtra and Gulbarga division merged with Karnataka. The rest of the two divisions of the state – Gulshanabad or Medak and Nizamabad merged with Andhra State.

Thus, the state of 'Andhra Pradesh' emerged merging all the districts of Coastal Andhra, Rayalaseema and Telangana on November 1, 1956, with Neelam Sanjiva Reddy as the Chief Minister and C.M Trivedi as the Governor.

8

India after Independence

A New and Divided Nation

When India became independent in August 1947, it faced a series of very great challenges. As a result of Partition, 8 million refugees had come into the country from what was now Pakistan. These people had to be found homes and jobs. Then there was the problem of the princely states, almost 500 of them, each ruled by a maharaja or a nawab, each of whom had to be persuaded to join the new nation. The problems of the refugees and of the princely states had to be addressed immediately. In the longer term, the new nation had to adopt a political system that would best serve the hopes and expectations of its population. home where you discuss what is likely to happen to India without the British. What would be your views about the future of India?

Franchise – The Right to Vote

India's population in 1947 was large, almost 345 million. It was also divided. There were divisions between high castes and low castes, between the majority Hindu community and Indians who practised other faiths. The citizens of this vast land spoke many different languages, wore many different kinds of dress, ate different kinds of food and practised different professions. How could they be made to live together in one nation-state?

To the problem of unity was added the problem of development. At Independence, the vast majority of Indians lived in the villages. Farmers and peasants depended on the monsoon for their survival. So did the non-farm sector of the rural economy, for if the crops failed, barbers, carpenters, weavers and other service groups would not get paid for their services either. In the cities, factory workers lived in crowded slums with little access to education or health care. Clearly, the new nation had to lift its masses out of poverty by increasing the productivity of agriculture and by promoting new, job-creating industries. Unity and development had to go hand in hand.

If the divisions between different sections of India were not healed, they could result in violent and costly conflicts – high castes fighting with low castes, Hindus with Muslims and so on. At the same time, if the fruits of economic development did not reach the broad masses of the population, it could create fresh divisions – for example, between the rich and the poor, between cities and the countryside, between regions of India that were prosperous and regions that lagged behind.

A Constitution is Written

Between December 1946 and November 1949, some three hundred Indians had a series of meetings on the country's political future. The meetings of this "Constituent Assembly" were held in New Delhi, but the participants came from all over India, and from different political parties. These discussions resulted in the framing of the Indian Constitution, which was adopted on 26 January 1950.

One feature of the Constitution was its adoption of universal adult franchise. All Indians above the age of 21 would be allowed to vote in state and national elections. This was a revolutionary step – for never before had Indians been allowed to choose their own leaders. In other countries, such as the United Kingdom and the United States, this right had been granted in stages. First only men of property had the vote. Then men who were educated were also added on. Working-class men got the vote only after a long struggle. Finally, after a bitter struggle of their own, American and British women were granted the vote.

On the other hand, soon after Independence, India chose to grant this right to all its citizens regardless of gender, class or education. A second feature of the Constitution was that it guaranteed equality before the law to all citizens, regardless of their caste or religious affiliation. There were some Indians who wished that the political system of the new nation be based on Hindu ideals, and that India itself be run as a Hindu state.

They pointed to the example of Pakistan, a country created explicitly to protect and further the interests of a particular religious community – the Muslims. However, the Indian Prime Minister, Jawaharlal Nehru, was of the opinion that India could not and must not become a "Hindu Pakistan". Besides Muslims, India also had large populations of Sikhs and Christians, as well as many Parsis and Jains. Under the new Constitution, they would have the same rights as Hindus – the same opportunities when it came to seeking jobs in government or the private sector, the same rights before the law.

A third feature of the Constitution was that it offered special privileges for the poorest and most disadvantaged Nehru wrote in a letter to the Chief Ministers of states:... we have a Muslim minority who are so large in numbers that they cannot, even if they want, go anywhere else. That is a basic fact about which there can be no argument. Whatever the provocation from Pakistan and whatever the indignities and horrors inflicted on non-Muslims there, we have got to deal with this minority in a civilised manner. We must give them security and the rights of citizens in a democratic State.

We Must give them Security and Rights Activity

Imagine a conversation between a father and son in a Muslim family. After Partition, the son thinks it would be wiser for them to move to Pakistan while the father believes that they should continue to live in India. Taking information from the chapter so far, act out what each would say.

Indians. The practice of untouchability, described as a "slur and a blot" on the "fair name of India", was abolished. Hindu temples, previously open to only the higher castes, were thrown open to all, including the former untouchables. After a long debate, the Constituent Assembly also recommended that a certain percentage of seats in legislatures as well as jobs in government be reserved for members of the lowest castes. It had been argued by some that Untouchable or as they were now known, Harijan, candidates did not have good enough grades to get into the prestigious Indian Administrative Service. But, as one member of the Constituent Assembly, H.J. Khandekar, argued, it was the upper castes who were responsible for the Harijans "being unfit today". Addressing his more privileged colleagues, Khandekar said: We were suppressed for thousands of years. You engaged us in your service to serve your own ends and suppressed us to such an extent that neither our minds nor our bodies and nor even our hearts work, nor are we able to march forward.

Along with the former Untouchables, the *adivasis* or Scheduled Tribes were also granted reservation in seats and jobs. Like the Scheduled Castes, these Indians too had been deprived and discriminated against. The tribals had been deprived of modern health care and education, while their lands and forests had been taken away by more powerful outsiders. The new privileges granted them by the Constitution were meant to make amends for this.

The Constituent Assembly spent many days discussing the powers of the central government versus those of the state governments. Some members thought that the Centre's interests should be foremost. Only a strong Centre, it was argued, "would be in a position to think and plan for the well-being of the country as a whole". Other members felt that the provinces should have greater autonomy and freedom. A member from Mysore feared that under the present system "democracy is centred in Delhi and it is not allowed to work in the same sense and spirit in the rest of the country". A member from Madras insisted that

Discuss in your class, one advantage and one disadvantage today of the decision to keep English as a language of India. "the initial responsibility for the well-being of the people of the provinces should rest with the Provincial Governments". The Constitution sought to balance these competing claims by providing three lists of subjects: a Union List, with subjects such as taxes, defence and foreign affairs, which would be the exclusive responsibility of the Centre; a State List of subjects, such as education and health, which would be taken care of principally by the states; a Concurrent List, under which would come subjects such as forests and agriculture, in which the Centre and the states would have joint responsibility.

Another major debate in the Constituent Assembly concerned language. Many members believed that the English language should leave India with the British rulers. Its place, they argued, should be taken by Hindi. However, those who did not speak Hindi were of a different opinion. Speaking in the Assembly, T.T. Krishnamachari conveyed "a warning on behalf of people of the

South", some of whom threatened to separate from India if Hindi was imposed on them. A compromise was finally arrived at: namely, that while Hindi would be the "official language" of India, English would be used in the courts, the services, and communications between one state and another. Many Indians contributed to the framing of the Constitution.

But perhaps the most important role was played by Dr B.R. Ambedkar, who was Chairman of the Drafting Committee, and under whose supervision the document was finalised. In his final speech to the Constituent Assembly, Dr Ambedkar pointed out that political democracy had to be accompanied by economic and social democracy. Giving the right to vote would not automatically lead to the removal of other inequalities such as between rich and poor, or between upper and lower castes.

With the new Constitution, he said, India was going to enter into a life of contradictions. In politics we will have equality and in social and economic life we will have inequality. In politics we will be recognising the principle of one man one vote and one value. In our social and economic life, we shall, by reason of our social and economic structure, continue to deny the principle of one man one value.

How were States to be Formed?

Back in the 1920s, the Indian National Congress – the main party of the freedom struggle – had promised that once the country won independence, each major linguistic group would have its own province. However, after independence the Congress did not take any steps to honour this promise. For India had been divided on the basis of religion: despite the wishes and efforts of Mahatma Gandhi, freedom had come not to one nation but to two. As a result of the partition of India, more than a million people had been killed in riots between Hindus and Muslims. Could the country afford further divisions on the basis of language?

Both Prime Minister Nehru and Deputy Prime Minister Vallabhbhai Patel were against the creation of linguistic states. After the Partition, Nehru said, "disruptionist tendencies had come to the fore"; to check them, the nation had to be strong and united. Or, as Patel put it:

... the first and last need of India at the present moment is that it should be made a nation ... Everything which helps the growth of nationalism has to go forward and everything which throws obstacles in its way has to be rejected ... We have applied this test to linguistic provinces also, and by this test, in our opinion [they] cannot be supported. That the Congress leaders would now go back on their promise created great disappointment. The Kannada speakers, Malayalam speakers, the Marathi speakers, had all looked forward to having their own state. The strongest protests, however, came from the Telugu-speaking districts of what was the Madras Presidency. When Nehru went to campaign there during the general elections of 1952, he was met with black flags and slogans demanding "We want Andhra".

In October of that year, a veteran Gandhian named Potti Sriramulu went on a hunger fast demanding the formation of Andhra state to protect the interests of Telugu speakers. As the fast went on, it attracted much support. *Hartals* and *bandhs* were observed in many towns. On 15 December 1952, fifty-eight days into his fast, Potti Sriramulu died. As a newspaper put it, "the news of the passing away of Sriramulu engulfed entire Andhra in chaos". The protests were so widespread and intense that the central government was forced to give in to the demand. Thus, on 1 October 1953, the new state of Andhra Pradesh came into being. After the creation of Andhra, other linguistic communities also demanded their own separate states. A States Reorganisation Commission was set up, which submitted its report in 1956, recommending the redrawing of district and provincial boundaries to form compact provinces of Assamese, Bengali, Oriya, Tamil, Malayalam, Kannada and Telugu speakers respectively. The large Hindi-speaking region of north India was broken up into several states. A little later, in 1960, the bilingual state of Bombay was divided into separate states for Marathi and Gujarati speakers. In 1966, the state of Punjab was also divided into Punjab and Haryana, the former for the Punjabi speakers (who were also mostly Sikhs), the latter for the rest (who spoke not Punjabi but versions of Haryanvi or Hindi).

The Making of Linguistic

Planning for Development

Lifting India and Indians out of poverty, and building a modern technical and industrial base were among the major objectives of the new nation. In 1950, the government set up a Planning Commission to help design and execute suitable policies for economic development. There was a broad agreement on what was called a "mixed economy" model. Here, both the State and the private sector would play important and complementary roles in increasing production and generating jobs. What, specifically, these roles were to be – which industries should be initiated by the state and which by the market, how to achieve a balance between the different regions and states – was to be defined by the Planning Commission.

In 1956, the Second Five Year Plan was formulated. This focused strongly on the development of heavy industries such as steel, and on the building of large dams. These sectors would be under the control of the State. This focus on heavy industry, and the effort at state regulation of the economy was to guide economic policy for the next few decades. This approach had many strong supporters, but also some vocal critics. State – Concerned with the government. (Note that used in this sense, the word does not refer.)

Nehru on the Five Year Plans

Prime Minister Jawaharlal Nehru was a great supporter of the planning process. He explained the ideals and purposes of planning in a series of letters he wrote to the chief ministers of the different states. In a letter of 22 December 1952, he said that:

... behind the First Five Year Plan lies the conception of India's unity and of a mighty cooperative effort of all the peoples of India ... We have to remember always that it is not merely the governmental machinery that counts in all this, but even more so the enthusiasm and cooperation of the people. Our people must have the sensation of partnership in a mighty enterprise, of being fellow-travellers towards the next goal that they and we have set before us.

The Plan may be, and has to be, based on the calculations of economists, statisticians and the like, but figures and statistics, very important as they are, do not give life to the scheme. That breath of life comes in other ways, and it is for us now to make this Plan, which is enshrined in cold print, something living, vital and dynamic, which captures the imagination of the people.

Activity

Discuss in your class whether Mira Behn was right in her view that science and machinery would create problems for human beings. You may like to think about examples of the effects of industrial pollution and Some felt that it had put inadequate emphasis on agriculture. Others argued that it had neglected primary education. Still others believed that it had not taken account of the environmental implications of economic policies. As Mahatma Gandhi's follower Mira Behn wrote in 1949, by "science and machinery he [mankind] may get huge returns for a time, but ultimately will come desolation. We have got to study Nature's balance, and develop our lives within her laws, if we are to survive as a physically healthy and morally decent species."

The Search for an Independent Foreign Policy

India gained freedom soon after the devastations of the Second World War. At that time a new international body – the United Nations – formed in 1945 was in its infancy. The 1950s and 1960s saw the emergence of the Cold War, that is, power rivalries and ideological conflicts between the USA and the USSR, with both countries creating military alliances. This was also the period when colonial empires were collapsing and many countries were attaining independence. Prime Minister Jawaharlal Nehru, who was also the foreign minister of newly independent India, developed free India's foreign policy in this context. Non-alignment formed the bedrock of this foreign policy.

Led by statesmen from Egypt, Yugoslavia, Indonesia, Ghana and India, the non-aligned movement urged countries not to join either of the two major alliances. But this policy of staying away from alliances was not a matter of remaining "isolated" or "neutral". The former means remaining aloof from world affairs whereas non-aligned countries such as India played an active role in mediating between the American and Soviet alliances. They tried to prevent war—often taking a humanitarian and moral stand against war. However, for one reason or another, many non-aligned countries including India got involved in wars.

The Nation, Sixty Years On

On 15 August 2007, India celebrated sixty years of its existence as a free nation. How well has the country done in this time? And to what extent has it fulfilled the ideals set out in its Constitution? That India is still united, and that it is still democratic, are achievements that we might justly be proud of. Many foreign observers had felt that India could not survive as a single country, that it would break up into many parts, with each region or linguistic group seeking to form a nation of its own. Others believed that it would come under military rule. However, as many as thirteen general elections have been held since Independence, as well as hundreds of state and local elections. There is a free press, as well as an independent judiciary. Finally, the fact that people speak different languages or practise different faiths has not come in the way of national unity.

On the other hand, deep divisions persist. Despite constitutional guarantees, the Untouchables or, as they are now referred to, the Dalits, face violence and discrimination. In many parts of rural India they are not allowed access to water sources, temples, parks and other public places. And despite the secular ideals enshrined in the Constitution, there have been clashes between different religious groups in many states. Above all, as many observers have noted, the gulf between the rich and the poor has grown over the years.

Some parts of India and some groups of Indians have benefited a great deal from economic development. They live in large houses and dine in expensive restaurants, send their children to expensive private schools and take expensive foreign holidays. At the same time many others continue to live below the poverty line. Housed in urban slums, or living in remote villages on lands that yield little, they cannot afford to send their children to school. The Constitution recognises equality before the law, but in real life some Indians are more equal than others. Judged by the standards it set itself at Independence, the Republic of India has not been a great success.

But it has not been a failure either.

Potti Sreeramulu

Potti Sreeramulu was an Indian revolutionary. He became famous for undertaking a fast-unto-death for achieving the Andhra State and losing his life in the process. His sacrifice became instrumental in the linguistic re-organisation of states. He is revered as *Amarajeevi* (Immortal being) in Andhra for his sacrifice. As a devout follower of Mahatma Gandhi, he worked life long to uphold principles such as truth and non-violence and objectives such as Harijan upliftment.

Early Life

Born to Guravayya and Mahalakshmamma at house no. 165, Annapillai street, Chennai. He studied in Madras till he was 20. Later, he studied Sanitary Engineering in the Victoria Jubilee Technical Institute in Bombay.

Career

Potti Sreeramulu joined the Great Indian Peninsular Railway and worked for about four years there. After the death of his wife in 1927 when he was only 26, he lost interest in the material world and resigned from his job. He divided property between his brothers and mother and joined Sabarmati Ashram as a follower of Mahatma Gandhi.

Independence Movement and Harijan Upliftment

He took part in the Indian Independence Movement. He was imprisoned for participating in the 1930 Salt Satyagraha. Between 1941-42 he participated in the individual satyagraha and the Quit India movement and was imprisoned thrice. He was involved in the village reconstruction programmes at Rajkot in Gujarat and Komaravolu in Krishna district, Andhra Pradesh. He joined the Gandhi Ashram established by Yerneni Subrahmanyam in Komaravolu.

Between 1943 and 1944 he worked for the widespread adoption of Charkha in Nellore district. He started partaking food from all houses without attaching importance to caste and creed. He undertook three fasts during 1946-48 for the entry of Harijans into religious places such as temples in Nellore. He fasted to gain entry for Harijans into the Venugopalaswamy temple in Moolapeta, Nellore and succeeded in achieving the objective. He again fasted to get favourable orders on Harijan upliftment passed by the Madras government.

As a result, the government instructed collectors to attend to measures of Harijan upliftment at least one day in a week. During the last stages of his life, he stayed in Nellore and worked for Harijan upliftment. He would wear placards with slogans on

Harijan upliftment and propagate the cause. He used to walk wearing these placards in the middle of the summer without wearing slippers or using an umbrella. People who did not know about his antecedents dismissed him as a mad man. He was chastied by the upper caste and his own caste for his support for Harijan upliftment.

Statehood for Andhra

In an effort to protect the interests of the Telugu people in Madras Presidency, and to preserve the unique culture of Telugu people, he attempted to force the government to listen to public demands for the separation of Andhra region from Madras Presidency based on linguistic lines. He went on a lengthy fast, and only stopped when Prime Minister Jawaharlal Nehru promised to support creation of Andhra State. However, there was no movement on the issue for a long time. He started fasting again for attaining statehood for Andhra in Maharshi Bulusu Sambamurthy's house in Madras on 19 October 1952. It started off without fanfare but steadily caught people's imagination despite the disavowal of the fast by the Andhra Congress committee.

The government of the day however did not make a clear statement about the formation of a new state despite several strikes and demonstrations by Telugu people. On the midnight of 15 December (i.e. early 16 December 1952), Potti Sreeramulu died and laid down his life trying to achieve his objective.

In his death procession, people shouted slogans praising his sacrifice. When the procession reached Mount Road, thousands of people joined and raised slogans hailing Sriramulu. Later, they went into a frenzy and resorted to destruction of public property. The news spread like wildfire and created an uproar among the people in far off places like Vizianagaram, Visakhapatnam, Vijayawada, Rajahmundry, Eluru, Guntur, Tenali, Ongole and Nellore. Seven people were killed in police firing in Anakapalle and Vijayawada. The popular agitation continued for three to four days disrupting normal life in Madras and Andhra regions. On 19 December, the Prime minister of the country Jawaharlal Nehru made an announcement about formation of a separate Andhra state.

On 1 October 1953, the state of Andhra was established with Kurnool as capital carving it out from Madras State. However, the

Telugu speaking Telangana was part of Hyderabad state until 1956. On November 1, 1956, Telangana was merged with Andhra and as a result Andhra Pradesh was formed with Hyderabad as its capital, against the recommendation of States Reorganization Commission (SRC). Kerala and Karnataka states were formed the same day in 1956, followed by Gujarat and Maharashtra in 1960. The formation of linguistic states is the single most important event in the history of South Indian languages, as it provided an opportunity for these languages to develop independently, each of them having a state to support.

Death

Potti Sreeramulu fasted in the heart of Madras (Chennai) city for over 58 days for an Andhra state with Madras as the capital. He described "Andhra without Madras as a dead body without a head. The reasons as to why the Rajaji government, Union government led by Nehru or police did not intervene to force feed or shift him to a hospital remain unclear. The intentions of Nehru and Rajaji governments to effectively homogenize the cultural and linguistic diversity of the Indian Union in the name of National Integration have seriously undermined the very federal spirit upon which India's foundation lies.. It is interesting to note that only one person before him in modern Indian history Jatin Das actually fasted to death; all the others either gave up or were arrested and force fed or hospitalised.

Gujrat and Maharastra Division

Gujarat is the most industrialized state in the Republic of India. Gujarat borders Pakistan, and the states of Rajasthan to the northeast, Madhya Pradesh to the east, Maharashtra and the Union territories of Diu, Daman, Dadra and Nagar Haveli to the south. The Arabian Sea makes up the state's western coast. Its capital, Gandhinagar is located near Ahmedabad, the former state capital and the current commercial centre of Gujarat.

Many settlements of the Indus Valley Civilization, also known as the Harappan Civilization, have been found in Gujarat. The most important of these are the trade port of Lothal in south eastern Gujarat and Dholavira in western Gujarat. Dholavira, The ancient metropolitan city, locally known as Kotada Timba, is one of the largest archaeological sites in India. It is located on the

Khadir island in the Kutch district of Gujarat-the island is surrounded by water in the monsoon season. The site was occupied from about 2900 BC for about a millennium, declining slowly after about 2100, briefly abandoned and then reoccupied, finally by villagers among its ruins, until about 1450.

The name of the state is derived from Gujjarâtta (Gurjar Râshtra), which means the land of the Gujjars. It is believed that a tribe of Gujjars migrated to India around the 5th century. Gujarat's coastal cities, chiefly Bharuch, served as ports and trading centres for the Maurya and Gupta empires. After the collapse of the Gupta empire in the 6th century, Gujarat flourished as an independent Hindu kingdom. The Maitraka dynasty, descended from a Gupta general, ruled from the 6th to the 8th centuries from their capital at Vallabhi, although they were ruled briefly by Harsha during the 7th century. In 775 the first Parsi (Zoroastrian) refugees arrived in Gujarat from Iran. The Arab rulers of Sindh sacked Vallabhi in 770, bringing the Maitraka dynasty to an end. A branch of the Pratihara clan ruled Gujarat after the eighth century.

Ethnically there are four groups of people who came to inhabit this land at different points of time and now form the majority here. These are Meghvals, Ahirs, Rabaris and Jats. The Patel of Gujarat are wealthy and landlords. The Banaskantha district, Mehsana, SabarKantha, Kheda, and Kutch have many Patel villages where a sizable population lives. The Ahirs came with Lord Krishna from Gokul in Uttar Pradesh. Most of the communities of Ahirs began with selling ghee and milk and are now spread all over the state.

The Rabaris are a nomadic tribe always wandering with their herds. The origin of this tribe has been traced back to Sindh and Afghanistan though many aspects of this tribe still remain a puzzle for anthropologists. They have been classified into three distinct groups, namely Vagadia, Dhabaria, and Kachhi. Women of this tribe engage themselves in making elaborate embroidery pieces while the men spend their time tending to their camels and sheep. There were also groups of Rajputs who settled in Gujarat, coming from Rajasthan. They played a very significant part in Gujarat's history, along with the Gujjars.

The Solanki clan of Rajputs ruled Gujarat from c. 960 to 1243. Gujarat was a major centre of Indian Ocean trade, and their capital at Anhilwara (Patan) was one of the largest cities in India, with a population estimated at 100,000 in the year 1000. In 1026, the famous Somnath temple in Gujarat was destroyed by Mahmud of Ghazni. After 1243, the Solkanis lost control of Gujarat to their feudatories, of whom the Vaghela chiefs of Dholka came to dominate Gujarat. In 1292 the Vaghelas became tributaries of the Yadava dynasty of Devagiri in the Deccan.

In 1297 to 1298 Ala ud din Khilji, Sultan of Delhi, destroyed Anhilwara and incorporated Gujarat into the Delhi Sultanate. After Timur's sacking of Delhi at the end of the 14th century weakened the Sultanate, Gujarat's Muslim governor Zafar Khan Muzaffar asserted his independence, and his son, Sultan Ahmed Shah (ruled 1411 to 1442), established Ahmedabad as the capital. Cambay eclipsed Bharuch as Gujarat's most important trade port. The Sultanate of Gujarat remained independent until 1576, when the Mughal emperor Akbar conquered it. It remained a province of the Mughal empire until the Marathas conquered eastern and central Gujarat in the 18th century; Western Gujarat (Kathiawar and Kutch) were divided among numerous local rulers.

Portugal was the first European power to arrive in Gujarat, acquiring several enclaves along the Gujarati coast, including Daman and Diu and Dadra and Nagar Haveli. The British East India Company established a factory in Surat in 1614, which formed their first base in India, but it was eclipsed by Bombay after the British acquired it from Portugal in 1668. The Company wrested control of much of Gujarat from the Marathas during the Second Anglo-Maratha War. Many local rulers, notably the Maratha Gaekwads of Baroda (Vadodara), made a separate peace with the British, and acknowledged British sovereignty in return for retaining local self-rule.

Gujarat was placed under the political authority of Bombay Presidency, with the exception of Baroda state, which had a direct relationship with the Governor-General of India. From 1818 to 1947, most of present-day Gujarat, including Kathiawar, Kutch, and northern and eastern Gujarat were divided into dozens of princely states, but several districts in central and southern Gujarat, namely Ahmedabad, Broach (Bharuch), Kaira, Panch Mahals, and Surat, were ruled directly by British officials.

The people of Gujarat were the most enthusiastic participants in India's struggle for freedom. Leaders like Mahatma Gandhi,

Sardar Vallabhbhai Patel, Morarji Desai, K.M. Munshi, Narhari Parikh, Mahadev Desai, Mohanlal Pandya and Ravi Shankar Vyas all hailed from Gujarat. In addition, Mohammed Ali Jinnah, Pakistan's first Governor-General, spoke Gujarati as his mother tongue and his father was from what later became Gujarat. Gujarat was also the site of some of the most popular revolts, including the Satyagrahas in Kheda, Bardoli, Borsad and the Salt Satyagraha.

After India's independence in 1947, 217 princely states of Kathiawar and Saurashtra, including the former kingdom of Junagadh, were grouped together to form the province of Saurashtra, with its capitol at Rajkot. On November 1, 1956, Saurashtra was merged into Bombay State. The modern state of Gujarat was created on May 1, 1960, out of the northern, predominantly Gujarati-speaking portion of Bombay State. The southern, predominantly Marathi-speaking portion became the state of Maharashtra.

After Indian independence and the partition of India in 1947, the new Indian government grouped the former princely states of Gujarat into three larger units; Saurashtra, which included the former princely states on the Kathiawar peninsula, Kutch, and Bombay state, which included the former British districts of Bombay Presidency together with most of Baroda state and the other former princely states of eastern Gujarat. In 1956, Bombay state was enlarged to include Kutch, Saurashtra, and parts of Hyderabad state and Madhya Pradesh in central India. The new state had a mostly Gujarati-speaking north and a Marathi-speaking south. Agitation by Marathi nationalists for their own state led to the split of Bombay state on linguistic lines; on 1 May 1960, it became the new states of Gujarat and Maharashtra. The first capital of Gujarat was Ahmedabad; the capital was moved to Gandhinagar in 1970. Surat is known as Diamond or Silk city of India and business city of India.

In Gujarat a few new towns have been established since Indian independence in 1947. Most of these are more like settlements established near existing urban centres. Gandhidham, Sardarnagar and Kubernagar are three rehabilitation towns more like refugee settlements than self-sufficient towns. The last two now form part of the city of Ahmedabad. Ankleshwar and Mithapur were two of the earlier industrial towns established in Gujarat. A complex of three small townships for the oil refinery, the Fertilizer Factory and Petro-chemicals plant also came up near Vadodara. Kandla is the only new port town established in the state.

Climate & Natural Features: The relief is low in the most parts of the state and involves diverse climate conditions. Though mostly dry, it is desertic in the northwest, and wet in the southern districts due to heavy monsoon season. With the construction of Sardar Sarovar on Narmada River, a result of the largest dam in India, irrigation facilities have improved immensely, with water being provided to the most dry areas of Kutch and Saurashtra through a 550 km long canal, an engineering marvel. With the Gulf of Kutch and the Gulf of Cambay, Gujarat has about 1600 km of coastline, which is the longest coastline of all Indian states.

Rivers: The major rivers flowing through the state include the Narmada, Sabarmati, and Mahi in central and northern Gujarat; Mithi, Khari, Bhadar, Shetrunji and Bhogavo in Saurashtra; Tapi, Purna, Ambika, Auranga and Damanganga in the south.

National Parks: Gujarat is home to four National Parks, including Gir Forest National Park, near Junagadh, Blackbuck National Park in Bhavnagar District, Vansda National Park in Navsari District, and Marine National Park on the Gulf of Kutch in Jamnagar District. In addition to these, there are twenty one Wildlife sanctuaries, which include: Nal Sarovar, Anjal, Balaram-Ambaji, Barda, Jambughoda, Jessore, Kachchh Desert, Khavda, Narayan Sarovar, Paniya, Purna, Rampura, Ratanmahal, and Surpaneshwar. Gir Forest is the only home of Asiatic Lions and the only natural habitat of lions outside Africa. This National Park in southwest part of the state covers only the part of lion's habitat. Besides lions, the other big cat can be found in the state are Panthers. Panthers are spread across large plains of Saurashtra and mountains of South Gujarat. The major cities in Gujarat are Ahmedabad, Vadodara (Baroda), Surat, Rajkot, Bhavnagar Jamnagar and Junagadh. Ahmedabad, the commercial capital of the state, is the sixth largest city of India. Other important cities include Nadiad, Anand and Ankleshwar in central Gujarat, Bharuch, Navsari, Vapi, and Valsad in the south; and Bhuj, and Surendranagar, Morbi, Dwarka in Saurashtra in the west.

Economy

The economy of Gujarat shows that it is one of the most prosperous states of the country, having a per-capita GDP 2.47

times India's average. Of all the states, Gujarat controls some of the largest businesses in India. According to the data published by "Centre for Monitoring Indian Economy" or CMIE, Gujarat ranked third among all the states of India in 2004, approximately same as Punjab and Maharashtra, at Rs. 15,800. Major Agricultural produce of the state include cotton, peanuts, dates, sugarcane, milk & milk products. Industrial products include cement, and petrol. Gujarat is the largest producer of milk in India. Amul, located at Anand is one of the largest milk product producer cooperatives in the world.

Surat is a hub of the global diamond trade. It is home to a thriving diamond trade and diamond cutting industry. Alang Ship Recycling Yard, located 50 km southeast of Bhavnagar, on the Gulf of Khambhat, is the world's largest ship breaking yard. Reliance Petroleum Limited, one of the group companies of Reliance Industries Limited operates the oil refinery at Jamnagar which is the world's largest grassroots' refinery.

Gujarat ranks first nationwide in gas-based thermal electricity generation with national market share of over 18% and second nationwide in nuclear electricity generation with national market share of over 16%. During the period 1960-90, Gujarat established itself as a leader in various industrial sectors-Textiles, Engineering, Chemicals, Petrochemicals. Drugs & Pharmaceuticals. Dairy, Cement & Ceramics. Gems & Jewellery, etc. Gujarat accounts for almost 21% share in the export basket of India. Gujarat's 1600 km coastline is dotted with 41 ports (1 major, 11 intermediate and 29 minor). Country's first private sector ports. Pipavav and Mundra are already in operation. In addition the liquid cargo (Chemicals) handling port at Dahej is also set up in joint sector and made operational.

On 1960-05-01, Gujarat was created out of the 17 northern districts of former State of Bombay. These districts were further subdivided later on. There are 25 administrative districts in the state (as of 2006).

Gujarat is governed by a Legislative Assembly of 182 members. Members of the Legislative Assembly (MLA) are elected on the basis of adult suffrage from one of 182 constituencies, of which 13 are reserved for scheduled castes and 26 for scheduled tribes. The term of office for a member of the Legislative Assembly is five years. The Legislative Assembly elects a speaker, who presides over the meetings of the legislature. A governor is appointed by the President of India, and is empowered to summon, prorogue, and dissolve the Legislative Assembly, and to address the House after every general election and the commencement of each year's first session of the Legislative Assembly.

The Leader of the Legislative Assembly is the leader of the majority party or coalition in the legislature (Chief Minister), or his or her designee. The Leader sets the dates of the legislative sessions, and decides what business is to be transacted in the legislature and what order it is taken up. The administration of the state is led by the Chief Minister.

Gujarat has 13 universities and 4 agricultural universities.

Engineering Colleges: L.D. College of Engineering, Dharmsinh Institute of Technology (DDIT) Nirma Institute of Technology and Dhirubhai Ambani Institute of Information and Communication Technology are among the premier engineering institutes of west India. Centre for Environment Planning and Technology is a well known institution for students of art and architecture. Gujarat also has a National Institute of Technology in Surat.

Research Organisations: Indian Space Research Organization is the premier space research institute located in the city of Ahmedabad. Known as the cradle of Space Sciences in India, the Physical Research Laboratory (PRL) was founded in 1947 by Dr. Vikram Sarabhai [7] in the city of Ahmedabad, near to Gujarat University and L. D. College of Engineering campuses. As a unit of the Department of Space, Government of India, PRL carries out fundamental research in select areas of Physics, Space & Atmospheric Sciences, Astronomy & Astrophysics and Planetary & Geosciences.

Institute for Plasma Research is an autonomous Physics research institute located in the capital city Gandhinagar, involved in research in various aspects of plasma science including basic plasma physics, research on magnetically confined hot plasmas and plasma technologies for industrial applications. Ahmedabad Textile and Industries' Research Association is also located in Ahmedabad, Gujarat.

Central Salt and Marine Chemicals Research Institute has been established under Council of Scientific & Industrial Research Govt.

of India at Bhavnagar. It was inaugurated in 1954 with a view to carry out research on marine salt, and salt from inland lakes and sub-soil brine. It is working on Reverse Osmosis, Electro Membrane Process, Salt and Marine Chemicals, Analytical Science, Marine Biotechnology and other related fields.

Indian Institute of Management Ahmadabad, one of the internationally reputed management research institute is located in Gujarat's commercial capital Ahmadabad. Indian Institute of Management Ahmadabad is one of the best management institutes in the world.

Its official and primary language is Gujarati, while Hindi is widely spoken and understood in urban areas. The religion of the majority of its residents is Hinduism, in addition to significant percentages following Islam, Jainism, Zoroastrianism and Christianity. Most of the Gujarati people are vegetarian. Amongst Hindus the deity of Krishna is famously worshipped in His form of Sri Nathji throughout Gujarat.

Temples: Palitana Temples is a complex of Jain temples situated 51 km south west of Bhavnagar. There are 863 temples from base to the peak of the Shatrunjaya hill, where the Palitana temples are located. Dwarkanath Temple: it is situated at Dwarka and is one of the important temples dedicated to lord Krishna. The Somnath Temple located in the Prabhas Kshetra near Veraval in Saurashtra, on the western coast of Gujarat, India is one of the twelve Jyotirlings (golden lingas) symbols of the God Shiva. It is mentioned in the Rig Veda. Somnath means "The Protector of Moon God".

The Somnath Temple is known as 'the Shrine Eternal', as although the temple has been destroyed six times it has been rebuilt every single time. The Swaminarayan Temple in Kalupur, Ahmedabad is the first built Swaminarayan Temple in the world, this temple is know to be very popular with tourists. The Modhera Sun Temple is famous for its rare position as specifically and uniquely designed for the worship of the Sun, Lord Surya. While the main temple is beautifully and intricately designed with complex architecture, painting and sculptures, there is a central pond and surrounding it stand 108 small temples for each of the Sun God's 108 names.

Dwarka city on the tip of the Arabian Sea is famous for being the legendary home of Lord Krishna, the eighth Avatara of Vishnu, hero of the Mahabharata epic. Ancient ruins of a city and temple complex found underwater suggest a historical basis for the legend. The Rann of Kutchch covers a large portion of western Gujarat, and is world-famous for its rare ecosystem, fossils, wildlife and terrain. Only 500 years earlier, the area was the Arabian Sea.

While the city of Ahmedabad is a large and fast-growing modern metropolis, it was also the home of the Indian Independence Movement, with the Sabarmati Ashram of Mahatma Gandhi a standing legacy. Other major tourist sites include Palitana, Diu, Kutch, Jamnagar, Junagadh, and Rajkot in the region of Saurashtra; and Champaner and Pavagarh in the Panchmahal district.

Bibliography

Adikaram, E. W.: *Early History of Buddhism in Ceylon,* D. S. Puswella, Migoda, 1946.

Agrawala, V. S.: *Shiva Mahadeva: The Great God,* Veda Academy, Varanasi, 1966.

Ahmad, Imtiaz: *State and Foreign Policy: India's Role in South Asia,* Vikas, New Delhi, 1993.

Ahmad, Jamil-ud-din: *Some Recent Speeches and Writings of Mr. Jinnah,* Lahore, Ashraf, 1952.

Aiyar, R. Krishnaswami: *Outlines of Vedaanta,* Chetana, Bombay, 1978.

Archer, W. G.: *The Kama Sutra,* Unwin Hyman, London, 1990.

Ashton, S.R. : *British Policy Towards the Indian States, 1905-1939,* London, Curzon, 1982.

Aurobindo, Sri: *Vyasa and Valmiki,* Acharya Press, Pondicherry, 1956.

Avalon, Arthur and Ellen: *Hymns to the Goddess,* Ganesh and Co., Madras, 1964.

Aziz, Ashraf: *Light of the Universe: Essays on Hindustani Film Music,* Three Essays Collective, New Delhi, 2003.

Bagchi, P. C.: *Studies in Dharmashastra,* University of Calcutta Press, Calcutta, 1939.

Bahadur, K.P.: *The Wisdom of Vedaanta,* Sterling Publishers Private Limited, New Delhi, 1996.

Banerjea, J. N.: *Pauranic and Vedanta Religion,* University of Calcutta, Calcutta, 1996.

Bankimchandra, C.: *Essentials of Dharma,* Sanskrit Book Depot, Calcutta 1979.

Basu, Manoranjan: *Dharmashastra: A General Study,* Shrimati Mira Basu, Calcutta, 1976.

Beaumont, Roger : *Sword of the Raj: The British Army in India, 1747-1947*, Indianapolis, Bobbs-Merrill, 1977.

Benjamin, Joseph : *Scheduled Castes in Indian Politics and Society*, New Delhi, Ess Ess Publications, 1989.

Bhattacharyya, B.: *Nispannayogavali of Mahapandita Abhyakara Gupta*, Oriental Institute, Baroda, 1949.

Borchert, Bruno: *Mysticism: Its History and Challenge*, Samuel Wiser, York Beach, 1994.

Bose, D. N.: *Dharmashastra: Their Philosophy and Occult Secrets*, Kali Press, Calcutta, 1965.

Bowle, John: *The Imperial Achievement: The Rise and Transformation of the British Empire*, Little, Brown, 1974.

Brockington, J. L.: *Righteous Rama: The Evolution of an Epic*, Oxford, London, 1984.

Bromley, D.: *Krishna Consciousness in the West*, Bucknell University Press, Lewisburg, 1989.

Brooks, E.: *The Original Analects: Sayings of Confucius and His Successors*. Columbia University Press, New York, 1988.

Bruhn, Klaus: *The Jina-Images of Deogarh*, MacMillan, Leiden, 1969.

Burke, Mary Louise: *Swami Vivekananda in America: New Discoveries*, Advaita Ashrama, Calcutta, 1966.

Chaudhary, M.: *Partition and the Curse of Rehabilitation*, Calcutta, Bengal Rehabilitation Organization, 1964.

Chaudhuri, Nirad: *Thy Hand, Great Anarch! India: 1921-1952*, London, Chatto & Windus, 1987.

Coomeraswamy, Ananda K.: *Buddha and the Gospel of Buddhism*, MacMillan, London, 1928.

Crawford, Cromwell S.: *Ram Mohan Roy: His Era and Ethics*, Acharya Press, New Delhi, 1984.

Dalton, Dennis : *Gandhi's Power : Nonviolence in Action*, New Delhi, OUP, 2001.

Danielou, Alain: *The Complete Kama Sutra*, Park Street Press, Rochester, 2000.

Dasgupta, Shahana: *Rani Lakshmibai: The Indian Heroine*, Rupa & Company, Calcutta, 2002.

Datta, V.N.: *Sati: Widow Burning in India*, Manohar, New Delhi, 1990.

David, M. D.: *John Wilson and his Institutions*, Mumbai, 1957.

De Bary: *Self and Society in Ming Thought*, Columbia University Press, New York, 1970.

De, Sushil Kumar: *Ancient Indian Erotics and Erotic Literature*, Firma K. L. Mukhopadhyay, Calcutta, 1959.

Deak, Istvan: *The Lawful Revolution: Louis Kossuth and the Hungarians 1848-1849*, Columbia University Press, 1979.

Dhar, Niranjan: *Vedanta and Bengal Renaissance*, Minerva Associates, Calcutta, 1977.

Dikshit, D.P. *Political History of the Chalukyas of Badami*. New Delhi: Abhinav, 1980.

Donat, K.: *Meditate the Tantric Yoga Way*, George Allen and Unwin, London, 1973.

Doniger, W.: *The Rig Veda: An Anthology*, Penguin, New York, 1981.

Duboi, Abbe: *Hindu Manners, Customs and Ceremonies*, Fifth Indian Impression, CUP, 1985.

Dwivedi, M.: *The Principal Upanishads*, Adyar Library, Madras, 1931.

Eaton, Richard M.: *Sufis of Bijapur, 1300-1700: Social Roles of Sufis in Medieval India*, Princeton University Press, Princeton, 1978.

Edwardes, Michael: *Battles of the Indian Mutiny*, London; B. T. Batsford Ltd., 1963.

Erickson, Erik H.: *Gandhi's Truth: On the Origins of Militant Nonviolence*, Norton, New York, 1970.

Farquhar, J.N.: *Modern Religious Movements in India*, Munshiram, New Delhi, 1967.

Fay, Peter Ward: *The Opium War, 1840-42*, University of North Carolina Press, 1975.

Fisher, Michael H.: *The Politics of British Annexation of India - 1757-1857*, Oxford, 1996.

Frauwallner, E..: *History of Indian Philosophy*, Motilal, Delhi, 1973.

Gambhirananda, S.: *Brahma Sutra Shamkar Bhasya*, Adavita Ashrama, Calcutta, 1977.

Gambhirananda, Swami: *Brahma Sutra Shamkar Bhasya*, Adavita Ashrama, Calcutta, 1977.

Gandhi, M. K.: *The Story of My Experiment With Trust*, Washington, Public Affairs Press, 1948.

Garbe, R.: *The Philosophy of Ancient India*, Chicago University Press, Chicago, 1899.

Goradia, Nayana: *Lord Curzon: The Last of the British Moghuls*, New Delhi, Oxford University Press, 1993.

Goudriaan, T.: *Ritual and Speculation in Early Tantrism*, State University of New York Press, New York, 1992.

Gough, A.E.: *The Philosophy of the Upanisads and Ancient Indian Metaphysics*, MacMillan, London, 1882.

Grant, G. P.: *Philosophy in the Mass Age*, Copp Clark, Toronto, 1959.

Grisenold, H.D.: *Insights into Modern Hinduism*, Oxford, New York, 1934.

Growse, F. S.: *The Ramayana of Tulasidasa*, Motilal Banarsidass, Delhi, 1995.

Gurumurthy, S. : *Hindu Heritage, Assimilative, Not Divisive*, Vigil, Madras 1993.

Haich, E.: *Sexual Energy and Yoga*, Aurora Press, New York, 1982.

Hasan, Murhirul: *Legacy of a Divided Nation: India's Muslims Since Independence*, New Delhi, Oxford, 1997.

Hasan, Mushirul: *India's Partition: Process, Strategy and Mobilization*, New Delhi, Oxford UP, 1993.

Heifetz, Hank: *The Origin of the Young God: Kalidasa's Kumarasambhava*, University of California Press, Berkeley, 1985.

Heimann, Betty: *Facets of Indian Thought*, Geroge Allen & Unwin, London, 1964.

Heinsath, Charles: *Indian Nationalism and Hindu Social Reform*, Princeton University Press, Princeton, 1964.

Heschel, J.: *God in Search of Man: A Philosophy of Judaism*, Noonday Press, New York, 1997.

Hirschman, Edwin: *White Mutiny: The Ilbert Bill Crisis in India and the Genesis of the Indian National Congress*, New Delhi, Heritage, 1980.

Hixon, L.: *Mother of the Universe: Visions of the Goddess, Tantric Hymns of Enlightenment*, Quest Books, Wheaton, 1994.

Hopkins, J.: *Kalachakra Tantra Rite of Initiation*, Wisdom Publications, Boston, 1982.

Hopkirk, Peter: *The Great Game: The Struggle for Empire in Central Asia*, Kodansha, 1992.

Hume, R.E.: *The Thirteen Principle Upanishads*, Oxford University Press, London, 1971.

Hutchins, Francis: *Spontaneous Revolution: The Quit India Movement*, New Delhi, Manohar, 1971.

Irene, S.: *Vedic Heritage Teaching Program*. Arsha Vidya Gurukulam, Coimbatore, 1994.

Iyar, K.: *Vedanta: The Science of Reality*, Ganesh and Co., Mardas, 1930.

Iyengar, B.K.S.: *Light on the Yoga Sutras of Patanjali*, Aquarian Press, London 1993.

Jacob, K.: *Religion and Ethics in Advaita*, C.M.S. Press, Kottayam, 1982.

Jafar, Malik Muhammad: *Jinnah as a Parliamentarian*, Lahore, Afzar Publications, 1977.

Jain, Kailash Chand, *Lord Mahavira and His Times*, Saraswati Press, Delhi, 1974.

James, Lawrence: *The Rise and Fall of the British Empire*, St. Martin's, 1997.

James, Robert Rhodes: *The British Revolution, 1880-1939*, New York, Knopf, 1976.

Jean, M.: *Tantrik Yoga*, The Aquarian Press, Wellingborough, 1970.

John, B.: *Mantras: Sacred Words of Power*, George Allen and Unwin, London, 1977.

John, Elsner: *Pilgrimage: Past and Present in the World Religions*, Harvard University Press, Cambridge, 1995.

John, K.: *The Origin and Development of the State Cult of Confucius*, Paragon Book, New York, 1966.

Karmarkar, D.: *Sankara's Advaita*, Karnatak University, Dharwar, 1976.

Kaushik, Asha : *Globalization, Democracy and Culture : Situating Gandhian Alternatives*, Jaipur, Pointer, 2002.

Kaviraj, G.: *Aspects of Indian Thought*, University of Burdwan, Calcutta, 1966.

Kavlekar, K.K. : *Non-Brahmin Movement in Southern India, 1873-1949*, Kolhapur, Shivaji University, 19790

Keith, A.B. : *Rigveda Brahmanas*, Harvard University Press, Cambridge, 1920.

Keith, Arthur Berriedale: *The Religion and Philosophy of the Veda and Upanishads*, MacMillan, Delhi, 1925.

Kishwar, Madhu : *Religion at the Service of Nationalism, and Other Essays*, OUP, Delhi, 1998.

Klaus, K.: *A Survey of Hinduism*, State University of New York Press, Albany, 1989.

Knipe, M.: *Hinduism: Experiments in the Sacred*, Harper, San Francisco, 1991.

Knott, K.: *Hinduism, A Very Short Introduction*, Oxford University Press, New York, 1998.

Kosambi, D. D. : *The Culture and Civilisation of Ancient India in Historical Outline*, London, Routledge and Kegan Paul, 1956.

Kottackal, Jacob: *Religion and Ethics in Advaita*, C.M.S. Press, Kottayam, 1982.

Kuiper, F.B.J. : *Aryans in the Rigveda*, Rodopi, Amsterdam, 1991.

Kuppuswamy, Sastri S.: *Compromises in the History of Advaitic Thought*, Kalyani Press, Madras, 1940.

Louis, Fischer: *Essential Gandhi: An Anthology of His Writings*, Vintage, New York, 1983.

Low, D. A. and Brasted, Howard: *Freedom, Trauma, Continuities: Northern India and Independence*, New Delhi, Sage Publications, 1998.

Maheshwari, Shriram: *Rural Development in India: A Public Policy Approach*, New Delhi, Sage, 1995.

Makhan, L.: *The Ramayana of Valmiki*, Munshiram Manoharlal, New Delhi, 1978.

Mathew, Arnold: *Culture and Anarchy*, The University Press, Cambridge, 1935.

Mayer, A. : *Caste in an Indian Village: Change and Continuity 1954-1992*, Delhi, OUP, 1996.

Mazumder, Sukhendu : *Politico-Economic Ideas of Mahatma Gandhi: Their Relevance in the Present Day*, New Delhi, Concept Pub., 2004.

Mearns, David J.: *Shiva's Other Children: Religion and Social Identity amongst Overseas Indians*, Sage, Walnut Creek, 1995.

Mearns, J.: *Shiva's Other Children: Religion and Social Identity amongst Overseas Indians*, Sage, Walnut Creek, 1995.

Mehra, Parshotam: *A Dictionary of Modern Indian History, 1707-1947*, New Delhi, Oxford University Press, 1985.

Metcalf, Thomas R.: *The Aftermath of the Revolt: India, 1857-1870*, Princeton, Princeton University, 1964.

Mohan, K.: *The Mahabharata*, Munshiram Manoharlal, Delhi 1997.

Mookerjee, Ajit: *Kali The Feminine Force*, Thames and Hudson, London, 1988.

Mookerji, Satkari: *Modern Polity and Vedanta*, Sanskrit College, Calcutta, 1972.

Moon, Penderel: *The British Conquest and Dominion of India*, London, Duckworth, 1989.

Morris-Jones, W.H.: *The Government and Politics of India*, London, Hutchinson, 1971.

Nanda, B. R. : *Gandhi and His Critics*, Oxford University Press, Delhi, 1993.

Neale, Walter C.: *Economic Change in Rural India: Land Tenure and Reform in the United Provinces, 1800-1955*, New Haven, 1962.

Nevile, P.: *Lahore: A Sentimental Journey*, New Delhi, Penguin, 1993.

Oddie, G.A. : *Hindu and Christian in South-East India*, London, Curzon Press, 1991.

Pathak, Dr S.P.: *Jhansi during the British Rule*, Ramanand Vidya Bhawan, Delhi, 1987.

Preston, Diana: *The Boxer Rebellion*, Berkley Books, 2000.

Raimundo Panikkar: *The Vedic Experience: Mantramanjari*, Longman Todd, London, 1977.

Raja, C. Kunhan : *The Taittiriya Sarvanukramani of Yaska*, Madras, 1931.

Ramamurti, A.: *Advaitic Mysticism of Sankara*, Visvabharati, Santiniketan, 1974.

Ranajit Guha: *A Construction of Humanism in Colonial India*, CASA, Amsterdam, 1993.

Renou, Louis: *The Nature of Dharmashastra*, Walker and Co., New York, 1997.

Robson, Brian: *Sir Hugh Rose and the Central India Campaign*, Sutton Publishing Ltd for the Army Records Society, UK, 2000.

Satyapal Verma: *Role of Reason in Sankara Vedanta*, Parimal Publication, Delhi, 1992.

Savarkar, Vinayak Damodar : *The Indian War of Independence* 1857 Rajdhani Granthagar, Delhi, 1988.

Scheftelowitz, Isidor : *Die Kasmirische Rezension von Katyayanas Sarvanukramani,* Zeitschrift fur Indologie und Iranistik, 1922.

Shukla, D. N.: *Vastu-Shastra,* Motilal Banarsidass, Delhi, 1966.

Singh, Birendra Kumar: *Early Chalukyas of Vatapi, circa A.D. 500 to 757,* Delhi, Eastern Book Linkers, 1991.

Smith, Col. J. T. : *Silver and the India Exchanges,* Effingham Wilson, London, 1876.

Strauss, L.: *Political Philosophy,* The Bobbs Merrill Co., New York, 1975.

Swami Vishnu Tirtha: *Devatma Shakti,* Swami Shivom Tirth, Rishikesh, 1962.

Talageri, Shrikant : *Aryan Invasion Theory and Indian Nationalism,* Voice of India, Delhi, 1993.

Tejomayananda, Swami: *Hindu Culture: An Introduction,* Chinmaya Publications, Piercy, 1993.

Thapar, Romila : *Ashoka and the Decline of the Mauryas,* London, Oxford University Press, 1961.

Thompson, Edward: *The Making of the Indian Princes,* Oxford University Press, London, 1943.

Trautmann, Thomas R.: *Kautilya and the Arthasastra: A Statistical Study,* Leiden, Brill, 1971.

Trimingham, J.: *Sufi Orders in Islam,* Oxford University Press, New York, 1998.

Utpat, V.N.: *Riddles of Buddha and Ambedkar,* Itihas Patrika Prakashan, Thane 1988.

Vable, D.: *The Arya Samaj. Hindu without Hinduism.* Vikas Publ., Delhi, 1983.

Vedalankar, Pandit Nardev : *Basic Teachings of Hinduism,* Veda Niketan, Durban, 1978.

Visvantha, K.: *Essentials of Hinduism,* Narosa Pub. House, New Delhi, 1989.

Wendy Doniger: *Siva: The Erotic Ascetic,* Oxford University Press, Delhi, 1998.

Zaidi, A. Moin: *Evolution of Muslim Political Thought in India,* New Delhi: S. Chand, 1975.

Index

F

G

H

I

J

L

M

N

O

P

Q

R

S

T

U

V

W

Z

□□□